# THE COLLECTOR'S HAYDN

# THE
# COLLECTOR'S
# HAYDN

## C. G. BURKE

### ADDENDUM BY
### ARTHUR COHN

**GREENWOOD PRESS, PUBLISHERS**
WESTPORT, CONNECTICUT

Library of Congress Cataloging in Publication Data

Burke, Cornelius G
  The collector's Haydn.

    Reprint of the 1959 ed. published by Lippincott,
Philadelphia, which was issued as no. KB 7 of Keystone
books in music.
    1.  Haydn, Joseph, 1732-1809--Discography.
2.  Haydn, Joseph, 1732-1809. Works.  I.  Cohn, Arthur,
1910-    II.  Title.  III.  Series: Keystone books
in music ; KB 7.
[ML156.5.H4B9  1978]    016.789'12        77-28259
ISBN 0-313-20239-7

This edition published by arrangement with J. B. Lippincott
Company, Philadelphia, New York.

Reprinted in 1978 by Greenwood Press, Inc.
51 Riverside Avenue, Westport, CT. 06880

Printed in the United States of America

10 9 8 7 6 5 4 3 2 1

# ACKNOWLEDGMENT

The Publisher, Mr. Charles Fowler, and the Editor, Mr. John M. Conly, of *High Fidelity*, very kindly permitted the use here of material that originally appeared in that magazine, and I am grateful to them. The various manufacturers of records have shown a pretty stoicism in maintaining composure in the face of sharp things I have frequently had to say about their products, and I am grateful to them.

C. G. B.

# PUBLISHER'S NOTE

After Mr. C. G. Burke had completed his work on the manuscript of this book in the summer of 1957, other commitments prevented him from bringing the work up to date in relation to new releases before the manuscript went to press. The publisher, therefore, enlisted the services of Mr. Arthur Cohn, formerly Curator of the Fleisher Collection of The Free Library of Philadelphia and Head of the Settlement Music School there, to make an Addendum of later Haydn releases. In the body of the book, music which is also discussed in the Addendum, is indicated by ***. The symbol of a dagger (†) in the body of the book indicates new titles recorded for the first time, which will be found in the Addendum.

# CONTENTS

# PREFACE

In 1948, Columbia Records, Inc., inaugurated a series of narrow-groove disks, recorded partly by new and partly by old procedures, that precipitated a new era in the reproduction of sound. The most obvious improvement in the new records was their extended* duration, obtained from the narrowing of the groove and a reduction of the revolving speed from 78 rpm to 33 rpm. This canceled most of the bother of changing disks and allowed long works of music to be reproduced without the exasperation of fifteen or twenty interruptions every hour. On

* At first they averaged less than twenty minutes to a twelve-inch side, against an average of less than four minutes for the twelve-inch side of the 78 rpm disk they almost immediately superseded. Technical ingenuity permitted subsequent extension to thirty and even thirty-five minutes, these not without sonic hazard; and the mean duration now favored is about twenty-five minutes a side. Collectors feel that a side shorter than twenty minutes is a cheat, the wealthier ones, however, making exception for Westminster's "Laboratory" series, in which for technical reasons duration is limited to seventeen minutes a side.

9

the long-playing records, LP as they are universally called, the forty-five interruptions in *Don Giovanni* on 78 rpm have been reduced to five. Thus LP, by merely justifying its name, immediately erased one of the most valid objections to the reproduction of music, and by improving the quality of recorded sound through the auxiliary of magnetic tape, forced its new eloquence on the public's attention indelibly, indeed extravagantly.

For Columbia's paragon not only spurred interest, but immediately began to stimulate the intensity and variety of recording, and gave irresistible impetus to the imagining, manufacture and distribution of reproductive apparatus. No need here to dilate on the fantastic expansion of the hobby, industry and passion known by the undefined term of "high fidelity," behind whose vague but honorable aspiration more rascals have covered inferior phonographs than chemical merchants have dosed man and dog with chlorophyll to eradicate their ineradicable effluvia. Fortunately other manufacturers were more expert and conscientious than those who sold and sell "hi-fi" automobile radios and "hi-fi" portable recordplayers, and the good houses made available to a public ever more swollen many types of reproducing equipment with a tonal glory hitherto unknown. LP fed consumers to the reproducers, and the good reproducers attracted consumers to LP.

There ensued a period, not yet ended, in which

a superb accomplishment of musical recording pursued its steady and sober development quite eclipsed by the glare radiated from an aggressive Festival of Noise, inaugurated by an unsuspected section of society awakening for the first time to Sound. The unprecedented audibility of fifteen thousand cycles stang into clanging life a brother-hood of electronic dervishes to whom any ex-plosion was good if it pierced and was heard through a loudspeaker. Suppressed since the first sonic cylinder, the extremes of the audial scope were revenged by excesses of outcry in which tinkle and boom were apotheosized via the power amplifier. No orchestra was in esteem to the devout unless triangle and piccolo dominated the rest, and to the rapt who could hear these countering bass tuba and bull fiddle thrice as large as life music was complete.

The sensitivity and portability of the tape-recorder made it easy to augment cymbals and big drum, percussion and concussion, by the aural "documentary," the recorder traveling any-where, and bringing back noise. The charac-teristic rackets of city streets, railroad yards, air-fields, industrial plants, metropolitan subways, athletic fields, telephone bells, insects' stridula-tions, afflictions of contemporary life even to the electronic dervish, are sources of reverent delight to him when reproduced in precincts where they do not belong.

It is hard to see on whom any permanent damage is inflicted by these oddities of sonic

taste. Undeniably some disrepute has been re-
flected on the reproduction of sound as a diver-
sion, but the phonograph has always encountered
disdain and survived it, and the extravagant ends
to which their equipment has been put have
encouraged manufacturers to enhance the sensitivity of their equipment, which when properly
adjusted is quite as veracious in the reproduction
of a string quintet as in that of a bray from a
jackass or a squeal on the sweet potato. And the
portability that makes a gnu's heartbeat and a
muezzin's wail relatively inexpensive and easy to
capture has vastly simplified the work of recording the world's leading musical organizations and
enormously increasing the recorded musical repertory.

The expansion of repertory, given its initial
force by the advent of LP, has incomputably
altered the domain of music. In a year or two
what may be called the standard concert repertory had been engraved on disks, and a great
number of the standard operas as well. The re-
searches of musical supervisors for the record
companies, especially of the crowd of companies
born since LP, led to the uncovering of music
buried in silence for years, decades, centuries.
The public found that concert and opera programs were a deceit prompted by economic considerations; that what was offered by impresarios
was an endless repetition of music, good or bad,
that had once evoked enthusiasm. LP supplemented the four Mozart symphonies in the stand-

ard American list by thirty more, and laid bare
the wonderful world of Mozart concertos, con-
ventionally represented in the American concert
hall by three or four. All the major works of
Beethoven were recorded, and the seven neglected symphonies of Schubert. Handel operas
were undertaken, and a procession without end
of the works of Bach and the sons of Bach. Boccherini, Dittersdorf, Méhul, Cornelius, Brunetti,
M. L. Charpentier, Cimarosa—where may these
be heard except on the phonograph? There is
more of Vivaldi and the two Scarlattis on records
than can be heard in twenty years of concertgoing. It was left to records to demonstrate the
great height and reach of Joseph Haydn.

The great bulk of this composer's music had
been buried under a complacent critical verbiage
that asserted its value to be no more than the
influence it had had on Mozart and Beethoven.
Token performances of a few symphonies out of
a hundred, a few quartets out of seventy-seven,
and devotional (cut) performances of two oratorios were felt sufficient, during the first fifty
years of this century, to illustrate a footnote in
musical history. Music reorganized itself in a
rather sorry direction after the end of the
Second* World War in 1918, giving first consideration to the virtuoso and the virtuoso
orchestra, with conductors valued in proportion
to the uproar they could incite in the *"Pathétique"* Symphony and the fragility of the whisper

* The First World War ended in 1763.

they could coax for Debussy's *Nuages*. In the era of self-disgust that followed the ruination of the Wilson aspirations and the delivery of the country to the statesmanship of Doctors Harding, Coolidge and Hoover, that part of the American people that felt the hurt most turned to noise as a palliative, and about the same time certain prominent French journalists, so much more eloquent but no more honorable than ours, completed their conquest of aesthetic thought in the United States by their lamentable discovery of a significant aesthetic in jazz, then as now being fabricated by the ton by every vagabond resourceful in plagiarism and respectful to the sway of the most fundamental rhythm. A composer-pianist perceived that more volume was possible from a piano when more keys were struck at once, and achieved some fame by flogging the instrument with his fists and forearms and his head, without any deterioration at all to the latter.

In such an uproarious disputation of clang, the gist of the music between Handel and Beethoven was too alien for admission, except as a proof of historical alertness. Such a candid and elegant sparkle as that of Haydn's symphony called "*La Reine*" would carry reproof with it into a concert program infested with contemporary music and post-Wagnerian romanticism, and the hearty power of Symphony No. 102, played next to a Shostakovich symphony, reveals too very clearly the difference between grandeur and grandiloquence. There are no copyrights on Haydn's music, no publishers ballyhooing for royalties on it. And *"La Reine"* requires an orchestra of no more than forty, in the proper place: what economic excuse can the modern virtuoso orchestra offer for wasting idle its trombones, tubas, celesta, harps, contrabassoons, alto flute, bass clarinet and glockenspiel, all well paid, for which a Haydn symphony provides no employment?*

* Far too many conductors, knowing just enough to be provoked into serious error, knowing that Haydn's orchestra often was a small one, consent to play him only after evicting three fifths of their players from the stage, their instruments in lonely sight disposed in empty chairs or desks. A sickening coyness generally characterizes the conductor's demeanor on these occasions, as if in belittling his better he were inviting his audience to share a quaint experience with him. A few conductors, knowing more, knowing that Haydn's orchestra (which in fact varied in size, according to circumstances, from a dozen to over a hundred) vented its strength in small enclosures, retain their full force of strings and double the wind parts, in order not to lose too much of the effect made in Haydn's time. The immense auditorium in which orchestra sonance is dissipated today did not exist in Haydn's time when concertgoers were a small and select class. Haydn's symphonies, and Mozart's and Beethoven's symphonies, were played under their composers' auspices in small theatres, ballrooms, assembly-rooms, the public hall of a university, clubrooms—wherever space could be rented or lent for a few hundred auditors. For example, the Hanover Square room, where Haydn's first London symphonies were introduced, measured ninety-five by thirty-five feet, which makes an area about four times as great as the living-room in which I hear Haydn from a phonograph; and the concert-room of King's Theatre, in which subsequent symphonies were presented, was

The record companies, more sensitive to the nature of public appetite than impresarios, discerned in the early years of electrical recording that the public's predilection for Haydn far exceeded the alacrity of the great symphony orchestras to satisfy it. Before LP, at least twenty-one Haydn symphonies had been recorded, and in the spurt of recording excited by the new method Haydn was given the greatest proportional gain of any composer, especially by the new and small companies, who found the economics of such recording (no royalties, fewer musicians to hire, a hungry public) singularly

the same length and only ten feet wider. Carnegie Hall could envelop from four to twenty of the enclosures in which Haydn's symphonies were played when young and for which their sonorities were calculated. In the small hall the *pianissimo* is quiveringly palpable, and the *fortissimos* and *sforzatos* take the breath like thunder. To re-create the dynamic impact of Haydn and Mozart symphonies as those composers planned them, a conductor in a place like Carnegie Hall would have to increase his orchestral forces at least two or three fold. I have never heard of this being done.

Unfortunately the dominant concept of the proper rôle for recorded music is that it reproduce the sound of public concerts, including their limitations, even when these are easy to evade or suppress. Thus most Haydn (and Mozart) symphonies as recorded utilize small orchestras in spacious halls, with a smaller but considerable number allotted to large orchestras in spacious halls, and a few laudable examples where the orchestras are proportioned to the scores and the halls are as small as the required suavity of tone will tolerate. It is Haydn that we want on records, not Carnegie Hall; and there are signs that more recording supervisors are beginning to realize this.

agreeable. The original Haydn Society led the
way, boldly putting on disks music not heard in
public for generations, and if economic pressure
did at last subdue the integrity and ambition
and scholarship of that organization to silence,
every music-lover owes it homage not only for
the heavy pile of excellent disks it testated, but
for the influence it exerted on other entre-
preneurs. Of the thirty Haydn symphonies
recorded by the Haydn Society three fourths
were obscure ones. The bigger companies, con-
tracted to the famous orchestras, prefer the most
celebrated works, whose printed parts are in the
orchestras' libraries, and which require no new
arduous preparation of study and trial; but they
have made a few tentative ventures into the
shadows, and will eventually have to induce
their conductors to heed the enormous volume
of unplayed great music waiting for registration.
Since the large companies imitate each other's
repertory doggedly, there have been at times as
many as a score of "Surprise" symphonies on
disks, and only two versions of No. 22 (none at
present), only two wretched versions of No. 86,
only one each of Nos. 77 and 78 (neither now
available).

The quartets have been treated the same way.
Suspended in mid-course, the great project of
the Haydn Society, of recording them all, has
contributed a large number of fine records, and
nearly the entirety of that part—the major part
—of the quartet repertory unfamiliar in the

concert hall. Duplications of recorded efforts abound in the eight or ten quartets most familiar.

This pattern of recording—fat here, lean there —extends in fact to all the categories of Haydn's work, as it does with all the great composers. It is dictated by habit and illusion first, mixed occasionally with a little musical judgment. It gives justification to a book like this—

Which is intended for use as a practical guide to collectors dismayed by the formidable difficulties of making a choice of the best Haydn records when there are so many. No one without time and professional facilities to spare would attempt to choose the best one or two versions out of the dozen phonographic "Surprises," "Militaries" and "Clocks," or the five "Creations," or the multiple editions of the quartets of Op. 76 and the keyboard concerto called Op. 21. This can be done only by comparison, under identical conditions of reproduction, of all those versions with each other.

I have undertaken to make those comparisons because someone must, and because Haydn discographies of mine, complete at the time they were written (but naturally much less extensive than this late one), were welcomed by collectors with enough warmth to justify a new and up-to-date survey. The first of those discographies was written in March, 1951, for *The Saturday Review*, and the second, naturally a more elaborate essay, appeared in *High Fidelity* for December, 1952. The latter has served as a basis for the present work, and wherever possible its text has been retained. This was not often, the total of Haydn records having in the meantime more than doubled. Regardless of the date of the text, the records themselves have in every case been re-examined, even when that was more painful.

I would not have the presumption to try to estimate the comparative value of these editions, man having no meter other than personal responses for the measure of art, if phonograph records did not have a complication for the critic that enables his criticism to be more definite and more valid while making it more difficult. This is the factor of sonics: when it is surpassingly good it can greatly increase the appeal of a mediocre performance and endow a good performance with irresistibility. A bad performance and bad sonics are equally mortal to the projection of music. When both are so-so, and when so-so parallels good, a record is not easy to evaluate.

Thus, to head and hand, or to perception and execution—the objects of scrutiny in the criticism of a performance—reproduction equipment or transmission must be added to the examination of a record. Judgment of the first, of the concept that prescribes the line, the pace, the fabric and the significance of music, must ultimately be determined by the nature of the judge's prejudices. The second, execution, is the easiest of the three to gauge unless it is tonally ugly (which may be a fault of engineering). The third, reproduction equipment, interposes an apparatus between the music and the critic, whose estimates must be based on a knowledge of the aptitudes and limitations of the machine. It is common in the criticism of records to find blame assigned to the disk that belongs to the reproducing equipment. This is unfair and regrettable, but less serious than the omission of blame that would have been allotted to the disk if the reproducer had been sensitive enough to expose the faults of recording.

In order to bring out the potential of a record, to leave nothing latent that ought to be sounded, I have used two complex, powerful and highly sensitive electronic assemblies throughout the examinations needed for this book. These were situated in two rooms of different acoustic properties, and one was used as a testifier for the other whenever either gave out extraordinary sound from a record, magnificent or miserable. I think that most people with good equipment will agree with the sonic judgments here, but those with inferior phonographs will be unable to hear what is particularly glorious or particularly execrable; no harm done, if they are contented.

Often, and especially in the case of older records, disks of acceptable quality or better are unable to show their mettle unless unusual concessions are made to their peculiarities. This is done by the control-unit if it is resourceful and the collector is bold enough to disregard conventional or recommended settings until he has found a balance of treble and bass that pleases his ears. I have not condemned records that respond satisfactorily when subjected to strong correction at the controls, but in general I have indicated when the correction was necessary. The machine makes possible a certain amount of objectivity in the contemplation of sonics, but since any opinion of a musical interpretation must result from the action of personal experience or personal chemistry, I think readers ought to have some knowledge of my preferences and prejudices in the matter of Haydn. I have never been able to resist his music: even the weakest I do not dislike. This is because he is the purest major exponent of the musical idiom I like most: clear design in motion, designed to beguile, whose images and narrative are abstract. Mozart broke out of this idiom often, and Beethoven very often, to make a music more powerful than Haydn's but foreign to any idiom except those of Mozart and Beethoven. Haydn was human and always shows it in levelheaded music true to the refined colloquialism of his time, a musical speech in competent hands nearly immune to fiasco.

Where one loves, one is sensitive to the treatment accorded the beloved. All the graces of his period cannot conceal the fact that Haydn was a plain man whose speech is to be interpreted literally. Subtleties are not a common feature of his music, and those we find were dictated by the time rather than the man. His effects are broad and must not be disguised: loud is *loud*, and soft is *soft*, especially when they alternate: *presto* and *adagio* are equally unambiguous; the harmonic structure, even at its boldest and most enticing, must not be allowed to obscure the thematic shape; and lurid colors must be delivered frankly and exuberantly. It must not be supposed that finesse is absent from the Haydn music, for it abounds there, but it is an element in his equipment and not a dominating characteristic.

Subtlety has been expunged from life in the age of the Bomb and of television, but is worshiped (along with extreme brutality) in the art of the age, whose interpreters too often try to transmute the transparency and spontaneity of Haydn to the self-conscious mystification now in aesthetic fashion. There is a persistent tendency to play the quick movements a little too slowly and the slow movements a little too fast, particularly the latter, lest they emanate feeling, deemed by our age, in its insistence on rigid definition, improper for classical music. I feel that Haydn should not be penalized by curt phrasing and brisked tempos for the sake of someone else's principles; that his slow movements should be given the pace most fitting to their shape or mood, determined by inspection of the score, not inspection of precedent. It is clear to anyone that Haydn needs hearty coöperation in his heartiest effusions (explosion in the "Surprise" Symphony, "*Und es ward Licht*," from *The Creation*, the epic banging of the added percussion in the "Military" Symphony), but whereas Haydn spiced the refinement of his times with such rousing vulgarities, our conductors seek to cover the vulgarity of our time with refinements, and shrink from showing a shameful sympathy with what is obvious and boisterous. Fortunately not all do.

Spare harmonic organization, clean rhythm, full phrasing, obedience to the obvious, and of course a gait never fancied up with extraneous accelerations and retards, compose the foundation of honorable representations of Haydn's music. Noble representation is an exaltation of the matter offered: there is no universality of opinion on how it is obtained.

Nor is there a formula for weighing the ingredients of a recorded performance against each other. The values are delicate, and I have been unable to be dogmatic in assaying the relative worth of say a beautiful phrase ideally turned by a pair of horns in mediocre reproduction and the same phrase played with casual competence by horns ideally reproduced. One choses among competing editions by the aid of the accumulation of impressions that parallel analysis. In my own case what is curious and comforting is that most of the impressions have stoutly maintained themselves against the trial of time.

I have tried to include in the discography every LP devoted to Haydn except those whose music is limited to fragments, excerpts or movements. No doubt there are omissions, and I shall be grateful to readers who call my attention to any that will help to make the next edition of this book more complete. The inclusion of everything, however bad, is intended as an indication to readers of the relative worth of their own versions, so that the poorer ones may be replaced. Discontinued records are noted because many are excellent and because the manufacturer's notice of withdrawal does not mean that dealers will not have them on their shelves, or that many will not suddenly reappear under a different label or altered to respond to a different curve of reproducing characteristics. Both practices are common, and the altered edition, the new product from the same tape that had made a previous product, is often a baffling element in the selection of records. It may be better than the pristine form, and yet sometimes it is worse and frequently it shows no real change in quality. The manufacturer may make a point of proudly announcing it or he may prefer discreetly not to announce a correction that after all admits obliquely that something was wrong with the original issue. Invariably in the discography I have based my opinion on the later edition when I know there are two, but it is only too possible that now and then two or more may exist without my knowing of more than one, in which case my estimate of sonic quality might be damaging to records since corrected.

Whenever clear evaluations of comparative value are confounded by conflicting faults and merits, I have tried to explain the nature of the conflict in the text. Whenever the text fails to describe the features of an edition, the omission is to be ascribed to deficiencies, usually of reproduction, too pronounced to justify the use of space in explanation.

A phonographic institution is the "phantom" orchestra, invisible on records, glorified on the label, and barren of social or civil status. Only on records will the music-lover be able to find the "Philharmonic Symphony Orchestra of London," the "Vienna State Philharmonia," the "Philharmonic Promenade Orchestra," "Pro Musica" orchestras of migratory estate, "Danube," "Warwick" and "Centennial" symphony orchestras. No limit is imposed on the number of such ephemeral titles, and the orchestras behind them may be very good indeed. Contractual restrictions and strategic considerations induce these more-or-less venial deceptions, and collectors gain by them when the mask hides a good countenance.

Collectors have, however, a right to be sharp at the ubiquitous distribution of the tricky sobriquet "Vienna State Opera Orchestra." Two operas in Vienna are subsidized by the state, the National Opera (*Staatsoper*) and the People's Opera (*Volksoper*). The Vienna Philharmonic Orchestra is the *Staatsoper's* orchestra and the *Volksoper's* orchestra bears the name of the company. "Vienna State Opera Orchestra" is generally applied by record manufacturers either

to the orchestra of the *Volksoper* or to a group
specially assembled for recording. Such a group
is not stable and may be composed of delegations
from all the orchestras in Vienna, or it may con-
sist almost entirely of members from any one of
them. I have not tried to identify the Viennese
assemblages ambiguously named, but I have de-
leted the word "State" whenever a label carries
it as descriptive of an opera orchestra from Vienna. Other pseudonyms I have either enclosed
in quotes, as a way of saying "*sic*," or, when the
identification is certain, replaced by the organiza-
tional name forbidden to the manufacturer but
not to us.

I have indicated the duration of every edition
to the nearest minute. This is not proof that I
listened to every record throughout (as in fact
I did, to many six or seven times), but it does
imply it. The feature may be of service in class-
rooms and broadcast studios where time must be
measured carefully.

Prices have not been printed because they
change often and capriciously, and I did not care
to risk contributing further confusion. At present
they are not unfair, but they have very little
relation to value. There are excellent records for
less than two dollars, and abominable ones for
nearly six. Recently there have been cautious
movements toward stabilization, with a norm
of four or five dollars for a twelve-inch disk. It
is worth noting that certain companies avoid the
norm, either for their entire production or for

a special series. Westminster has a "Laboratory" series whose records are the most expensive in the United States, and Decca's "Archive" series, a product of Deutsche Grammophon, commands an extra price. Camden records are very cheap. Columbia has a very cheap series, "Entré," coded RL, which in spite of what we might expect from the misspelling, contains many admirable plums in addition to the expected lemons. RCA's intermediate series, "Bluebird," coded LBC, has a high average quality.

# HAYDN: BIOGRAPHICAL
# SKETCH

IN THE SMALL group of composers so vastly gifted that one feels genuine awe in contemplating them through their musical monuments, three figures are found whose eminence was wrested away from hostile circumstances completely unpromising to greatness. These unlikely figures are Bach, Gluck and Haydn.

When we say "genius" we mean a power of expression too great to be explained. It is a mystery, perhaps of human chemistry, that we acknowledge with admiration, humility, or resentment. Still, although we cannot explain it, we like to account for it—we have a need to find something rational in its origin or development.

It is easy enough to find an accounting for some of this genius, and while the accountancy may not satisfy the head, it satisfies the sentiments of people. Despite the deficiency of Beethoven's parentage as a mould for genius, his glittering environments and associates, and the turbulence of his unkempt ways, are gratifyingly compatible with most notions of the background of genius; and the penurious, carefree Schubert, inhaling music and sweating it, fits ideally into the general concept. No need to insist on the perfection of the Mozart fit, snug almost to burlesque, nor the fit of Wagner, who lived an integrity of exalted criminal romanticism in frank emulation of the glorious rascalities of his music-dramas. The life, character and surroundings of Handel seem just right for his music.

Whereas Bach was clearly destined by the conditions of his existence to be a scholastic hack, drab and hopeless. In his household, and his ancestors', collaterals' and descendants' households, music was a trade prescribed for Bachs, a trade plied as a tailor would ply his, cutting material to fixed standards. The Bach we call Bach composed for the Christian calendar in the knowledge that if he failed to provide a cantata or prelude for a churchly occasion he would be dismissed from his post in the provincial church that held his genius captive. He was a hack writing under the most appalling conditions, and that out of the enormous production of his dutiful travail a good one third belongs with the highest manifestations of the human spirit simply cannot be explained.

And Gluck, the only man ever to have become a great composer after having been a miserable one. The conventional trivialities of his early operas had carried him through a limping career until he was nearly fifty: what happened to erase the vaudeville from this soul that suddenly gave

out a musical Hellenism to this day unchallenged
as the essence of what Greek art ought to be?

Haydn, finally, whose origin and first four
decades seem even less propitious for the creation
of any kind of true art than the restrictions con-
fining Bach. There was no music in his ancestry
of peasants and artisans and only a dismally coun-
trified sort of music in the villages where he
spent his earliest years. His organized education,
musical and general, was slipshod and short. The
opportunities offered by travel were withheld
from him until his musical sophistication had
advanced beyond a need for them. He was a
liveried recluse in the train of a nobleman who
stipulated in detail the duties of his household,
including the musical. His marriage burdened
him with an ignorant wife for forty years, and
his love affairs were decidedly circumspect. He
was benevolent and honorable, and modest although not ignorant of his merit. Nearing
seventy he was a far greater man than he was, or
promised to become, at thirty-five; and during
his last thirty years he was recognized—as nearly
universally as that is possible—as the leader of
the world's music. His music had such enormous
authority that it imposed itself as a standard
when it appeared. The controversy or the indifference that beset other men's music was not
the fate of his. His works had the painful honor
of being imitated, plagiarized or pirated with
minimum delay after their introduction. And a
hundred and fifty years after his death more of

his vast production is known and remembered and loved, thanks to the phonograph, than at any period of history.

Scrutinizing Haydn, we are confronted by the fact of genius, and the only accounting usually offered for it is shamefully lame: he was born with an inextinguishable seed-germ of music and a huge reservoir of diligence. Manured by diligence, the germ developed and flourished, as if music were cereal. This is dangerous, sententious cant whose circulation encourages every blockhead with a germ to be industrious in bringing it to flower in the form of tedium. Let's confine ourselves to saying that Haydn was and his music is, and in a quick examination of his life look not for clues but for information, information being always interesting when it is about the great.

Haydn was born in the duchy of Lower Austria, the soul of the Hapsburg domain and (since it contained Vienna) one of the largest of the four hundred states and statelets comprising the tragic expedient called the Holy Roman Empire. The birthdate was April 1, 1732, not quite six weeks later than that of another man short of education but destined to be noted: George Washington. Haydn's father was a wheelwright and his mother helped in the kitchen of the neighboring *seigneur*, like Beethoven's. In his natal hamlet of Rohrau and the larger village of Hainburg Franz Joseph Haydn passed the first eight years of his impoverished youth in a material misery from which he would be long in escaping.

But in Hainburg he was housed with a school-teacher who also was master of the choir and taught him. The boy, all his life a worker, learned to sing and to play a little on the violin and harpsichord. His soprano was good enough to make a place for him in the choir of St. Stephen's, Vienna, whither he departed, on the recommendation of his Hainburg teacher, in 1740, the year in which Maria Theresa half ascended the throne of the Hapsburgs and her nemesis Frederick the Great mounted his own parvenu seat and began to eye her inheritance. The child had hardly settled into the rigorous routine of the choir school when the War of the Austrian Succession precipitated the empire, Europe and the world into the great series of great wars that with only minor intermission were to last six years longer than the composer, and among whose results was to be the termination of the Holy Roman Empire itself. Haydn's roots were in the first half of the eighteenth century, and like his contemporaries he ignored in his music the political and social transformations of the second half. The courtliness of the brilliant Grétry does not waver a jot in its progress from a Bourbon setting through a French Revolution setting to a Napoleonic setting, and Haydn's most turbulent music was composed during Europe's longest period of peace in his lifetime. The true classicists did not compose autobiography.

The world has never seen another choirboy both so apt and so industrious as little Haydn. In return for food, clothing and a roof he was obliged to sing and to attend classes, but he surpassed the obligation by studying hard and by learning what he was taught and a good deal more that he investigated for himself. He acquired church Latin and a close familiarity with church music and strict counterpoint. He learned the Italian that thereafter was to be his preferred speech, since his German was dialectal and Italian was the speech of music. He practised the violin and harpsichord, on neither of which was he ever to achieve more than competence, and made some attempts at composition.

He came out of St. Stephen's—dismissed when his soprano underwent the pangs of manhood—with a musical equipment far superior to that of an ordinary graduate and sufficient to earn for him a living in music ever afterwards. His history during this time is obscure but has been enlivened by anecdotes, most of them untrue but some enlightening, true or not. One story concerns an escape from the Worse than Death: when his voice began to break and the hoots attracted consternation, someone of authority made the practical recommendation that for the greater glory of God, Franz Joseph Haydn's soprano be salvaged by the venerable process of gelding its owner. The boy's father intervened to preserve the son's body and talent intact, but the thought of this near-miss draws out the sweat from lovers of music. The composer himself used to tell the story.

The four years between his dismissal from the Cathedral and his twenty-first birthday were passed in the unsavory underworld of music. To eat, he sang with bands of street musicians who infested Vienna's precincts, and he gave harpsichord lessons for a pittance. But he met the poet and librettist Metastasio, and the singing-master Porpora, who also composed, and who instructed the young man in return for menial services. Haydn began to compose, and through his new connections met others influential in the world and in music. He obtained more pupils, who led to other associations that aided him, and he gradually escaped from indigence. A countess presented him to a baron who presented him to a count who employed him as conductor and composer at an annual salary. The composer was then twenty-five years old.

His existence until 1757 seemed to promise at most a career as a rather disreputable hack, but two characteristics help solve the enigma of his transformation. One is the diligence, noted above, that kept him studying even while he fell asleep, and the other is the desire he aroused in people to do something for him. Someone with the proper influence was always at hand when Haydn needed him, and this must be attributed to the liking inspired for his sturdy, honest character. Not for him the fatal hostilities of Mozart or the magnetic truculence of Beethoven,

the one inviting opposition and the other over-
riding it—Haydn's simple warmth and unpre-
tentiousness brought friends to him clamoring
with offers of help.

In 1761 he entered the household of Prince
Paul Anton Esterházy as assistant *Kapellmeister*,
and, after the death of that nobleman in the
following year, remained in the service of the
decedent's brother Nicholas. For nearly thirty
years Haydn was the latter's musical factotum,
a trusted upper servant who trained the musicians
and singers of the prince's establishment, conducted the orchestra, gave lessons to the prince
and the prince's family, supervised the care of
the instruments, and composed music for the
prince's pleasure. He was cloistered for most of
the months of every year at the Esterházy country place, first at Eisenstadt, then at the miniature
Versailles called Esterház, constructed in the
swamps south of the Neusiedler See just over
the border into Hungary. It was a cushioned
prison advantageous to Haydn's temperament,
although he repined at being separated from
Vienna, for what was expected from him was
music, and he had absolute authority in its presentation and skillful musicians, their every trait
familiar to him, with whom he could practise
experiments and innovations without fear of rebuke. He entered the Esterházy service an industrious but tentative hack, and emerged from
it a consummate and confident master.

Thus both obligation and opportunity second

inclination and diligence during these decades of wonderful growth. It was Haydn's duty to do what he most wanted to do, and perhaps this is the most fortunate fate that man can have. When he pleased himself most he most pleased his employer, and if such encouragement did not improve the quality of his production it increased the quantity and authority of it. The Esterházys, vastly rich, and favored by the Hapsburgs whom they served well in the army and in diplomacy, had great influence, and their patronage of Haydn spread his reputation and ultimately salvaged their own, generations after their power had all leaked away.

Esterház was in effect a minor court, where the prince received his vassals and peers and entertained his empress. The entertainments were the hunt and the shoot, parade and manoeuvre; and those more imaginative diversions requiring a stage: church, theatre and music. Haydn was occupied with all three, and composed besides field music for the troops and dance music for who would dance. He was the provisioner of music for the glittering palace in the princely swamp, and if the prince required a Mass Haydn made one. If it was the season for an opera, Haydn composed it. He provided symphonies with remarkable regularity, and chamber music of one type or another almost continuously. To mollify the lust of Prince Nicholas for the baryton, or viola bastarda, a string instrument now obsolete but in mid-eighteenth century popular with German musical amateurs, he composed more than a hundred divertimentos exploiting the instrument, and he wrote sonatas or concertos for piano, organ, harpsichord, flute, violin, horn, string bass or violone, cello, lute and lira organizzata.

Much of this mass of music traveled, although Haydn did not. His symphonies and quartets particularly acquired renown and were pirated and copied all over Europe. He was an international celebrity before he had ever been a hundred miles from his rustic refuge. No composer was so widely imitated as Haydn, and it is possible for modern writers on music to say with some accuracy of a thousand pieces of music composed after 1775 that they "sound like Haydn," because from that date until the revelation of Beethoven's Second Symphony in 1803 his prescriptions were followed by most of the capable—and incapable, too—composers of Europe. His music and his person were in demand in most of the great capitals, and although he steadfastly refused the second as long as his patron Esterházy lived, the first became international property with or without his connivance.

But the prince died in 1790, and Haydn then surrendered to an offer by a German impresario domiciled in England that, for a very large honorarium, he visit London to compose and conduct there, the richest city in the world. He visited the English capital not once but two times, each a sojourn of about eighteen months. The first was a conquest such as no musician except Handel had ever had there, and the second was a confirmation of the first. Stimulated by the love accorded to his being and his music, he composed, for the rich and cultivated London burghers who went to concerts, his last twelve symphonies, those numbered now 93 through 104, a consecution of manly masterpieces that no one before or since has equaled. It is impossible not to find in the vital imaginativeness of these wonderful works evidence of the honorable gratitude of the guest-composer on his mettle to repay the honors bestowed on him. Haydn was a man who filled his contracts, real or implied; and he has been belittled for possession of such a middle-class virtue, as if it were common in the middle class or any other. Great existences are scrutinized and their faults laid bare: no one bothers to scrutinize the routine vices of the ordinary. Everyone commends Haydn warmly for having had a mistress or two, as if this expression of normality were an aberration; and most commentators deplore his honesty and plain-dealing as if they were intolerable in a great artist.

After London, Vienna became his home, that Vienna where his boyhood and young manhood had been imprisoned in bruising penury, but where during the long comfortable years of honored serfdom at Esterház he had always wanted to live. He was sixty-three years old, and in music everyone deferred to him. It is true that a new litter of young composers, stirred by the tremendous events and even greater hopes of the French Revolution then assailing all the institutions of the old Europe, were restless under the formal restrictions of the music that Haydn's imitators had made paramount, but their restlessness did not effect a tonal revolution until the old composer had laid down his quill. The least patient of them all, Beethoven, had imitated Haydn like the rest and had actually taken lessons in composing from the older master whom he disparaged and respected, and whose musical temperament was strikingly like his own. But these young men were the outposts of the eighteenth century and Haydn was *par excellence* of the eighteenth. Until the new century expunged the Holy Roman Empire, Haydn in the imperial metropolis was an adored imperial property, and in his pleasant house held a musical court of the highest influence. During the two French occupations of Vienna, in 1805 and 1809, the old man was honored by the conquerors as one of the chief glories of Europe. His preëminence was not openly deprecated anywhere, no one daring to presume rivalry with a man who was not only Austria's most enduring institution but a personality of disarming and nearly unshakable equanimity.

His creative powers failed during the last six years of his long life, and at seventy-seven he died in Vienna on the last day of May, 1809, a few days after the unprecedented victory of his countrymen at Aspern-Essling, a few weeks before the expected catastrophe of his countrymen at Wagram.

There was little strife in the career of this professional. He was quilted in music against the ferment of ideas and the struggles of armies that tore asunder the traditions of his age. In a spectacular era of disputation this composer without truculence composed; and however admirable and valuable his relentless pertinacity was to music, it was fatal to biography, which to be dramatic needs a larger field than a cloister and a desk. Among all the commanding figures in music Haydn was the most aloof from the great events of his day. He acquiesced in the currents consecrated by the court of Vienna. He was devout without being particularly religious. (He prefixed *In nomine Domini* and appended *Laus Deo* to every one of his symphonic scores, an amusing ritual that touches a little, in its mixture of faith and prudence.) His dabble in freemasonry has the opposite of revolutionary significance, since among the membership was Joseph II, Holy Roman Emperor.

He was not a student except in music, his curiosity being idle rather than sustained, so that what he learned was generally unimportant or wrong. He read little, and was a poor linguist at a time when three, four or five languages were customary in the equipment of men who had accomplished something. His German was bad, and he spoke by preference Italian, the language of music. He had perhaps the human minimum of waspishness, seldom speaking in denigration of anyone (although he would not speak favorably of music he considered bad), and a surpassing capacity for loyalty, attested by his continuance with the Esterházys long after the patronage had become unnecessary to him, his toleration of an awful wife, his maintenance of a tiresome mistress, his devotion to Mozart and his cleaving to old friends.

It was not hard to impose on a nature that wanted to be friendly, but it was hard to make a gull out of this son of the land whose gumption made him a successful courtier. Accepting an occasional imposition without resentment was part of the *Kapellmeister's* work, just as an ability to put to use his human attractiveness was an advantage he had no reason to reject. His benignity was real and not assumed: he had risen high and was grateful for it, but knowledge of his own merit and a dry dignity protected him completely from the offensive state of the parvenu ashamed of his arrival. The nickname "Papa," given to him at Esterház when he was young, has colored no doubt unduly the most popular concepts of Haydn, for this was merely a way of saying the "Boss," like the designation of the "Old Man" applied by troops to the commanding officer, no matter his age. The young Haydn, despite the responsibilities that he bore so manfully, clung to a boyishness far beyond its usual time, and his love of a joke is emphasized in his music from every period of his production.

As a whole, a levelheaded fellow with a normal streak of fun, faithful, discreet, capable and obstinate. An agreeable but unexciting companion, a recluse from the vital stream of eighteenth century thought, an accepter of whatever was, a conservative—not by thought but by bent— in an age when the aspirations of mankind were all directed fiercely at perfection, Haydn in himself had none of the heated stuff indispensable to a biography in itself worth writing or reading. The music was the essential stuff of this man. Haydn's excitement was poured into insatiable myriads of staves and measures, and very little overflowed to exhilarate the conditions of his physical being.

In the shockingly lazy musical writing of thirty years ago Haydn was invariably called the "Father of the Symphony," the implication being that he had invented the form. Not to venture a tiresome discursion on the mutations of meaning suffered by the word "symphony," it may be said that Haydn did not invent the word or the thing, whatever it is, but that he did compose more than a hundred musical works to which he assigned the title, that he developed the form and expanded it, and that his influence was so great that his innovations were copied and the form obtained a measure of stability when he, after eighty efforts, finally found satisfaction in the externals as he had wrought them.

Examining without pomposity Haydn's symphonic contribution, we see that it was of great importance and still is. What we ought to mean by "importance" is primarily the pleasure it gives, the basic function of music. Haydn has left a larger total of great symphonic music than any three composers combined. We can acknowledge the symphonic evolution in which Haydn influenced Mozart, gave a discipline to Beethoven and prepared a route for Schubert, without denigrating Haydn's symphonies considered as an end in themselves. Music is composed to be heard, and even the weakest of Haydn's hundred-plus symphonies have enough stamina to command attention, while perhaps seventy-five of them are safely and entirely beyond the reach of mortality as long as new music persists in thwarting the hopes once entertained for it.

When Haydn started composing, the world of music was abandoning the venerable certitudes of polyphony and fumbling for a more plastic, urbane and skeptical logic. The ascendancy of polyphony had been dictated by the superiority of the human voice to other instruments, but throughout the eighteenth century remarkable improvements were achieved in the fabrication and design of string, wind and keyboard instruments, to the encouragement of non-vocal music and simultaneously to the creation of a new type of instrumental music liberated from processes originally ordained by the qualities and limitations of the voice. Furthermore, in the second half of the eighteenth century, when churches were so severely scrutinized that all had to undergo reform, polyphony, nowhere so much at home as in the cathedral, was slighted because it implied reaction. Polyphony was not evicted— there has never been a composer who did not turn to fugue in his later years—but it was displaced as an end in itself and relegated to a more modest place in the collection of devices at a composer's disposal.

The music nourished by the new conditions emerged slowly and tentatively nearly everywhere in Europe, without proclamation but under the compulsion of the new ideals of clarity promulgated with such eloquence by the authors of the great French *Encyclopédie*, which began the intellectual subjugation of Europe in 1751. No one could possibly be further from the spirit of the ruthless interrogations, the intrepid conclusions and the rebellious recommendations of d'Alembert, Diderot and their predecessor Bayle than young Franz Joseph Haydn seeking princely patronage for a living; but in following the current of music as he found it, the composer not only obeyed directions mandatory on a new man, but did so in full ignorance that Voltaire had a greater influence on his work than Maria Theresa.

This Age of Enlightenment believed in the invincibility of reason. What could not be proved was to be laughed at; and while this incipient worship of science invited the perpetration of ludicrous hoaxes, it did diminish the fascination of older hoaxes, and in promoting a healthy skepticism it did offer nourishment to inquiry, wit, freedom of discussion and directness of examination and report. The authority of authority was denied: ideas that could not support themselves without leaning on an institution were rejected.

The air was new, fresh and exciting. Manners and the arts stepped out of the shadows and with firm vivacity substituted point and grace for decorum. As the ceremonial wig shrank in size throughout the eighteenth century and eventually disappeared, the head beneath it became less and less stuffy and dictated thoughts intended to be apprehended before they were repeated.

In music, an old word, "sonata," was given to a new product, which Haydn helped to develop. His help was principally to the symphony—sonata for orchestra—for he was not a virtuoso, and he did have an orchestra at his autocratic command. In its incipience fluctuating and tentative, this new form neverthless showed at once, and continued to show until romanticism overheated it, a liking for light, decision and directness. It established the hegemony of the Tune, a hegemony the musical public has liked better than any other. Melody henceforth was not properly to be swathed in competition: diatonic in its purest form, in a major key by perference, definite and positive in shape, it became the chief actor in the great music composed after 1760. In the preceding age the melody had been less tuneful, more a theme for contrapuntal exploitation. It was now to have the character to permit the composer full sway in its use, so that, regardless of its changed shape in embellishments of any kind, it retained its identity, and could be recognized. The enormous melodic difference between the two periods is this, that in the earlier period the nature of the exercise determined the shape of the tunes, while in the later time the shape of the tune dictated the nature of the exercise.

While the hegemony of the tune prescribed the tone of the music, its form developed by a series of adjustments and was never for long unshakably fixed. The various component traditions of sonata-form were accepted one at a time, and the experimentation and authority of Haydn were of first importance in the maintenance of sonata and symphony and quartet in a gracious and logical mould of singular plasticity. It was the lesser men of the century who let their music congeal or gasp within a framework they tried to keep obdurately tight. Haydn although a good musical scholar was never under the spell of any kind of scholasticism, and his symphonies were not composed to be parsed, but to be enjoyed by a specific and critical audience.

It is for his hundred-odd symphonies that we

love Haydn most. It is the aggregate of fresh
and versatile music in these that matters first,
but the procession of his symphonies constitutes
a perfect history of the form from the time he
found it naked until he had expanded it to fitness
for the mighty voice of Beethoven. In the very
early works the orchestra has four string parts
colored by a pair of horns or a pair each of horns
and oboes. A harpsichord supports the bass
throughout the three or four movements, which
in some cases are played without pause. There
is an abundance of writing for instruments in
solo, a relic of the baroque period just ending,
and one that Haydn was to retain, with the
abundance diminished, in most of his symphonies,
even the ones culminating his work. Few among
the first twenty symphonies last longer than
fifteen minutes, and several last less than ten.
The first movements are usually in a simple
binary form, and do not display that contrast
of themes that later characterized nearly all
sonata-allegros. The themes themselves, although
invariably clear and straightforward, are often
more easily remembered by their meter than by
their tune. The symphonies of fifty of his contemporaries resemble these early ones by Haydn,
and it would be unfair to the best of them to
assert that Haydn's were consistently better.

But if Johann Stamitz, Karl Stamitz, Cannabich
and Wagenseil wrote symphonies on a par with
those of Haydn's youth, and two sons of Bach,
John Christian and Karl Philip, rose above

Haydn's early standard, Haydn's unremitting growth fostered a progressive eloquence of symphonic expression whose like was not approached by those excellent composers. In taking the lead in symphonic development Haydn did not mark time until he had reached a plateau of his own making. His symphonies comprise the biography of the Symphony.

Mozart, who wrote a dozen symphonies that Haydn could not surpass, had no corresponding symphonic influence; for the younger composer, in his improvements on the Haydn model, was imitating that model, whereas Haydn provided his own innovations. It is quite possible that no one composed so much music to which the word "amiable" may be accurately applied as Haydn, and he has been derided for this, musical thinking esteeming heartbreak more highly than heartbeat; but Haydn it was who interrupted his amiability half a dozen times with symphonies of dark staccato passion against Mozart's two imitative ventures; and Haydn again who in fifty works proved the diversity of charm inherent in witty, humorous and funny episodes. As for technical advances, they are very impressive to who will listen to say a dozen symphonies each composed in a different year, and reproduced in the order of their composition. As an example of mastery promoted by experience, there is nothing quite like this demonstration in art. The increasing authority of harmonic progressions, the growth of naturalness in thematic development, and the mounting *rightness* of orchestration evoke immediate recognition, while behind them are sensed as positively, if less demonstrably, the agile controls of a musical mind remarkably, sensitive to and ever more learned in the niceties of cohesiveness and proportion.

So, too, with the quartets for strings. Haydn's donation to this form exceeded that of anyone else in the line of its development and in the quantity of great exemplars. His influence made the string quartet peculiarly the music of his time, to a degree that every quartet composed since Beethoven and Schubert seems an anachronism, lame or labored or pretentious. The quartets existing when Haydn was very young, and that he set himself to emulate until he perceived their barrenness, were in general divertimentos or suites in which a violin was accompanied by the dependent other strings. He made this unpromising and colorless field to flower. His seventy-seven quartets, issued in pushes usually of six or three at a time, irregularly but with about half appearing after he was fifty—and these are the best—constitute a history to give the greatest gratification to creator and auditor, for every push is an obvious ascent, and the last, the two quartets of Op. 77, when compared to the first, Op. 1, composed forty years earlier, soars infinitely higher than anyone could have dared to hope.

So much space has been devoted to symphony and quartet because Haydn's contribution to those forms is his principal glory. The vocal music, especially that written in his maturity, is not inferior but has more formidable rivalry from other composers. Out of more than twenty operas none holds the stage today despite a musical beauty that would have crowned a number as masterpieces if they had had more fortunate librettos. Much of the church music is characterized by the infectious liveliness of a man rejoicing that belief came easily to him, and *The Creation* and *The Seasons* are established in human affections like old family dogs. In the thirteen* Masses extant at least twelve are far more generous with jubilation than with sanctimony, and the exuberant scoring of several won for them that manna of churchly prohibition on which great art thrives. These Masses, and particularly the last six, express a virile, unashamed conviction of an ultimate all-powerful, all-knowing, all-loving Father that transfigures the shopworn rote of the liturgy. In another period this could seem less extraordinary, but the superior church music then most esteemed by the cultivated class was marked less by adoration than by urbanity, and the glorification of godhood in music has no more inner concern with piety than the swapping of benefices. Haydn's Masses enthrall the music-lover without repelling the devout. The consummate musicianship of these culminating works—the "Windband" Mass, No.

* One of two that had been lost has recently been found by Mr. H. C. Robbins Landon.

14, was the last major composition completed by Haydn—is invariably admired and needs no further eulogy, but the epic counterpoint earns a special word of awe-struck praise for its statement of universality without obtrusion, permitting the most elaborate interweaving to hide its learning and to sound natural and indeed inevitable.

The concertos have had to suffer a good deal of condescension from the criticism, long in vogue, that would not tolerate what was not distended. It was said that they had no importance. Neither has a pretty girl, considered cosmically, and described in such a lexicon. The concertos are diversions designed to captivate, and justify no graver reproach from hearers than that it is shameful to infatuate so effortlessly. Except those with wind instruments solo they are in general disdained by virtuosos, whose livelihood comes from showier music, and only one each among those for keyboard and those for violin may be found on conventional programs. That is why so many people depend on records.

The attraction of the instrumental music of less than orchestral scope is greatest in the quartets and in some of the trios. Interest in the sonatas and the many divertimentos in which the baryton was originally featured is naturally dispersed and uneven. The triple handicap of being *pièces de circonstance*, of being fitted to the capacity of the prince who had ordered and would play them, and of submitting to the limitations of a short-lived, freakish thing like the viola bastarda has kept most of the baryton pieces on the shelf, while the best of the sonatas are a small world of ingenious but by no means obvious invention, with an initial appeal in general too slight to persuade the idle listener that patience will bring a real and growing enjoyment.

Strewn among the works of large dimension, which comprise by far the greater part of Haydn's production, are several hundred smaller things for voice or instrument, chorus or orchestra. The few to which a reluctant hearing is granted incite an appetite for more, for the veriest tyro in Haydn has learned that what impresarios offer the public of this composer is no better than what they keep silent. The appalling old patterns of selection held a dictatorship for more than a hundred years and are now discredited: we no longer rely on eight * symphonies and a dozen quartets and abridgements of two oratorios for the entertainment offered by the composer of a thousand works. The symphonic creation is put at the top of the Haydn list not because of the consummate art of a few, but because so many are consummate. We have learned not to despise the songs just because the symphonies are greater, and we no longer sniff at the shorter pieces because they are short. The

---

* No. 45, "Farewell"; No. 88, "Letter V"; No. 92, "Oxford"; No. 94, "Surprise"; No. 100, "Military"; No. 101, "Clock"; No. 103, "Drumroll"; No. 104, "London."

earlier quartets are not now dismissed as mere preparations for the later ones, and we are even gradually learning that Nicholas Esterházy's prisoner composed great music for the stage.

The grandeur, the poignancy, the manhood, the wit, the learning and the struggle distributed in his music have been hidden or diluted in a fragmentary presentation and by the contagion of an obstinate, fulsome and slobbering folktale that has depicted the mighty artist as a "Papa" Haydn born old and slavish, the composer of a long simper. We know better now, musical writing having improved here and there to affirm what the phonograph proves. No one who has heard half the Haydn recorded will ever condescend to him again.

The music of Haydn is herein divided for convenience into these general classes, alphabetically
presented: Chamber Music, Instrumental Music,
Miscellaneous, Orchestral Music, Vocal Music.
Each of these classes is subdivided alphabetically
into its titular elements, like this, under Orchestral Music: Concertos, Dances, Overtures, Symphonies.

The relative placing of an edition in its listing
reflects the relative rank ascribed to it here.
When several editions are considered of equivalent value the text so says. The black line
employed wherever conditions permit, dividing
the various editions into two sections, must always be interpreted to mean that the editions
above it are unmistakably and convincingly more
attractive than the ones below it. It is important
to note that the sections are relative to each
other and not to an absolute, for some of the
editions below the line are in fact very good
albeit overshadowed by what must be, in such
cases, outstanding records. The separation is
devised to let readers know, in a wink, whether
it is worth while to replace one version by another: if their edition is listed below the line
readers would do well to replace it by an edition
above.

All records are twelve-inch, two-faced, 33⅓
rpm LP's unless noted to be other.

The abbreviations used ought to be self-explanatory.

The duration indicated refers only to the work under immediate consideration, and does not include other music on the same record or in the same album. Such associated material, when it appears, is indicated within parentheses following the manufacturer's code number.

# CHAMBER MUSIC*

THAT THIS SECTION is virtually limited to the
quartets and trios is not meant to imply that
Haydn's chamber music contains nothing else.
He composed more than two hundred other
works that could be embraced by the rubric,
most of them called "divertimentos" and a number called by several titles, but in Haydn "divertimento" covers many pieces that are decidedly
not chamber music, and on records a confusion
of transcriptions joins a chaos of titles in a carni-
val of bafflement impossible to rationalize except
by the creation of a special catch-all section,
"Miscellaneous," designed to include all the music
whose titles are not exactly or completely or
satisfactorily destined to be somewhere else.
Many of Haydn's cozy instrumental combinations were intended for use outdoors, and one
balks at calling such things chamber music; while
a number of true pieces of chamber music bear
the same titles as the outdoor works. Among the

* Music for three or more instruments, but not of
orchestral scope.

57

things heaped together under "Miscellaneous" are divertimentos, field-partitas (*Feldpartien*), nocturnes, marches, serenades and scherzandos.

## QUARTETS FOR STRINGS

How many quartets Haydn composed is a matter of definition. How they should be numbered depends on definition and expediency. Where there are so many we must have a method of identification, and several methods of numeration have been tried without unanimous acceptance. Helpful nicknames are sparse, and a designation like "Op. 76, No. 6" is cumbersome. Furthermore, the opus numbers assigned by Haydn's publishers are misleading in the failure of the opus indications to reflect the correct chronology of Haydn's quartets. We need a corrective to the inaccurate impression left by these opus numbers; and if we call Op. 3, No. 6 the Nineteenth Quartet we shall efface the illusion that the low opus number denotes the music of a tyro.

Years ago it was conceded that Haydn composed seventy-six quartets. Later is was assumed that the total should be eighty-three: was not each of *The Seven Last Words* in the quartet version assigned one seventh of Op. 51? Then Miss Marion Scott uncovered an early effort (No. 1 in E-flat) written before the eighty-three (or seventy-six), and there was some agreement that the definitive total of Haydn quartets is eighty-four. But musicology is never static, and concerned itself at once with Op. 1, No. 5, which is no more than the string parts of what had first been a primitive symphony: back to eighty-three.

In influential circles this kind of learned monkeyshines often arouses a choked excitement that can cause mischief. What we want is the convenience of a fixed numeration that is in fact a system of appellation, the numbers taking on significance from the music. We do not want the numbers engraved in quicksand. We accept the convenience of the official order of 104 symphonies (the product of the research made by Mandyczewski, in connection with the complete edition of Haydn's music, which was only partially published) although we know now that there are actually 107 symphonies and that some of the original total are chronologically misplaced. We do not need to remember which those are: musicologists will know, because of the extraordinary scholarship of H. C. Robbins Landon, who has proven the authenticity of the new total of symphonies, and others will not much care. A Haydn Appendix might be of service as the Köchel Appendix to Mozart and the Grove Appendix to Beethoven have been. *Leonora III* as a title has acquired a magic that no one thinks of dispelling by correcting it to *Leonora II*. And there is no convenience in instability.

The numeration used here is quite simply the one before the last of the more-or-less accepted, with the addition of Miss Scott's discovery introduced as Number One (Op. 0), and with the retention of Op. 1, No. 5. Opus 1 was published in a set of six, and the omission of Op. 1, No. 5—because of its wind parts—would create a gratuitous mystification. Here it is called No. 6.* Op. 51, *The Seven Last Words*, in its quartet form could be listed acceptably as a quartet, but it seems better to list it as supplementary, as the quartet version of *The Seven Last Words*. We then have seventy-seven quartets, and Op. 103, the last, unfinished, one, is No. 77.

Record labels will not often be found in agreement with this system, or with any.

No. 1, IN E-FLAT
No. 2, IN B-FLAT, OP. 1, No. 1, "LA CHASSE"
No. 3, IN E-FLAT, OP. 1, No. 2
No. 4, IN D, OP. 1, No. 3
No. 5, IN G, OP. 1, No. 4
No. 7, IN C, OP. 1, No. 6

These are treated as a group because they were so issued and because there are no competing versions.

It is natural in music-lovers to think of these very early works as divertimentos, with their five movements that include a second Minuet,

---

* Quartet No. 6, the fifth of Op, 1, is not included in the recordings of the Schneider Quartet, but exists in an edition of its symphonic original.

their superficial and pleasing song, their casual
resistance to the enormous potentiality of the
four instruments in congress, which Haydn himself more than any other was to elucidate during
the next fifty years. There is a certain inevitable
similarity among the tentative essays, a default
of distinctive character that could make one or
another salient from the rest. But we note incipient traits that Haydn later glorified, and an
uncluttered melodic clarity which in later years
was to be apotheosized into the most brilliant
light even when most elaborately embellished.

Schneider records are the principal conveyors
of Haydn quartets: one of the dearest projects of
the original Haydn Society was the registration
of all seventy-seven confided to this group, and
when financial night dimmed that society's bright
hopes, time had been found for forty-five of the
quartets and *The Seven Last Words.* A large
majority of these exist only in the Schneider
records, and the good judgment of the Haydn
Society in choosing those musicians for the bold
undertaking is the good fortune of music-lovers.
I do not know in what direction one might wish
changed their performance of these lively, affable
and unassuming early quartets. It is significant
that no one else has essayed them on records—
any of the first seventeen. Collectors to whom
the form is intimidating will find very little that
can be called austere in the frank and infectious
playing of the four instruments. I am inclined
to say that the group undertook in advance to

avoid any appearance of recherché fussing in their delivery of the forthright formations of eminently perspicuous music, so positive are the vigor and clarity of their attack.

These records date from 1952 and are superior in sound to most quartet records made before or since. Probably resemblance to the original is more admired in this kind of recording than in any other except of the piano; and here the engineers have managed a crisp and smooth reality with imperceptible help from the dangerous factor of reverberation. One would call the reproduction matter of fact; and in the half art of recording the art of music, one calls the matter of fact excellent.

—Schneider Qt. Three 12-in HAYDN SOCIETY HSQ-A. 18, 16, 18, 14, 21, 19 min. (The disks are available separately, with the Quartets in consecutive pairs, on HSQ-1, 2 and 3.)

## No. 18, IN F, OP. 3, No. 5

This is a quartet with which to begin a novitiate in chamber music. It is all fragrant and agile charm, disarming in rhythmic simplicity and melodic grace, light in construction but durable in its attraction. The second movement, *andante cantabile*, an airy song sung by the muted first violin over the other instruments plucked, is often played alone in transcription. It is hard for good musicians to spoil this music, and the recorded versions are satisfactory although dis-

tinctly different. I like the natural responses of
the Amadeus group best, and the rather hurried,
rather weak (but silken) delivery of the Grillers
least. The Quartetto Italiano, best of the world's
quartets on those occasions when their style does
not affront the music they are playing, introduce
some suave and subtle languors into a piece not in
need of any, and weaken the Minuet a little, but
in compensation give a variety of expression and
of tonal glow not heard from their rivals. They
and the Grillers have been accorded satisfactory
reproduction, the Grillers' with better bite, while
a very strong reverberation unfortunately tints
the Amadeus edition with artificiality. This big,
round, reënforced sound is not unpleasant in itself, but our knowledge that it is wrong makes it
seem unpleasant.

—Quartetto Italiano. ANGEL 35185 (with _Qt. No.
70_).* 17 min.              ,   ,

—Griller Qt. 10-in. LONDON LS-656 (with _Mo-
zart: Qt. No. 6_). 12 min.

——Amadeus Qt. 12-in. WESTMINSTER XWN
18609 (with _Qt. 77 and String Trios, Op. 53,
Nos. 1, 2 and 3_). 14 min.

## No. 20, IN C, OP. 9, No. 1 †

* Obviously the nature of the music and the quality of
the recording of items joined in a single issue to the work
under immediate consideration will affect the selections
made by readers. The writer has rigorously avoided any
consideration whatever of such collateral material in his
estimates of comparative value. In all cases these refer
only to the work under scrutiny in its place in the discography—in the present instance to Quartet No. 18.

No. 21, IN E-FLAT, OP. 9, No. 2 †
No. 22, IN G, OP. 9, No. 3 †
No. 23, IN D MINOR, OP. 9, No. 4 †
No. 24, IN B-FLAT, OP. 9, No. 5 †
No. 25, IN A, OP. 9, No. 6 †


No. 26, IN E, OP. 17, No. 1
No. 27, IN F, OP. 17, No. 2
No. 28, IN E-FLAT, OP. 17, No. 3
No. 29, IN C MINOR, OP. 17, No. 4
No. 30, IN G, OP. 17, No. 5
No. 31, IN D, OP. 17, No. 6

Have more originality, much more profundity
and a more elaborate organization than any of
the preceding quartets, and feature carefully
worked and thoughtful slow movements (in
every case following the Minuet). Haydn was
nearly forty when he composed them, and we
can feel him reaching toward a deeper expressiveness in a form still unfixed and docile to who
would control it. I do not think he controls it
here: the spontaneity of the breezier early works
has been compromised by preoccupations with
betterment. These quartets are spotted with dis-
continuous beauties that betray their position of
transition between divertimento and sonata: the
architect is in conflict with the decorator. Few
of the movements except the very lively finales,
the opening *moderato* of No. 29, its dashing
Minuet, and three of the four in No. 30, sustain
a deep interest unless we are fascinated by an

unparalleled opportunity to hear a man thinking his way to greatness.

Alone again, the Schneider Quartet have undertaken to have performances recorded. In view of the relative unfamiliarity of the music and its failure to conform consistently to any dominant style, the mellow good sense of the playing deserves to be called remarkable. The problems are not evaded or mollified but are given as Haydn left them, with warm honesty and pleasant tone. There is an excess of recitative and declamation in these quartets, much of it leading nowhere, and it seems to me that the players show nice discrimination in allowing just enough eloquence to expose the intent without emphasizing the shortcoming. Sonically the records are agreeable and respond easily to the old Columbia curve, but the bass loses authority and force in a vague articulation. Some collectors like the euphony generally a product of this slighting of crispness.

Those intending to buy these quartets two at a time are warned of the curious distribution of the first four in the set.

—Schneider Qt. Three 12-in. HAYDN SOCIETY HSQ-E. 20, 18, 20, 20, 20, 17 min. (The disks are available separately, with *Qts. No. 26 and 29* on HSQ-13, *Nos. 27 and 28* on HSQ-14; *Nos. 30 and 31* on HSQ-15.)

No. 32, IN E-FLAT, OP. 20, No. 1
No. 33, IN C, OP. 20, No. 2

No. 34, in G minor, Op. 20, No. 3
No. 35, in D, Op. 20, No. 4
No. 36, in F minor, Op. 20, No. 5
No. 37, in A, Op. 20, No. 6

Known as the "Sun" Quartets from an engraving, on an early title-page, of the sun mounting, the imposing set comprising Op. 20 were called in Haydn's lifetime quite naturally the "Great" Quartets, so greatly and so obviously did they transcend existing works in the form. Composed in 1772, only a year later than those of Op. 17, they are free of the tentatives that make those less than completely satisfying, and strike out boldly into the domain of feeling. They seem to be—and quite possibly were in fact—guided by scenarios, from which the stronger emotions are not excluded, but they are not labored and they are relieved by long sections and whole movements of pure design. There is a stinging variety of mood and movement, with one quartet (No. 4) almost entirely gay, another (No. 5) persistently somber, three utilizing fugues in their finales, one whose *Adagio* is called *capriccio*, one with a gypsy Minuet, and several with prankish episodes. I cannot find grounds to favor one consistently over the others, but Nos. 32, 33 and 37 have in their first movements the quickest enticement.

The records of the Schneider Quartet are of a quality to have terrified all competitors, except one, into silence, and the one challenge, in the F Minor Quartet, is strongly only in the central movements, slipping into routine for the allegros. The heartiness of participation in the Schneider disks is an uncommon virtue in such unfamiliar music as that of Op. 20. The care in preparation and gusto in delivery are what we should expect in performances of the "Emperor" and "Lark" quartets, and the intelligent point of the phrasing, the good proportions among the instruments, the sensitivity to subtle variation, are what we find only in the best organizations. Bold, clean reproduction of unusual merit confirms the value of the playing and compels the strongest recommendation for the records; with the proviso, however, that they be reproduced without cutting their high volume to a soft emission that blurs their incisiveness.

—Schneider Qt. Three 12-in. HAYDN SOCIETY HSQ-F. 19, 22, 21, 21, 22, 17 min. (Records are available separately, the Quartets in consecutive pairs, as HSQ-16, 17 and 18.)

—Vienna Philharmonic Qt. (*No. 36* only). TELEFUNKEN 66034 (with *Schubert: Qt., No. 10*). 18 min.

"RUSSIAN" QUARTETS ("THE JOKES")

The six quartets of Op. 33 are known as the "Russian" Quartets or as *The Jokes* (*Gli Scherzi*), the latter because their capering minuets were designated by the composer either *scherzo* or *scherzando*. Nothing is Russian in them but their dedication to a grand duke, who as Tsar Paul I became the saddest figure among the tormented and reeling monarchs who saw the French Revolution explode. (Rather prepossessing son of the Great Catherine, his equanimity was disturbed by such jocularities of his hating mother as her professed dismay at the circumstances of his paternity, which she could not quite vouch for, torn as she was between the reasonable probability of several, including her husband, Peter III, whom she had suppressed, and a few close friends. Madness distinguished his short reign, which ceased by strangulation; and Haydn's six quartets are the best memory we have of him.) Composed nine years after Op. 20, they flourish a startling progress in sonata form, especially the first, which adheres recognizably to the pattern in three of its four movements.

### No. 38, in B minor, Op. 33, No. 1 ***

Like the rest of Op. 33 this No. 38 flashes strong contrasts of disposition shamelessly, and one of the admirable features of the Schneider Quartet is their gusto in stipulating such contrasts. Their playing for the record is knowing and healthy, and the strong reproduction, with full value to viola and cello, is excellent.

—Schneider Qt. HAYDN SOCIETY HSQ-19 (with *Qt. No. 39*). 18 min.

### No. 39, in E-flat, "The Joke," Op. 33, No. 2 ***

The special joke of this one, earning the special title within the general nickname, is some enter-

taining foolishness in the Finale, a portentous
balking in a flurry of confetti. Only the Largo is
serious in a good-natured and animated quartet
of which the phonograph has three praiseworthy .
editions fundamentally alike. Robustness and candor, more palpable from the strong registration,
distinguish the Schneider essay; candor and comfort and a mellower stroke feature the Pascal,
and refinement the Budapest; but the principal
contours are the same in all. The various indi-
vidualities are not overworked, and I do not
believe that in this music any one style is intrinsi-
cally superior to any other when none is exag-
gerated. Comparative sound is not a determinant
since the three records are of high and approxi-
mately equal order, although the Schneider is
most forceful and most notable in articulation,
the Budapest has a delicate warmth, and the
Pascal, rich in the lower instruments, is entirely
free of strain. My own preference fluctuates between Schneider and Pascal, but it is easy to sum-
mon a plausible reasoning in favor of any.
—Schneider Qt. HAYDN SOCIETY HSQ-19 (with
*Qt. No. 38*). 19 min.
—Pascal Qt. 10-in. MMS 47 (with *Qt. No. 70*).
15 min.
—Budapest Qt. Two 12-in. COLUMBIA SL-225
(with *Brahms: Qts. Nos. 1, 2 and 3*). 17 min.

No. 40, IN C, "THE BIRD," OP. 33, No. 3 ***
Plaintive, whimsical chirps in the first movement
and cuckoo-clucks in the last give this charming

quartet its name and a popularity not vouchsafed to the other elements of Op. 33. We shall encounter this suasion of the sobriquet often, particularly in the symphonies. Both records here are beguiling, and I have several times reversed my opinion on which is better. At present I am inclined to the feeling that the admirably distinct etching of the sound given to the Schneiders gives an advantage to their disk that the highly competent but less compelling sonics of the other cannot dispute. The Italians offer a heated grace and very strong sweep of dynamics against a steadier and neater performance in which the Schneiders achieve a marked distinction of line.
—Schneider Qt. HAYDN SOCIETY HSQ-20 (with *Qt. No. 41*). 19 min.
—Quartetto Italiano. ANGEL 35297 (with *Qt. No. 72*). 20 min.

### No. 41, IN B-FLAT, OP. 33, No. 4 ***

The neglect of this characteristic quartet, loaded with good humor and easily assimilable, is typical of the treatment accorded to much of Haydn's best work when it has no literary or anecdotal auxiliary like the single record's overside, the "Bird." That record is recommended for its playing and recording although neither has the overside's assurance.
—Schneider Qt. HAYDN SOCIETY HSQ-20 (with *Qt. No. 40*). 17 min.

### No. 42, IN G, OP. 33, No. 5 ***

The central movements of this stunning quartet patently had a sway on Beethoven, the *scherzo* particularly. I find the grave contemplation of the G minor *largo cantabile*, its song largely entrusted to the first violin, a little casual in the Schneider version, as if the musician feared to be maudlin; but elsewhere the performance is sturdy and intelligent, and the sound is excellent. —Schneider Qt. HAYDN SOCIETY HSQ-21 (with *Qt. No. 43*). 20 min.

### No. 43, IN D, OP. 33, No. 6 ***

The reproduction of the last of the "Russian" Quartets, which is profuse with tricky inventiveness, demands in the Schneider version careful setting of the controls, in view of the high volume of this record and the abundance of material for the violins high and loud. Unusually effective under proper adjustment, the sound can cause distress through an apparatus not adjusted to its difficulties. The performance is forceful and convincing. —Schneider Qt. HAYDN SOCIETY HSQ-21 (with *Qt. No. 42*). (The three records of the Schneider version of Op. 33 may be had as a unit in HAYDN SOCIETY HSQ-G, with an album and notes.)

### No. 44, IN D MINOR, OP. 42

The only complete quartet of Haydn's published alone, No. 44 is simple but not guileless, glibly self-confident but not assertive, as appealing as a May breeze. I take mild exception to the Adagio as the Schneiders give it, a rich adjustment of the vertical values and a constriction of the innate tenderness of its musing theme, since I prefer the essence to the aura and they could well have lingered a trifle; but they make a capital entertainment out of the rest. Competent sonics although a little strained, and the least striking reproduction noticed for this group so far.

—Schneider Qt. HAYDN SOCIETY HSQ-37 (with *Qt. No. 75*). 15 min. (Also available in HSQ-M, with *Qts. No. 75, 76 and 77*, two 12-in. with album and notes.)

No. 45, IN B-FLAT, OP. 50, No. 1
No. 46, IN C, OP. 50, No. 2
No. 47, IN E-FLAT, OP. 50, No. 3
No. 48, IN F-SHARP MINOR, OP. 50, No. 4
No. 49, IN F, OP. 50, No. 5
No. 50, IN D, OP. 50, No. 6

Frederick the Great, who died in 1786, played the flute. He was succeeded by his nephew Frederick William II, who played the cello. This is the only respect in which the nephew improved on his uncle. The cellist was a Rosicrucian, whose mysticism failed to prevail against stern rational swords wielded by the Generals Hoche and Jourdan, who cut away the Rhine provinces from Prussia for the benefit of revolutionary France. Frederick William expired be-

fore this work was complete, leaving a remarkably anomalous impression as the guy of all Europe except the musical, of which he was the
darling. Haydn dedicated these quartets to the
king and Mozart was to dedicate his last three to
the same monarch, who tried to employ the best
musicians of the time, along with the queerest
philosophers and the worst generals.

So Haydn's quartets are the "Prussian" Quartets. They are sophisticated and esteemed and
rarely played. We have found out by this time
that frequency of performance has nothing to
do with the merit of Haydn's music: musicians
follow an obedient road ordained by unreflecting
custom. It is disagreeable to realize that the
audacity and devotion that prompted the Haydn
Society to issue this music resulted in financial
distress. This means that there are Haydnists
without this edition of the "Prussian" quartets,
probably because the Schneider Quartet's patent
abilities have not received the publicity invariably lavished on those who do not deserve it.

These are splendid records, a clear and strong
sound according well with the direct bowing
and transparent delineation of the nimble, resourceful counterpoint so abundant in Op. 50.
Good records are superior in this particular to
good concerts unless the latter are in intimacy:
the lines are more easily distinguishable. Note
that the sonic characteristics are not identical
in the six quartets. Several have an incipient edgi-
ness that must be blunted by the controls at the

reproducer. Try the third of the set as an apéritif for the rest.

—Schneider Qt. Three 12-in. HAYDN SOCIETY HSQ-H. 20, 21, 19, 23, 16, 19 min. (Records available separately, the Quartets in consecutive pairs, as HSQ-22, 23 and 24.)

## No. 51, IN G, OP. 54, No. 1 †

## No. 52, IN C, OP. 54, No. 2 ***

Few of Haydn's quartets are easier to like than this one that mingles a certain harmonic boldness with positive and clean-cut melodies. The Kroll Quartet are almost invariably persuasive in music essentially classical, warming the content while keeping the form chaste, and this would be a saliently attractive record were it not for some oddity in the sound. The absence of reverberation gives a real sense of proximity but cramps the violins, and after passages in which cello and viola are impressively lifelike appear sections where the tone is denatured.

—Kroll Qt. ALLEGRO 58 (with *Qt. No. 75*). 17 min.

## No. 57, IN C, OP. 64, No. 1

Unexpected tricks and a general airy inconsequence are diverting but need more understanding than the musicians give them in the only recording. One longs for an occasional whiplash in the long relaxation. Whining, wiry violins spoil the sonics.

—Vienna Konzerthaus Qt. Westminster XWN 18603 (with *Qt. No. 58*). 25 min.

## No. 58, in B minor, Op. 64, No. 2

There is so much spaciousness to the sound of the one record here that the violins rattle metallically and the control-unit can mollify but not cure them. Too bad; the performance is vivacious and the music full of harsh and cheerful fancies mixed.
—Vienna Konzerthaus Qt. Westminster XWN 18603 (with *Qt. No. 57*). 19 min.

## No. 59, in B-flat, Op. 64, No. 3

Wonderful music, good performance, violins ugly in reproduction. I think collectors would be wise to wait for new editions before deciding on the sad Wesminster versions of Op. 64 (except No. 6) in which the violins are at best unpretty.
—Vienna Konzerthaus Qt. Westminster XWN 18604 (with *Qt. No. 60*). 23 min.

## No. 60, in G, Op. 64, No. 4

The note under No. 59, immediately above, applies here.
—Vienna Konzerthaus Qt. Westminster XWN 18604 (with *Qt. No. 59*). 20 min.

## No. 61, in D, "Lark," Op. 64, No. 5 ***

Strange that the most often played and most persistently lyrical of the Haydn quartets should still be waiting for a thoroughly satisfactory record. That three of the four editions have been withdrawn points to a certain discontent in the reception of them, but the one remaining in the catalogues is as a whole as bad as any.

The best sound, given to the American Art Quartet on an inexpensive RCA Bluebird, is not first class; and the best performance (by far) is carried by the oldest sonics. This is the Budapest, the only interpretation to get beneath the skin. Next are the Americans, with poetry in their *adagio cantabile* and a nimbly scurried Finale alternating with a routine presentation of the other two movements. The Vienna effort is merely proficient, and in reproduction the violins hurt, while the Hungarian Quartet are a little weak and their sound is a little tame. Thus the Budapest record is the only possible choice in spite of mediocre sound. However, it serves, its faults of age being unaggressive, the most serious a weakness of instrumental definition.

—Budapest Qt. COLUMBIA ML-4216 (with *Qt. No. 72*), discontinued. 18 min.

---

—American Art Qt. RCA LBC-1073 (with *Beethoven: Qt. No. 10*), discontinued. 17 min.
—Vienna Konzerthaus Qt. WESTMINSTER 18015 (with *Qt. No. 58*). 18 min.
—Hungarian Qt. RCA LM-1076 (with *Mozart: Qt. No. 15*), discontinued. 18 Min.

No. 62, in E-flat, Op. 64, No. 6

The Italians have all the better of it in the playing of this luscious thing, and the Viennese win hands down in the sound. The quick imagination and taut organization of the first are sensed but incompletely heard through a woolly and toneless old disk, while the comfortable and fleshy procedure of the second is incomparably more effective in the detail allowed by the engineers and above all in the tonal suavity denied by electronics to the superior performance. The Konzerthaus performance is a good one until the other is heard; and in consequence readers are urged not to hear the other record, which will torment by hinting at a mastery it cannot reveal.

—Vienna Konzerthaus Qt. Westminster 5034 (with *Qt. No. 80*), discontinued. 22 min.

---

—Quartetto Italiano. London LL-320 (with *Boccherini: Qt., Op. 6, No. 1*), discontinued. 17 min.

No. 66, in C, Op. 74, No. 1 †

No. 67, in F, Op. 74, No. 2

The only recorded example is venerable in terms of LP and its sound is precarious. The orderly performance seems primmer and shorter in phrase than I think it really was, for the absence of reverberation, advantageous for showing articulation in the bass, thins the violins and cur-

tails their audible vibrations. The sound is small, and when brought to an effective level distorts. A curious and discomfiting record as a whole.
—Baroque Qt. PERIOD 503 (with *Mozart: Qt. No. 15*), discontinued. 18 min.

### No. 68, IN G MINOR, "HORSEMAN," OP. 74, No. 3

The catalogues groan with twenty-five proclamations of the exultant misery called the *Symphonie Pathétique,* but refuse a present place to the inexhaustible fancies of this great quartet. We need a version recorded with the modern competence of LP, for both of the retired editions are below standard, although not impossible. The Urania disk has the better, cleaner, sound, but must be reproduced at moderate volume lest the violins bare their wire; but the Roman players, capable and alert, have not the finesse of the Budapesters nor their suppleness. Nevertheless it is not unlikely that many collectors will be more impressed by the comparative crispness of the Roman totality than by the union of murkiness and acid that compromises the more masterly playing. We would all be grateful for a new Budapest edition.
—Budapest Qt. COLUMBIA ML-4029 (with *Beethoven: Qt. No. 4*), discontinued. 17 min.
—Quartetto di Roma. URANIA RS-720 (with *Verdi: Qt.*), discontinued. 18 min.

### No. 69, IN G, OP. 76, No. 1

There are more annual public performances of

the quartets of Op. 76 than of all the other Haydn quartets. This does not mean that they are uniformly the best, but it does imply the truth that only Beethoven's Op. 18 challenges this Op. 76 in offering between one pair of covers so many masterpieces of the quartet literature. Haydn composed his at sixty-five; and pray let's not dispel the miracle by trying to explain it.

The first of these quartets was composed in 1797, and its first and third movements contain noticeable bits of Franz Schubert, born that same year. It has one of those ineffable slow movements, here *adagio sostenuto, mezza voce,* that the composer lavished so incredibly in his later years; a symphonic first movement, a flip and lovely Minuet-Scherzo, and a Finale baited with surprise. The recorded performances are imposing although dissimilar, and the sonics are quite as dissimilar and a good deal less imposing. An unsympathetic chamber* dried up the Buda-

* In the Library of Congress reposes a set of Stradivari instruments whose value is so exalted that they are in effect chained within those halls fecund in learning for the occasional Congressman who might care to read. For Haydn's Op. 76 and other music the Budapest Quartet have been equally chained to the instruments, and thus imprisoned in the Library. The Elizabeth Sprague Coolidge Auditorium bears a name honored in music, but Columbia's experience with its acoustics for recording purposes offers no proof that a boxcar or a bathysphere might not be better. The Budapesters have been putting into disks the greatest masterpieces of quartet literature played on those Stradivaris in that hall, and not one of those disks has sound to compare with what Columbia can produce in less Olympian

pest sound, throttled its articulation, and coarsened its fabric at every *fort:* it is unpleasant without being striking. The best sound has been given to the taut and (comparatively) nervous playing of the Schneiders, although this bright, clean sound may be less effective than the broad and warm reproduction to be obtained from the Konzerthausers when very drastic reduction is made from the treble output, which will be ugly if the maker's recommendation to follow the RIAA curve is observed. This big spaciousness of sonics (with a pretty strong reverbation) is decidedly appropriate to a bold performance in which nothing is diminished: it is in places the most energetic of interpretations, and in the Adagio and Minuet the most sensuous. As a whole, my own taste is most satisfied by the Viennese record, but the hazards of its reproduction are abesnt from the Schneider, which I am consequently putting in the highest place. The Barchet record is worth more consideration than I originally gave it, construing its serene proportions as lassitude of the imagination. It improves with time, or perhaps I have. Its clean lines now seem admirable, and the sound is satisfactory if not faultless.

quarters. What good the Stradivaris if their blood is chilled by four wrong walls? What matter the Budapest sentience and knowledge if their strings chirp when they should sing, if viola and cello sound exhausted and desiccated? Columbia facilities and Columbia personnel produced the Schneider Quartet records for the Haydn Society, excellent records for the most part, but not made in the Library of Congress.

—Schneider Qt. HAYDN SOCIETY HSQ-34 (with *Qt. No. 70*). 19 min.

—Vienna Konzerthaus Qt. WESTMINSTER XWN 18606 (with *Qt. No. 70*). 24 min.

—Barchet Qt. RENAISSANCE 33 (with *Qt. No. 74*). 19 min.

---

—Budapest Qt. COLUMBIA ML-4922 (with *Qt. No. 70*). 18 min.

## No. 70, IN D MINOR, "QUINTET," OP. 76, No. 2 ***

In matters of tempo and phrasing I find the Budapest Quartet realizing every opportunity and every implication with spellbinding address, but the Quartetto Italiano, with whose ideas in the same respects one is more likely to disagree, give out a tone of seductive smoothness, at all intensities, to overcome resistance; for only a handful of records so sweetly present the string quartet, without scratch or strain. Admittedly the playing is not of the firmest and one must sacrifice to have this tone unless one takes a second version. Completely opposite is the brave, tense and enthusiastic attack of the Galimir group, outstanding as a unified concept, but least attractive of all in texture, perhaps because of the close recording that makes the bass real (and perhaps overstrong) and the violins tenuous. Both the Schneider and Konzerthaus records are commendable, but they lack the saliency in performance of those mentioned above, although their sound is superior to Galimir and Budapest. Please note that the Budapest registration is much more satisfactory than the Budapest of No. 69. The Pascals, never bothered by a personalized style, make a firm, strong and undeviating exposition, and the clear, spacious sonics applied to their record are almost excellent. I am constantly aware of the reverberation backing their attack, and intermittently aware of background noise.

The quartet's nickname comes from the vehement, falling fifths out of which the first movement is constructed. This is a perfect little model of contrapuntal resourcefulness, but the central movements are something more: the entrancing Andante composed with that calm mastery of fluent contemplation that characterizes Haydn's late slow movements and suggests spontaneous generation; and the evil, ungainly, fascinating Minuet, a frolic of murderers and trulls. It may not be the best of Op. 76, but none is better.

—Quartetto Italiano. ANGEL 35185 (with *Qt. No. 18*). 22 min.

—Budapest Qt. COLUMBIA ML-4922 (with *Qt. No. 69*). 19 min.

—Galimir Qt. PERIOD 504 (with *Qt. No. 71*). 17 min.

—Pascal Qt. 10-in. MMS-47 (with *Qt. No. 39*). 18 min.

—Schneider Qt. HAYDN SOCIETY HSQ-34 (with *Qt. No. 69*). 19 min.

—Vienna Konzerthaus Qt. WESTMINSTER XWN 18606 (with *Qt. No. 69*). 21 min.

No. 71, in C, "Emperor," Op. 76, No. 3

Francis II, last Holy Roman Emperor and as Francis I first emperor of Austria, Haydn's sixth monarch and a young one in 1797, received a birthday present that year from the composer, a fervent religious tune intended to fortify Austrian resistance against the spectacular encroachments in Italy of a tatterdemalion French army inspired by a general even younger than the emperor. The tune did not prevail against the soldier, but it has prevailed and flourished against time. *"Gott erhalte Franz den Kaiser"* was the Austrian anthem as long as the Austrian empire lasted, and it was pilfered by various churches for hard use under several titles (like "Glorious things of Thee are spoken") and by German nationalists who called it *"Deutschland über Alles,"* which everyone who does not know it thinks is a brazen assertion of German supremacy. It is a great tune, and Haydn wrote four variations on it for use as the slow movement of Op. 76, No. 3. The repute of this *poco adagio cantabile* has militated against the renown of the rest, three splendid movements brilliantly devised and rather uncommonly placed, the jocularity in front and the problem as Finale.

Eliminate the Konzerthaus version for its wry and unnatural sound. Eliminate the Budapest for a failure to transmit a sense of vital experience and for repeated sonic seepage ("pre-echo," "precho") from adjacent grooves. Note that the

Amadeus are the most consistently responsive to *all* the moods of the quartet, but that their reproduction will be less incisive and less pure than the Schneiders'. The latter have the best sound of all and give a convincing performance. Galimir, bright, positive and forceful, neat and imperious, are compelling except in the Adagio, which needs more oil than their style accords. Again a close and vivid sound from this group, arresting but not pretty.

—Schneider Qt. HAYDN SOCIETY HSQ-35 (with *Qt. No. 72*). 22 min.

—Amadeus Qt. RCA LHMV-1039 (with *Mozart: Qt. No. 14*), discontinued. 22 min.

—Galimir Qt. PERIOD 504 (with *Qt. No. 70*). 19 min.

---

—Budapest Qt. COLUMBIA ML-4923 (with *Qt. No. 72*). 21 min.

—Vienna Konzerthaus Qt. WESTMINSTER XWN 18607 (with *Qt. No. 72*). 27 min.

## No. 72, IN B-FLAT, "SUNRISE," OP. 76, No. 4

Above a dark accompaniment the violin soars high, and this is the "Sunrise," in the first movement. The nickname is helpful, like most of those in Haydn, and does not fit badly until we note that sonata form requires the sun to rise repeatedly. The awe and the musing regret of the Adagio hold the essence of a composer who had not yet published a quartet, Beethoven. Both Minuet and Finale are lively and assertive, giving the unusual formation of a second half all action opposed to a first half mainly contemplation.

Limbo for the Konzerthaus record, too metallic for correction. Ditto for Budapest 1954, overnice in statement and seldom agreeable in tone. The remaining three have different claims to consideration, old Budapest for its clarity and force, its straight hewing; Italian for its gift of nuance, especially in the first two movements, most especially for its ravishing Adagio; and Schneider for sustained intelligent proficiency. The last has the best sound. The Angel sonics trespass into harshness when the play is louder than *mf*, and the old Columbia sonics of the old Budapest are hearty and sonorous, impressive in the strong cello, but unpolished and not uncoarse. I think that there can be no question that the Schneiders' is the best record as a whole, but the best has not the élan of the old Budapest, and no version is quite in position to dispute the suave and successful finesse of the Italian Quartet in the two movements that contain the deeper soul of the music.

—Schneider Qt. HAYDN SOCIETY HSQ-35 (with *Qt. No. 71*). 22 min.

—Budapest Qt. (LP, 1949). COLUMBIA ML-4216 (with *Qt. No. 61*), discontinued. 22 min.

—Quartetto Italiano. ANGEL 35297 (with *Qt. No. 40*). 24 min.

---

—Budapest Qt. (LP, 1954). COLUMBIA ML-4923 (with *Qt. No. 71*). 19 min.

—Vienna Konzerthaus Qt. WESTMINSTER XWN 18607 (with *Qt. No. 71*). 24 min.

## No. 73, IN D, OP. 76, No. 5

The second movement is the great heart of this music. A Largo nearly as long as the other three movements together, it bears the admonition *cantabile e mesto*, not to be neglected; and is written in F-sharp, not an aid to intonation. It is a deep but tranquil elegy to days gone, and almost ideally apt to the broad, cordial romanticism of the Konzerthaus Quartet, whose unabashed, lingering and juicy stroke here provides one of the richest fulfillments in the Haydn quartets. The other movements I find superior in the sharper Schneider treatment, and I think that Budapest conquer in the Finale. Otherwise the last record is disappointing both in what the players convey and in what the sound makes of the conveyance. Again the Schneiders have the most thorough and the truest registration, that of the Konzerthaus, beautifully full and glowing in the Largo, inclining to coarseness in the external movements. One must choose between one version with a steadily high average and another whose erratic values include an irresistible offering of the heart of this music. I do not know how the irresistible can be resisted.

—Vienna Konzerthaus Qt. WESTMINSTER XWN 18608 (with *Qt. No. 74*). 23 min.

—Schneider Qt. HAYDN SOCIETY HSQ-36 (with *Qt. No. 74*). 21 min.

—Budapest Qt. COLUMBIA ML-4924 (with *Qt. No. 74*). 19 min.

## No. 74, IN E-FLAT, OP. 76, No. 6

Is a curious venture into repetition essayed as a constructive end in itself. Unfortunately the material is not attractive, and mere resourcefulness is not enough: otherwise Swinburne would have Shakespeare's place. Interest is not continuous and not intense, but curiously the work is not dull and it has a frail, chilly charm to offer when one has learned to expect nothing more. It is hard to say how it should be played. The Budapesters hurry through it in a way to impart some disdain, and maybe that is right. The Schneiders and the Barchets put a good deal more apparent heart into their efforts, and the Konzerthausers find more matter for serious concern than any of the others. Sonic values descend in this order: Schneider, Budapest, Barchet, Konzerthaus; which may be respectively characterized excellent, good, variable, difficult. In this case I think that the sonics are in accord with the over-all values.

—Schneider Qt. HAYDN SOCIETY HSQ-36 (with *Qt. No. 73*). 23 min.

—Budapest Qt. COLUMBIA ML-4924 (with *Qt. No. 73*). 20 min.

—Barchet Qt. RENAISSANCE 33 (with *Qt. No. 69*). 24 min.

—Vienna Konzerthaus Qt. WESTMINSTER XWN 18608 (with *Qt. No. 73*). 25 min.

(The six quartets of Op. 76 in the Schneider playing have been collected in an album as HAYDN
SOCIETY HSQ-L, and the complete Budapest version of three disks fills COLUMBIA SL-203.)

## No. 75, IN G, OP. 77, No. 1 ***

Haydn is becoming old. Intending six quartets
for dedication to Josef Franz Maximilian von
Lobkowitz, most musical ever of musical princes,
he has strength, at sixty-seven, for only two:
those are Op. 77. The prince was not cheated, for
the actual two are worth any six conceivable
after the two had drawn off their tremendous
quota of creative power. In the hierarchy of
Haydn quartets No. 75 must give precedence
only to No. 76, and anyone who is not enthralled
by it, from the breezy confidence of its opening
prance to the flippancy of the final ta-ta, is wasting his time listening to chamber music.

The three records are variously faulted in reproduction and variously admirable in performance. Schneider and Heifetz both have some
effect of dilation from their environment, more
of this in the latter; and both have too much wire
in the violins. This can be soothed away via the
control-unit in the case of Schneider, but there
is a residue of asperity in the Heifetz which re-
sists any therapy, afflicting the naturally ingrati-
ating tone of these musicians with strips of hard
cicatrice. At their best, they have the suavest
strings when the hazards of recording are able
to reveal them; and their dexterity and under-

standing are not inferior to their rivals'. I find
them and the Schneiders enough alike not to have
a preference in the playing, but the Schneiders'
sound is better although not the Schneiders' best.
The taut, muscular exposition of the Krolls is
denied the full vibrancy of the strings by a confined and rather dry sound. (The eponym of
the Heifetz Quartet is a cellist of remarkable address in chamber music, Mr. Benar Heifetz.)
—Schneider Qt. HAYDN SOCIETY HSQ-37 (with
*Qt. No. 44*). 21 min. (Also available in HSQ-M,
with *Qts. No. 44, 76 and 77*, two 12-in. with
album and notes.)
—Heifetz Qt. EMS 301 (with *Qt. No. 76*). 24
min.
Kroll Qt. ALLEGRO 58 (with *Qt. No. 52*). 20 min.

No. 76, IN F, OP. 77, No. 2
This is Haydn's last complete quartet, and although one dare not say that among the seventy-
six complete there is an indisputable best, everyone agrees that there is none better. Its greatness
is continuous, its artistry as grand in one movement as in another, all of those movements endowed with indelible distinction of character.
The miracle is that none of them makes a special
protrusion into memory as an entity: we remember the sublime Andante, as beautiful as a slow
movement can be, not of extraordinary grandeur
—like the Largo of Quartet No. 73—but as an
inherent part of a union in which no beauty is
special.

It is a surprise but not a regret that the most fashionable performers have avoided Op. 77, No. 2, for records: the two performances we have will not be abashed by competition. Between these two the differences are of minor detail and are much less significant than the differences between their respective sonics, which notably favor the Schneider disk, more cleanly chiseled, more outright and free of the violin-scratch at *forte* or louder that cannot be eliminated from the Heifetz record. Played at moderate volume, the Haydn Society effort is exceptionally true to the real values of the four instruments. It will not easily be superseded by another version.

—Schneider Qt. HAYDN SOCIETY HSQ-38 (with *Qt. No.* 77). 22 min. (Also available in HSQ-M, with *Qts. No. 44, 75 and* 77, two 12-in. with album and notes.)

—Heifetz Qt. EMS 301 (with *Qt. No. 75*). 25 min.

No. 77 (UNFINISHED), IN B-FLAT, OP. 103 ***

Two aspects of a septuagenarian's regret—part revolt and part acceptance—at his lassitude after fifty years of making music. An Andante in B-flat and a *menuetto* in D minor, the central movements of a string quartet still unfinished three years after its commencement, signal Haydn's retirement from composing. He sent the manuscript in 1806 to his publisher, with the sad visiting-card he had recently adopted, that quoted his song "The Old Man":

Gone is all my strength,
Old and weak am I.

Nothing weak in the music. Its content is philo-
sophical and its hue is dark, but the fatigue behind its creation remains concealed in the expert
ease of its construction.

The Schneider is as a whole a better record
than the Amadeus, but I am not sure that it makes
a greater musical effect. The Amadeus Quartet
have been given a registration, backed by reverberation, that suggests something larger than a
string quartet and thus is artificial; but listeners
who are not dismayed by that adjective may
find in the deep blend of the strong tone a
warmth more comfortable to their taste than
the analytic, detailed and fresh sound contrived
for Schneider. Again it is the sonics which
will decide, rather than differences of performance of less importance.

—Schneider Qt. HAYDN SOCIETY HSQ-38 (with
*Qt. No. 76*). 12 min. (Also available in HSQ-M,
with *Qts. No. 44, 75 and 76*, two 12-in. with
album and notes.)

—Amadeus Qt. 12-in. WESTMINSTER XWN
18609 (with *Qt. No. 18 and String Trios, Op.
53, Nos. 1, 2 and 3*). 11 min.

THE SEVEN LAST WORDS OF THE SAVIOUR ON THE
CROSS (Quartet Version), Op. 51 ***

In 1785 Haydn composed an amazing devotion
for orchestra, and two years later transcribed it
for string quartet. In 1796 it was converted into

an oratorio. Most accessible as a quartet, it is most often heard in that form, where indeed it is most poignant. There are nine movements: Introduction, the Seven Words and Cataclysm. The nine make a unity that should never be divided; a principle frustrated when the nine elements are considered as seven—or any other number than one—separate works.

The text, from the Vulgate, is implicit in the quartet and is easily followed, in the rhythms and inflections of the strings, by the listener who has the printed words at hand. It is enough for most of us to know the sense of each Word (meaning Sentence) in English to gather the entire tragic substance from the music. The Agony on the Cross was awfully real to Haydn, who in putting his professional mastery at the disposal of his belief made a dramatic narrative of consummate tenderness, compassion and fright. *The Seven Last Words* is not to be enjoyed merely as music. Unless one is willing to be a spectator at Calvary one will hear a solemn procession of *graves, largos, adagios* and *lentos* punctuated by strident spasms of temporary haste, and unless the musicians play under the full compulsion of the Christian epos a solemn procession of small feeling is all they will be able to produce. Not that non-Christians have to believe, any more than a sentient baritone has to believe himself Wotan, but they do have to be enthralled to be convincing, whereas an intelligent baritone does

not, to be convincing as Wotan, who inspires no
conviction.

The two editions of the Amadeus Quartet are
made from the same tape, and in spite of the
increased duration per side, the newer edition, on
one disk instead of two, is sonically somewhat
superior to the older. This version has the most
intensity of playing and the warmest organization
of the strings. It would be the best beyond cavil
if hall-tone had not enlarged the sound beyond
the reality of a string quartet. Here, however,
the enlargement is less likely to hurt critical sensibilities, *The Seven Last Words* not being purely
music, and the sound being agreeable, albeit in-
correct. The Schneiders as usual benefit from the
best registration, and although they play at a
speed faster than Haydn's indications, they have
not deformed the contours or noticeably diluted
the sentiments in doing so, a rare feat.

In expressiveness of phrase the Guilets are
second to no one here, but what ails their records
is a sparse adjustment that gives constant pre-
eminence to the first violin and alleviates the
tragedy. I do not think that this characteristic
was inflicted by the engineers, who have done
pretty well. The Boston performance is tight,
supercilious and elegant, finely filigreed without
feeling by an immaculate first violin after whom
the others trot in the background of a thin and
gutless recording.

—Amadeus Qt. WESTMINSTER 18055. 58 min.

—Schneider Qt. HAYDN SOCIETY HSQ-39. 52 min.

---

—Guilet Qt. Two 12-in. CONCERT HALL 1084 (with *Beethoven: Elegiac Song*). 63 min.
—Boston Symphony Qt. RCA LM-1949. 54 min.

## TRIOS FOR KEYBOARD AND OTHER INSTRUMENTS

The music composed by Haydn for three instruments lies largely undisturbed in a disheveled and discouraging heap comprising about two hundred items. Well more than half of these are "divertimentos" for baryton, viola and cello, not one of which has been recorded in its correct form, although there are a few recordings of some in transcription. There are about fifty trios for the classic combination of violin, viola and cello, in the main ignored by records as they are in concert; a few trios for strings and wind, and about thirty for piano, violin and cello. Of the last, the most authoritative edition that of Breitkopf and Härtel, contains thirty-one, including two perhaps not by Haydn. Because these have a homogeneity of ensemble much more pronounced than we can find in the trios lacking a keyboard (except those for baryton) they have been grouped here, and all the others recorded have been assembled below (beginning on page 102).

With one or two exceptions the piano trios are in fact piano sonatas with accompaniment by the strings. They were so published, and many can be played as piano solos. Most of the works belong to Haydn's full maturity. The numbers applied to them in the edition published by C. F. Peters have been used here because several are thoroughly indentified with the works they designate, but they represent musical numeration at its very worst, yielding to scrutiny no clue of the system that inspired it. No. 8 is the trio generally believed to be the last composed. No. 1 is very late, and No. 26 is one of the earliest.

(The trios in the following discography are all for piano, violin and cello except where otherwise stated. The players are listed in this instrumental order.)

### No. 1, in G ***

The only Haydn trio that may be called familiar is a coruscating work of very high art, fluent and entirely unassuming, whose final gypsy Rondo is known to everyone who has ever labored at piano lessons. Admittedly that dreadful usage has attracted relentless enmity.

Recording honors are to the Westminster version. Mr. Badura-Skoda is a formidable pianist, solo or in company, and the line fashioned by Mr. Fournier's violin is a charm of elegant grace. A little more go in the Rondo would not have been detrimental, and the same observation may be applied to the Trieste performance, a well-drilled essay leaner in the two slow movements than need be. Both these versions have accurate and pleasing sound, the Westminster riper. The Almas manipulate the music capably, but their close reproduction gives out a quantity of rasp to negate the effect obtained by strong and sweet realism. It is a very old record.

—P. Badura-Skoda, J. Fournier, A. Janigro WESTMINSTER XWN 18610 (with *Trios No. 28 and 30*). 16 min.

—Trio di Trieste. LONDON LL-1176 (with *Brahms: Trio No. 2*). 13 min.

---

—Alma Trio. ALLEGRO 4 (with *Beethoven: Trio No. 5*), discontinued. 15 min.

### No. 2, IN F-SHARP MINOR

The Adagio of this beautiful trio is either mother or daughter of the Adagio of Symphony No. 102. It is time someone made a new recording, for the only one existing is an old transfer from old 78 rpm's, and its sound is no longer acceptable. Amidst the harshness, the clatter and the murk we can nevertheless distinguish playing of lofty quality.

—L. Kraus, S. Goldberg, A. Pini. Two 12-in. DECCA DX-104 (with *Trios No. 3 and 5, and Andante con variazioni in F minor*). 15 min.

### No. 3, IN C

Excellent performances and inadequate sonics emanate from the three editions of a trio all good humor and infectious brilliance. No one will find fault with the celebrated Russians' expert delivery until the K-G-P combination is heard in its knowing and alert stylization. That is the result of a sympathetic study that transfigures mere musicianship. Unfortunately the registration is brittle and cannot be recommended. The Westminster sound is the best, and is satisfactorily pure, but is thoroughly shallow. Colosseum, engraving the same performance, have neglected the purity and eliminated bass in a recording not quite of one dimension.

—L. Kraus, S. Goldberg, A. Pini. Two 12-in. Decca DX-104 (with *Trios No. 2 and 5, and Andante con variazioni in F minor*). 17 min.

—L. Oborin, D. Oistrakh, S. Knushevitsky. Westminster 18176 (with *Dvořák: Trio No. 3*). 20 min.

---

—L. Oborin, D. Oistrakh, S. Knushevitsky. Colosseum 248 (with *Trio No. 17 and Locatelli: Sonata "Au Tombeau"*). 19 min.

No. 4, in E

Barring some awkwardness from the violin in the tricky Finale, the only performance is professionally competent, and something more from the pianist. Good sound, above average for this combination, after the treble has been subjected to strong reduction.

—P. Badura-Skoda, J. Fournier, A. Janigro.

WESTMINSTER XWN 18611 (with *Trios No. 16, 27 and 29*). 14 min.

### No. 5, IN E-FLAT

Two placid, slowish movements leading to a fitful *allemande* quite unlike what composers of the preceding generation had led us to expect from this dance, offer more importance to the violin part than in most of the trios, and Mr. Goldberg makes the most of it. Outstanding in performance, the disk has an easier sound than we find in the two other trios in this Decca series, and will pass if we do not insist on bright clarity or deep substance.

—L. Kraus, S. Goldberg, A. Pini. Two 12-in. DECCA DX-104 (with *Trios No. 2 and 3, and Andante con variazioni in F minor*). 16 min.

### No. 7, IN E MINOR

This trio was composed seven or eight years earlier than the ones listed above. It is notable for a fine Rondo, the two other movements being perfunctorily serious. The one record, containing two other trios, is accurate and spacious in sound for all three, and if the playing of Trio No. 7 seems less convincing than that accorded to the others, I think that the music is to blame. (Note that this disk bears the B. & H. numbers 10, 16 and 24 while the listing here is 7, 19 and 11 for the same trios. One system is as bad as the other, but the latter is more frequently used.)

—P. Badura-Skoda, J. Fournier, A. Janigro.

WESTMINSTER 18054 (with *Trios No. 11 and 19*). 14 min.

### No. 11, IN A-FLAT

A prepossessing trifle mixing sweetness and stimulation, beautifully played, with rare nuance for such a little thing, and neatly registered.
—P. Badura-Skoda, J. Fournier, A. Janigro. WESTMINSTER 18054 (with *Trios No. 7 and 19*). 16 min.

### No. 16, IN G MINOR

Lively in performance and sound (reduce the treble), this record of a dashing little work cannot displease anyone.
—P. Badura-Skoda, J. Fournier, A. Janigro. WESTMINSTER XWN 18611 (with *Trios No. 4, 27 and 29*). 9 min.

### No. 17, IN E-FLAT

The atrocious sound is an outrage on one of Hadyn's most distinguished trios.
—E. Gilels, L. Kogan, M. Rostropovitch. COLOSSEUM 248 (with *Trio No. 3 and Locatelli: Sonata "Au Tombeau"*). 15 min.

### No. 19, IN G MINOR

Composed earlier than any other of the trios recorded, this is richly imaginative and in facile interest surpasses many written much later. Enthusiastic but well-shaded performance, excellent reproduction.

—P. Badura-Skoda, J. Fournier, A. Janigro. WESTMINSTER 18054 (with *Trios No. 7 and 11*). 11 min.

## No. 27, IN F

Does not sound like Haydn, and there is good reason to believe that its femininity, agreeable but just a little contemptible, is the product of the great man's brother Michael. Here it has a performance perhaps above its worth, in slightly disappointing sonics inclined to give a clatter to the upper half of the piano.

—P. Badura-Skoda, J. Fournier, A. Janigro. WESTMINSTER XWN 18611 (with *Trios No. 4, 16 and 29*). 12 min.

## No. 28, IN G

Fluffy, beguiling music played with sensitive grace and reproduced with true, strong character in the three instruments.

—P. Badura-Skoda, J. Fournier, A. Janigro. WESTMINSTER XWN 18610 (with *Trios No. 1 and 30*). 14 min.

## No. 29, IN F

Nos. 29, 30 and 31 allow either flute or violin in the secondary part. All three have been recorded in the flute version, and two in the violin. I have tried to ignore the difference of color and texture as a decisive element in making my comparisons. In No. 29 my slight preference for the

Oiseau-Lyre disk is based on some slight superiority in reproduction; not that that disk is remarkable, but the Westminster piano is a little explosive and the violin is hard. I think the playing values go somewhat in the opposite direction, but not enough to balance the difference in sound. In general the Westminster players are suaver, juicier, the Frenchmen more nervous and impatient.

—R. Veyron-Lacroix, J-P. Rampal (flute), J. Huchot. OISEAU-LYRE 50036 (with *Trios No. 30 and 31*). 11 min.

—P. Badura-Skoda, J. Fournier, A. Janigro. WESTMINSTER XWN 1811 (with *Trios No. 4, 16 and 27*). 12 min.

### No. 30, IN D

It is hard to choose between the two Westminsters, which offer different emphases in this catchy, glib and courtly trio. Mr. Badura-Skoda *et al.* rather surprisingly treat it with a warm seriousness which I do not think is in it, but this registration has a mellow substance to make the contention plausible, and collectors who are influenced by quality of sound will prefer it, although Comrade Gilels, *et al.*, have been engraved with a crisper purity, with the Kogan violin a silken joy. It is depth that is deficient here, not badly. The alert and elegant aloofness of the Russians' playing impresses me as being exactly right. The Frenchmen are not far from the same concept and are indeed admirable in everything except ripeness of sound as it comes from their record a little dry.

—E. Gilels, L. Kogan, M. Rostropovitch. WEST-MINSTER 18181 (with *Brahms: Horn Trio*). 19 min.

—P. Badura-Skoda, J. Fournier, A. Janigro. WESTMINSTER XWN 18610 (with *Trios No. 1 and 28*). 14 min.

—R. Veyron-Lacroix, J-P. Rampal (flute), J. Huchot. OISEAU-LYRE 50036 (with *Trios No. 28 and 29*). 17 min.

### No. 31, IN G

One of the most brilliant and assimilable of the trios, delivered with skillful dash by the players to the engineers, who have responded with sonics vaguely obscure and uncomfortable, brittle in the piano, cramped for the flute and gracious nowhere.

—R. Veyron-Lacroix, J-P. Rampal (flute), J. Huchot. OISEAU-LYRE 50036 (with *Trios No. 29 and 30*). 22 min.

## TRIOS WITHOUT KEYBOARD

FLUTES (OR FLUTE AND VIOLIN) AND VIOLONCELLO

There are ten of these, of which the first six, composed in 1784, were called divertimentos, and the last four, composed in London ten years later, include one consisting of an isolated Allegro.

No. 1, in D ***
No. 2, in G ***
No. 3, in C ***
No. 4, in G ***
No. 5, in A ***
No. 6, in D ***


No. 7, in C
No. 8, in G
No. 9, in G
No. 10 (ALLEGRO), in G

Amiable trifles from Haydn's finest era, played with spirited skill by Mr. Kaplan, *et al.*, but recorded close, giving strong realism including the flutist's gasps, plus more harshness than the flutes would have given with more room for expansion. The Decca, just a snip, is less artfully played, a little more artfully recorded.

—P. Kaplan (flute), L. Schaefer (flute), S. Mayes. 10-in. ALLEGRO 48, discontinued. 8, 5, 7, 5 min.

—Flutes and cello from the London Baroque Ensemble (*No. 10* only). 10-in. DECCA DL-4076 (with *Field-Partita in F and 2 Marches*). 3 min.

HORN, VIOLIN AND VIOLONCELLO, IN E-FLAT ***
Easy on the ears but musically frail although a fearful ordeal for the horn-player, this is an early work here played from manuscript, masterfully by the horn, carefully by the strings, with a big and very bright registration.

—F. Koch, W. Schneiderhan, N. Huebner. HAYDN SOCIETY 1044 (with *Nocturnes No. 3, 5 and 6*). 10 min.

LUTE, VIOLIN AND VIOLONCELLO †

VIOLIN, VIOLA AND VIOLONCELLO:
G, OP. 53, No. 1 ***
B-FLAT, OP. 53, No. 2 ***
D, OP. 53, No. 3 ***

The loving conscience of the players can almost convince the hearer that these short pieces are something more than routine late eighteenth century. In essence violin solos decorated by the deeper strings, they contain some pretty, and some pretty ordinary, passages. No. 1 is the most interesting. The disk gives out a good gliding sound after the amplifier has taken edge away from the violin.
—J. Pougnet, F. Riddle, A. Pini. WESTMINSTER XWN 18609 (with *Qts. No. 18 and* 77). 8, 9, 8 min.

# INSTRUMENTAL MUSIC*

## MISCELLANY—PIANO

ANDANTE CON VARIAZIONI, FOR PIANO, IN F-MINOR
Haydn's most famous work for piano solo, composed in 1793, presents a kind of variation writing
that Beethoven could not help imitating. The
double theme is a contest between good and bad
cheer (F major and minor) which the variations
multiply into more complex moods of quickly
changing color. Its three recordings all have some
sonic bother: the old Decca is percussive and bad;
the Remington needs more retention of bass to
be truly good; and the Westminster, chiseled
with delicate exactness, is plagued by precho.
Even for collectors particularly sensitive to that
defect, it is the record to have, in the transparency both of Miss Reisenberg's playing and
of the sound. Sonics aside, the Dohnanyi performance, swift, elegant and authoritative, is
worth hearing.
—N. Reisenberg. WESTMINSTER 18057 (a Haydn
miscellany). 16 min.
—E. von Dohnanyi. REMINGTON 199-16 (with

* Music for one or two instruments.

*Beethoven: Sonata No. 17 and Andante Favori*).
10 min.

---

—L. Kraus. Two 12-in. DECCA DX-104 (with
*Trios No. 2, 3 and 5*). 16 min.

ARIETTA AND VARIATIONS, FOR PIANO, IN A
A simple piece constantly diverting, played here
with transparent nimbleness and a taste for neat-
ness, beautifully registered without a frayed edge
anywhere.
—N. Reisenberg. WESTMINSTER 18057 (a Haydn
miscellany). 16 min.

ARIETTA AND VARIATIONS, FOR PIANO, IN E-FLAT
—N. Reisenberg. WESTMINSTER 18057 (a Haydn
miscellany). 7 min.

CAPRICCIO, FOR PIANO, IN G
A Rondo, mildly fanciful and cheerfully attractive, given an exercise of remarkable clarity and
refinement that permits us to condone some over-
reliance on restraint. Finely detailed sound.
—N. Reisenberg. WESTMINSTER 18057 (a Haydn
miscellany). 7 min.

FANTASY, FOR PIANO, IN C
After hearing the erratic bounce of this extraordinary piece, as pat as it is capricious, one must
regret that Haydn did not exploit further the
province of the piano whim. The recording is

a small jewel, twinkling primness carried by washed sonics.
—N. Reisenberg. Westminster 18057 (a Haydn miscellany). 6 min.

THEME AND VARIATIONS, FOR PIANO, IN C

An appealing late trifle, beautifully played and recorded, save for its continuous and clear double precho.
—N. Reisenberg. Westminster 18057 (a Haydn miscellany). 4 min.

## SONATAS FOR KEYBOARD (Piano or Harpsichord)

No. 1, IN C
No. 2, IN B-FLAT
No. 3, IN C
No. 4, IN D
No. 5, IN A
No. 6, IN G
No. 7, IN C
No. 8, IN G
No. 9, IN F
No. 10, IN C

Haydn and others of the time, with an exasperating indifference to the requirements of a musicology not yet born, referred to his music for "clavier"—keyboard. Besides the organ, a special instrument that like the brown thrasher aspires to include all others, he had three keyboards at his disposal during his life: clavichord, harpsichord and piano. The first, so greatly admired by Beethoven, by John Sebastian and Philip Bach, was apparently no favorite of Haydn, and the second was supplanted in his creation by the third rather early in his career. We do not know exactly when: we do know that with a few startling exceptions most of his keyboard music is more effective on the piano, and the later Haydn declared that his keyboard pieces were composed for the piano, meaning the ones he was writing then. Nowadays many people love the harpsichord and many hate it, the latter unfairly, since no two of our modern reconstructions sound alike, and disparagement of the type often proceeds from dislike for a particular example. It is my lot to esteem the harpsichord in music for which it is fit, and I think that the ten sonatas recorded by Miss Marlowe are apt to her instrument. My tepid appraisal of those records is entirely divorced from any considerations on harpsichord versus piano.

It is important to note that I have used the rational B. & H. numeration for the piano sonatas thereby following the proven order of sequence made by Breitkopf and Härtel, the publishers of the projected complete edition. Record labels use various systems—and sometimes different systems on the labels and jacket of the same record—of reversed chronology which I have corrected. The last sonata is often called No. 1, but B. & H. and I prefer No. 52, a designation without mischief.

Since everyone admits that Haydn imitated in his early sonatas the keyboard works of Philip Bach, there is no gain in disputing it. What is not usually said is that whatever the technical indebtedness of the South German Haydn to the North German Bach, their music has very little similarity of temperament, and that the debonair shadow of John Christian Bach prevails over the soberer outlines of his elder brother in the pages of the young sonatas of Haydn. (This Christian Bach was hard to resist: his influence on Mozart lasted from the latter's childhood until his death.)

The sound of the harpsichord in the Marlowe records is exceptionally clear and solid; no hint of artificiality in it. In saying I do not like the playing I mean as a whole, for there are a number of movements to satisfy my taste. But in almost every sonata I note a mildness of thrust, a deficiency of froth, a habit of sameness, and a broad, square-toed cut that to my irritated sensibility seems deliberately contrived to demonstrate how just too dear and primitive and quaint these lovely old nosegays by dear old "Papa" Haydn are on this adorable old instrument. I feel that the lady played archly, in costume, lighted by a candelabrum assuredly authentic Louis XV. It is to be hoped that this baneful impression is mine exclusively. In any event everyone must applaud the player's ability as a colorist.

Miss Reisenberg, who has offered testimony elsewhere of high skill in Haydn, and who has been scheduled to record all the sonatas for Westminster, makes a handsome start with No. 6, well felt, alert, variable, light and lively, with the piano sound imposingly seized by the engineers.

—N. Reisenberg (*No. 6* only). WESTMINSTER 18357 (with *Sonatas No. 37 and 50*). 15 min.
—S. Marlowe (harpsichord). (*Nos. 1-10*) Two 12-in. HADYN SOCIETY 3037, discontinued. 9, 14, 5, 6, 9, 14, 6, 6, 5, 8 min.

## No. 13, IN E

An attractive, spirited piece (as so many of the early sonatas are), played with slighted expression and little grace, in a registration pretty good when given extra volume.

—S. Stravinsky. ALLEGRO 3040 (with *Sonatas No. 19, 31, and 32*), discontinued. 8 min.

## No. 19, IN D

One of the most confidently fanciful of piano sonatas, by anybody. Mr. Stravinsky, son of a great father, makes something, in an unkempt, forceful way, of the Finale, but the rest is far too awkward. Satisfactory reproduction in this, decidedly inferior to the close, clear and substantial sound given to Miss Kraus's deft and protean attack.

This Educo disk is a good one, but it can cause some confusion from its inclusion of four tiny snips from longer works along with its two sonatas. The four together last a few seconds more than six minutes.

—L. Kraus. EDUCO 3005 (with *Sonata No. 35 and 4 snips*). 21 min.

---

—S. Stravinsky. ALLEGRO 3040 (with *Sonatas No. 13, 31 and 32*), discontinued. 13 min.

### No. 20, IN C MINOR

The three movements are more concerned with tense feelings than any of the preceding sonatas. More flexible manipulation makes Miss Long more persuasive in the angry external movements, and she benefits from the crisper reproduction. Hers is the better record, but Mrs. Pleasants is a very honorable musician whose concepts, less completely realized, are in places more moving.

—K. Long. LONDON LL-1380 (with *Sonatas No. 31, 40 and 46*). 12 min.

—V. Pleasants. 10-in. HAYDN SOCIETY 3013 (with *Sonata No. 50*). 15 min.

### No. 23, IN F

There is more glib sport in Mr. Anda's lithe scooting than in the measured trot of the other in this shallow, engaging and worldly little sonata obviously conceived for the harpsichord. Sonics are a minor factor where both records are more than satisfactory, but the Telefunken piano is more sharply etched.

—G. Anda. 10-in. TELEFUNKEN 68023 (with *Mozart: Sonata No. 17*). 10 min.
—R. Wallenborn. 10-in. HAYDN SOCIETY 3035 (with *Sonata No. 32*). 12 min.

## No. 24, IN D

Compact and cozy, with a dab of feeling in the Adagio, this harpsichord sonata—which became a sonata for keyboard and violin—is just a little too cozy in a careful, symmetrical treatment that precludes any conveyance of enjoyment. Acceptable sound.

—R. Wallenborn. 10-in. HAYDN SOCIETY 3036 (with *Sonata No. 30*). 11 min.

## No. 30, IN A

Polite sonata, dutiful playing, fair reproduction.

—R. Wallenborn. 10-in. HAYDN SOCIETY 3036 (with *Sonata No. 24*). 13 min.

## No. 31, IN E

The honors of performance and recording are very easily London's in a short, whimful sonata wherein Miss Long's display is clean and luminous, her rival's unsure and rude.

—K. Long. LONDON LL-1380 (with *Sonatas No. 20, 40 and 46*). 8 min.
—S. Stravinsky. ALLEGRO 3040 (with *Sonatas No. 13, 19 and 32*), discontinued. 5 min.

## No. 32, IN B MINOR

The flushed, impatient and demanding music

here extorts more compliance from Mr. Wallenborn than he chose to offer in his less rugged
recordings, and Mr. Stravinsky shows a good
understanding of the musical obligation. Un-
luckily his good intentions are rather blowsily
translated. Mr. Levy is as convincing as the first
and more presentable than the second; and he
has been accorded a sound of deep, vibrant and
startling realism.

—E. Levy. Unicorn 1036 (with *Sonatas No. 46,
50 and 51*). 10 min.

—R. Wallenborn. 10-in. Haydn Society 3035
(with *Sonata No. 23*). 10 min.

—S. Stravinsky. Allegro 3040 (with *Sonatas
No. 13, 19 and 31*), discontinued. 10 min.

No. 34, in E minor †

No. 35, in C***

A word ought to be said for Miss Dumont's
nicety of play in this attractive sonata whose pert
outside movements scoff at the halfhearted
seriousness of the Adagio, but the sound carrying
that nicety is old and poor and the record is best
forgotten. Nothing halfhearted in Miss Kraus's
brilliant participation, entirely manifest in clear,
strong reproduction.

—L. Kraus. Educo 3005 (with *Sonata No. 19
and 4 snips*). 13 min.

—L. Dumont. Concert Hall 18 (with *Sonata
No. 40*), discontinued. 14 min.

No. 37, IN D

Extraordinary sound, substantial and transparent, underlines the value of Miss Reisenberg's sensitive playing of a sonata loaded with devices proleptic of Beethoven. Miss Kraus is a nimbler frisker, and I would hate to say that her performance is inferior to any of these. Since her record, although old, gives a full and accurate piano, I think it is fair to call the contest a toss-up. Mr. Hambro's light dexterity is abetted by a light recording, and the combination belittles the sonata.

—L. Kraus. 10-in. Vox 1740 (with *Sonata No. 52*), discontinued. 9 min.

—N. Reisenberg. WESTMINSTER 18357 (with *Sonatas No. 6 and 50*). 10 min.

---

—L. Hambro. REMINGTON 199-135 (with *Sonata No. 52 and Mozart: Sonata No. 11*). 9 min.

No. 40, IN G ***

Again Miss Dumont is let down by erratic acoustics, not improved by the not-so-narrow grooves of a ten-minute side. I prefer her work in the first movement of this sly, animated sonata, but Miss Long's lesser expressiveness has the aid of first-class recording, and she is admirable in the swirling Finale.

—K. Long. LONDON LL-1380 (with *Sonatas No. 20, 31 and 46*). 6 min.

—L. Dumont. CONCERT HALL 18 (with *Sonata No. 35*), discontinued. 10 min.

### No. 43, IN A-FLAT ***

Played with a disarming naturalness, the lively external movements are decidedly attractive in the only recording, but I feel that the commendable taste summoned for their exposition excludes full value from the phrasing in the dangerous simplicity of the Adagio. But excellent in sum, in a reproduction light and fine at its best, the treble here and there uneasy.
—C. Rosen. EMS 3 (with *Sonata No. 51 and Nocturne No. 4*). 15 min.

### No. 44, IN G MINOR

A competent account of a wistful, rather plain sonata in fair sonics.
—V. Pleasants. 10-in. HAYDN SOCIETY 3033 (with *Sonata No. 45*). 13 min.

### No. 45, IN E-FLAT

An early work, demure and appealing, played with an evenness of restraint in need of some punctuation of enjoyment. Pleasant piano sound when reproduced at moderate volume.
—V. Pleasants. 10-in. HAYDN SOCIETY 3033 (with *Sonata No. 44*). 14 min.

### No. 46, IN A-FLAT

The high style and supple manipulation of Miss

Long in this beautiful, albeit early, sonata have received a registration of imposing, luminous accuracy and the record is hard to beat. Nevertheless, the arresting roll and crystal spank of the Unicorn piano will excite adherents for the blunter Levy performance. Sonically the choice is between a chaste and an aggressive realism, between the unquestionable and the unanswerable. Mrs. Pleasants is calmly eloquent in her best recorded performance, and the Haydn Society sound is of very good quality, if less compelling than the others'. I prefer as a whole the Long-London, but collectors possessing any of the three versions do not need really to replace it by either of the others.

—K. Long. LONDON LL-1380 (with *Sonatas No. 20, 31 and 40*). 13 min.

—E. Levy. UNICORN 1036 (with *Sonatas No. 32, 50 and 51*). 15 min.

—V. Pleasants. HAYDN SOCIETY 3034 (with *Sonata No. 49*). 17 min.

## No. 48, IN C ***

Two movements, a thoughtful and stimulating set of variations which finds Mrs. Pleasants in thorough command of its spirit, and a half-gay Rondo more soberly delivered than I believe is best. This is a pretty old record, but it has a plump and caressing sound for its piano.

—V. Pleasants. 10-in. HAYDN SOCIETY 3032 (with *Sonata No. 51*). 13 min.

No. 49, IN E-FLAT ***

Composed as a gift for his dear friend Marianne
von Genzinger, this sonata carries Haydn's profound affection in its *adagio cantabile* and subtle
minuet. The playing is capable but not illumi-
nating—perhaps it is too much to have to explain to the satisfaction of outsiders so personal a communication—and the sound is fair as
a whole.
—V. Pleasants. HAYDN SOCIETY 3034 (with
*Sonata No. 46*). 19 min.

No. 50, IN C

This is one of the last three sonatas, all composed
for Thérèse Jansen, a pianist of imposing measure if she could play what she inspired. It seems
tailored to the fine talents of Nadia Reisenberg,
all fresh vivacity and telling finesse here. With
the refinement and strength of the Westminster
sound to support her, it is needless to have concern for the other records, in spite of Mr. Levy's
intelligent exposition and the rich Unicorn
sound. The Haydn Society's record is not in the
class of these.
—N. Reisenberg. WESTMINSTER 18357 (with
*Sonatas No. 6 and 37*). 17 min.
—E. Levy. UNICORN 1036 (with *Sonatas No. 32,
46 and 51*). 16 min.

---

—V. Pleasants. 10-in. HAYDN SOCIETY 3013 (with
*Sonata No. 20*). 14 min.

No. 51, IN D

No music of Haydn's invites Beethoven more
than this model of compression in design and
sentiment. The records are good, save for the
Haydn Society's fatuity in offering as LP a side
less than six minutes in duration; but I think that
the Levy performance and sound, superior in
force and more direct on their target, are the
inevitable choice for everyone. Next I rather
hesitantly prefer the Pleasants, but I would
counsel everyone to boycott all disks two-thirds
empty.

—E. Levy. UNICORN 1036 (with *Sonatas No. 32,
46 and 50*). 6 min.

—C. Rosen. EMS 3 (with *Sonata No. 43 and
Nocturne No. 4*). 6 min.

—V. Pleasants. 10-in. HAYDN SOCIETY 3032 (with
*Sonata No. 48*). 6 min.

No. 52, IN E-FLAT ***

For two movements Haydn's greatest sonata, in
spite of the bravura elements with which it
bristles, is bold in compelling excursions into
fancy. That there are only two recordings,
neither good enough, is one of those mysteries
so commonplace in the scheduling of disks. I
suggest that readers wait to hear what Miss
Reisenberg will do with this in her complete
edition of the sonatas. We have here a brilliant,
potent and expressive statement from Mr. Hambro, in a reproduction in which the bell cannot
be evicted from the piano high and loud; and a

brilliant, far less potent and much less expressive display from Miss Kraus, in sonics of thoroughly decent quality. The less successful performance occupies the more successful record and must be preferred.

(A note on the perils of bad numeration and the hazards of reading jacket notes: the Remington jacket, in a single vivid sentence sage with three errors, coaxes our enthusiasm for the composer's boldness ". . . in the very first . . . of the sonatas." This E-flat Sonata is Haydn's last or nearly, but in a number of cheap editions it is No. 1.)

—L. Kraus. 10-in. Vox 1740 (with *Sonata No. 37*), discontinued. 20 min.

—L. Hambro. REMINGTON 199-135 (with *Sonata No. 37 and Mozart: Sonata No. 11*). 16 min.

SONATA FOR PIANO AND FLUTE (OR VIOLIN), No. 7, IN G

This is a transcription of the wonderful Quartet No. 75, Op. 77, No. 1, with the Minuet omitted. Grateful music for the flute is very rare after Handel and Bach, and we will not denounce the two excellent flutists who made these records for trying their skills at something delightful, although the original is terribly weakened as any organism must be by the removal of half its vitals. I could not find the old Oxford disk, but the old Concert Hall is played with catchy animation and is surprisingly well registered, bright in the flute and firm, almost commanding, in the piano.

—P. Loyonnet, R. LeRoy (flute). CONCERT HALL 1082 (with *Pergolesi: Flute Concerto No. 2*), discontinued. 16 min.

—J. Arnold, J. Baker (flute). OXFORD 106 (with *Mozart: Clarinet Trio*), discontinued.

SONATA FOR VIOLIN AND VIOLA, No. 6, IN C

Sounds good even in the unlikely transcription for piano and cello, used here, that darkens a light fabric and alters its mood and texture. One would prefer the original but one takes what there is, and this cellist is so smooth in song and so rich in voice that we can almost condone the pianist's having been pushed back into a far corner. Superior reproduction.

—S. Pearlman (piano), S. Mayes (cello). BOSTON 210 (with arcana by Beethoven, Bréval and Mozart). 13 min.

# MISCELLANEOUS*

## DIVERTIMENTOS

Haydn applied this title to several hundred
works, including many of the string quartets and
piano trios, and many of his things are called
divertimento in one edition, field-partita in another, serenade in another, etc. Where he used
"divertimento," and it suits the modern notion
of the term, and does not suit another title better, I have retained the word. The distinction
between field-partita and divertimento, in his
mind and ours, is that the former covers music
for wind instruments exclusively while the latter
usually includes strings.

* Under this dubious rubric I have put all the music
that would be insecure under another. A field-partita is
not chamber music and it is not orchestral. The nocturnes are closer to orchestral than to chamber music.
Most of the things here are short and many are trifling.
Many are transcriptions and a number are not easily
identified exactly. I have not tried to establish the
status of a piece when it seemed not worth the trouble.

### BARYTON, VIOLA AND VIOLONCELLO, No. 6, IN D
### BARYTON, VIOLA AND VIOLONCELLO, No. 82, IN C

For this combination Haydn composed more than a hundred divertimentos, his patron Nicholas Esterházy being enamored of the baryton, a bass instrument of six strings supplemented by an unfixed number of tuned wires in sympathetic vibration. The baryton is obsolete, and the only possibility of hearing a few of these divertimentos is in a transcribed form. Haydn may have arranged some of the works for other instruments, but we have no proof at the present time. Various movements have been put together by editors in settings for modern string instruments. Without considering the matter of a close substitute for the baryton, the material is available to anyone, choosing any instrument that will balance with the viola and cello. In this recorded pair a trombone virtuoso assumes the baryton part, skilfully and with seductive tone; no harm done except to the viola, nearly inaudible, and to the cello, half audible, and neither attractive in a dry registration.

—D. Shuman (trombone), M. Johnson, B. Greenhouse. 10-in. PARADOX 10002. 10, 9 min.

### BARYTON, VIOLA AND VIOLONCELLO, IN D (SYNTHETIC)

Six movements assembled from five divertimentos, and played by instruments archaic or obsolescing when Haydn composed the originals. No

doubt factitiously cute and distasteful to con-
template, the synthesis has nevertheless a simple
charm of distinct flavor, and conjures spurious
but pretty images like Lully and Christian Bach
strolling together. Unpretentious playing, easy
reproduction.
—H. Kirschner (tenor viol), F. Beyer (viola
d'amore), W. Biller (viola da gamba). RENAIS-
SANCE 40 (with 18th century miscellany). 20 min.

CLARINETS, HORNS, VIOLINS, VIOLAS AND
    CONTINUO, IN C

A young man composed this wide-ranging, un-
settled and robust divertimento, although from
the use of clarinets we should infer that it is a
late work. The recorded performance is from
manuscripts collected and compared by that
spectacular Haydnist, Mr. H. C. Robbins Landon, and has a surprising soar in view of the unfamiliarity of the notes. The sound is a puzzle—
weak and obscure in the strings, outward in the
winds, excellent in the difficult horns. Extra volume is required to make it satisfactory, and to
make the *fortes* absolutely first rate.

On the jacket, the music is called both serenade
and divertimento (*a nove stromenti*).
—Players from a Vienna Opera Orch. STRADI-
VARI 622 (with *2 Field-Partitas and Mozart: 2
Divertimentos*). 20 min.

OBOES, HORNS AND STRINGS, IN G

Although very early in the Haydn creation, this

lively divertimento, with a symphonic first movement and two Minuets, is one of the works that
most deserve the title: it fulfils the obligation of
being unimportant in an engaging way. Very
good but rather cool playing and big, clean sound
slightly edgy in the violins are the essential qualities of the one recording.
—Ch. Orch. of the Danish National Radio, M.
Wöldike. LONDON LL-1308 (with works by J. C.
Bach, Dittersdorf and Mozart).

HORNS AND STRINGS, IN. E-FLAT
There is a remarkably fine bloom in the sound of
the rich horns in this invigorating little work
composing one fourth of the best record in existence of Haydn's essays in the type. Played to
transmit facile enjoyment and very solidly registered with an easy display of accurate timbres,
all four pieces on Westminster 5227 are warmly
recommended.
—London Baroque Ensemble, K. Haas. WEST-
MINSTER XWN 18612 (with *Divertimentos in
A minor and G; Scherzando in F*). 13 min.

FLUTE, HORNS AND STRINGS, IN A MINOR
FLUTE, HORNS AND STRINGS, IN G
This pair are later works than the divertimentos
already listed here, and are much more assured,
inventive and resourceful. They are included on
the Westminster disk extolled immediately above,
and are the best part of an outstanding record of
captivating froth.

—London Baroque Ensemble, K. Haas. WEST-MINSTER XWN 18612 (with *Divertimentos in E-flat and Scherzando in F*). 15, 10 min.

FLUTE, HORNS AND STRINGS, IN G
Ought not to be confounded with the Divertimento in G immediately above. It is part of the same series and is in no way inferior in musical potential or performance to the other two recorded, but its sound lacks the smooth firm flesh of that pair and will be satisfactory only when reproduced through an apparatus capable of taming the shrillness of the violins.
—London Baroque Ensemble, K. Haas. 10-in. DECCA DL-4066 (with *Field-Partita in B-flat*). 10 min.

HORNS, ENGLISH HORNS, BASSOONS AND VIOLINS, IN F
Has the essentially lively and staccato quality of a field-partita, a title forbidden by the inclusion of a pair of violins with the three pairs of winds. It is a very early work and very charming in its colored bravery; played here with gusto and understanding, in a sound acceptable but imprecise in timbre and sharp in the violins.
—London Baroque Ensemble, K. Haas. 10-in. DECCA DL-4076 (with a Haydn miscellany). 11 min.

CELLO AND PIANO, IN D (TRANSCRIBED BY PIATIGORSKY)†

## FIELD-PARTITAS

This is one of the rarer titles in music, but apter than most when it is used only where it really fits: in works of several movements without strings in the scoring.

OBOES, BASSOONS AND HORNS, IN C
OBOES, BASSOONS AND HORNS, IN F
The difficulties of nomenclature are delightfully revealed by the editorial freedom of this disk, labeling the two pieces respectively "Serenade (Feld Parthie) in C," and "Serenade in F for Wind Band," designations repeated on the obverse of the jacket but on the reverse transformed for both works into divertimentos. (If we tire of those, we can apply "cassation" and "scherzando.") At any rate, they are both jolly, early pieces with decided bounce, performed with happy alacrity and registered with good timbre and clarity, without trouble from the troublesome horns.
—Wind Sextet from Vienna Opera Orch. 10-in. STRADIVARI 622 (with *Divertimento for Clarinets, etc., in C and Mozart: 2 Divertimentos*). 10 min.

TWO OBOES, TWO HORNS, THREE BASSOONS AND SERPENT, IN B-FLAT, "ST. ANTHONY" ***
Better known by Brahms's borrowing of the chorale tune of its second movement as the basis

of his Variations on a Theme by Haydn than by any frequency of performance, this vigorous music is itself a set of variations on the same tune, scattered through the other three movements. The brilliantly played and beautifully recorded Columbia version is an emasculation cut to fit a virtuoso ensemble and to display in a salon. The Decca record preserves the requisite guttural tone and beery aura of the instrumentation, and is the more valuable product. (The serpent is dead, and so is its heir the ophicleide. A tuba was probably used for the Londoners' performance, but I was unable to distinguish it.)

—London Baroque Ensemble, K. Haas. 10-in. Decca DL-4066 (with *Divertimento for Flute, etc., in G*). 10 min.

—Philadelphia Woodwind Quintet (flute, oboe, clarinet, bassoon and horn). Columbia ML-5093 (with a wood-wind miscellany). 7 min.

## MARCHES

Four have been recorded, two of them twice, enlivening fanfares of more interest than worth. The same players have been employed by two companies, and it is amusing to note that they blew twice as fast for Westminster in one of the Esterházy marches as for Decca—infantrymen will prefer the latter. No choice in play or sound, both competent on both disks.

—London Baroque Ensemble, K. Haas (*Ester-*

*házy March in E-flat; Esterházy March in C; London March in E-flat; London March in B-flat*). WESTMINSTER 5080 (with *Nocturne No. 1;* and works by Boccherini and M. Haydn). 6 min. (all). Discontinued.

—London Baroque Ensemble, K. Haas (*Esterházy March in E-flat; London March in E-flat*). 10-in. DECCA DL-4076 with *Divertimento for Horns, etc., in F*, and snip from a *Flute Trio*). 5 min. (both).

## NOCTURNES

Such was the original title of the eight mellow and sophisticated divertimentos that Haydn composed in 1790 for Ferdinand IV of Naples (I of the Two Sicilies), king for one of the longest and most dreadful reigns in European history. This Spanish Bourbon—whose wife was a sister of Marie Antoinette—had an insatiable passion for the lira organizzata, a hybrid begot by the hurdy-gurdy out of the bastard of a guitar and a viol. He admired Haydn and in 1790 tried to employ him. Haydn went to London instead, but sent to the monarch the eight nocturnes, scored for two liras, two clarinets, two horns, two violas and bass. Resourcefully he retained copies for himself, and in London the nocturnes, rechristened divertimentos, were played to great applause in a new scoring that substituted flute and oboe for the liras which the English were happily unable to find. He also authorized the use of either clarinets or violins.

The eight pieces, of which seven have been recorded, ought to have an honored prominent place in the composer's gallery of secondary attractions. Among the divertimentos, field-partitas and other diffident attractions the nocturnes have a deeper, more resourceful and above all more varied appeal than the rest. They hover between a realm of thought and a realm of dream, and have a most seductive way of implying that they could be serious, if they liked, or trivial, if they chose; and why should anyone insist that they be tied to any prosaic singleness of purpose?

On records I like best No. 1, in the juicily played and neatly engraved version on Westminster 5080, perhaps because clarinets are used instead of violins. Nos. 1, 2, 4 and 7, on the earlier of two Haydn Society disks devoted to the first seven of the nocturnes, are attractive in performance and sound and an obligation to Haydnists. The supplementary and later disk, containing Nos. 3, 5 and 6, is the product of a more pretentious kind of recording, lushly echoic and ringing-bright, that becomes distasteful with repetition. No. 4, beautifully played by a decad from the NBC Orchestra for EMS, begins to show the age of the sonics applied to it, commendable in their time.

—London Baroque Ensemble, K. Haas. *No. 1.*

WESTMINSTER 5080 (with *4 Marches* and works by Boccherini and M. Haydn). 13 min. Discontinued.

—Vienna Ch. Orch., F. Litschauer. *Nos. 1, 2, 4, 7.* HAYDN SOCIETY 1023. 11, 10, 14, 11 min.

—Vienna Ch. Orch., F. Litschauer. *Nos. 3, 5, 6.* HAYDN SOCIETY 1044 (with *Horn Trio*). 16, 10, 7 min.

—Ten from NBC Orch., E. Fendler. *No. 4.* EMS 3 (with *Piano Sonatas No. 43 and 51*). 16 min.

## OCTET FOR OBOES, CLARINETS, BASSOONS AND HORNS, IN F

In spite of enduring learned opinion contesting his authorship, Haydn does seem to have been the composer of this bold and brilliant festivity, a field-partita in fact, although so often labeled as plain octet that I have preferred to list it where it will be identified. The single edition enjoys excellent playing and enjoys less a rather pale and smoky sound much less satisfying than it once seemed.

—Wind Octet from the Vienna Philharmonic Orch. WESTMINSTER XWN 18058 (with *4 Marches and M. Haydn: Turkish Suite*). 19 min.

## SCHERZANDO IN F

Four short movements in an insistent romp, a gusty exhibition for flutes, oboes, horns, violins and bass, composed very early in Haydn's career, and endowed with lively powers to amuse. The

recording is included on the best realized of all
disks containing music of this sort by Haydn.
—London Baroque Ensemble, K. Haas. WEST-
MINSTER XWN 18612 (with *3 Divertimentos*).
8 min.

HAYDN: HIS LIFE—HIS TIME—HIS MUSIC †

# ORCHESTRAL MUSIC

## CONCERTOS

FLUTE AND ORCHESTRA, IN D ***

Alas, there is no evidence at all that Haydn composed it, and strong indication that he did not. The cascading Finale is copied from Mozart in a way that Haydn never copied except from himself, and Miss Rosemary Hughes, a Haydnist to be heeded, deposes flatly that the author was Leopold Hoffmann, a competent composer who in Vienna held one of the lucrative employments that Mozart coveted and could not obtain. I have included the records in this discography because the music has a healthy and mettlesome appeal, and because I mistrust all verdicts based on investigations long after the event, including my own. The MMS disk is by far the best, the only one satisfactory sonically, and displaying to boot the most cohesive orchestral playing and a solo flute quite as convincing as the others.

—W. Urfer; Winterthur Symph. Orch., C. Dahinden. 10-in. MMS 55 (with *Trumpet Con-certo*). 17 min.

---

—H. Barwahser; Vienna Symph. Orch., B. Paum-gartner. Epic LC-3075 (with *Telemann: Suite in A minor*). 24 min.
—Scheck-Wenzinger Ch. Group. Urania 7031 (with *Telemann: Suite in D*). 19 min.

Horn and Orchestra, No. 1, in D
From about 1770 to the Congress of Vienna, music had the wonderful knack of assimilating the display in its display-pieces. The breath tak-ing acrobatics of the horn in this concerto do not seem extrinsic but inherent in the design, so that listeners feel no interruption of fluency (no mat-ter what the poor soloist may feel) when the horn is called to prove his mettle. This is early Haydn, good mid-eighteenth century divertisse-ment, on the record bravely handled by the solo horn and depressingly by the conductor. Good plump sound for both horn and orchestra, no trifle to achieve for the former.
—F. Koch; Vienna Symph. Orch., A. Heiller. Haydn Society 1038 (with *Trumpet Concerto*). 16 min.

Horn and Orchestra, No. 2, in D
Authorship is disputed, but there is nothing in this piece, livelier than No. 1 but less pungent, incompatible with Haydn's inclinations. The per-formance is admirable, with an infectious whip

to the supporting strings; and the sound, with a push upward at the volume-control, is decidely agreeable for the orchestra and cramped for the solo.

—A. Brain; Janssen Symph. Orch., W. Janssen. CAPITOL P-8137 (with *Handel: 2 Concertos*). 15 min.

### KEYBOARD AND ORCHESTRA, IN C (1756)

No one dares to provide a numeration for the keyboard concertos until the authenticity of several has been clarified. Those recorded are listed here in the order of their composition, starting with this one in C, described in Haydn's catalogues as a concerto for harpsichord, with the qualifying note in pencil, "*per l'organo.*" Two other concertos, one of them lost, were composed with the solo primarily for organ. The rest are for harpsichord or piano; and we find a curious fact here, that the style of writing is consistently more effective on the first, the contrary of what we have found to be true for the majority of the keyboard sonatas.

The first of all the concertos by Haydn is a slender pastime docile to the conventions of the 1750's, but equipped with mannerisms that the composer was to keep for thirty years. It is discreet but agreeable, and the recorded performance, featuring a singularly sweet old organ, is persuasive in style and execution, forthright in untroubled sound.

—A. Heiller (organ of the Franziskaner Church,

Vienna); Vienna Symph. Orch., H. Gillesberger.
HAYDN SOCIETY 1043 (with *Organ Concerto in C*,
1760). 19 min.

### KEYBOARD AND ORCHESTRA, IN C (1760)†

### KEYBOARD (ORGAN) AND ORCHESTRA, IN C (1760)

Haydn referred to this as an organ work primarily. It is far more stimulating than its predecessor and far less tentative. Lusty exercises for trumpets and drums make the sport exhilarating, and its delivery by players and engineers is considerably above standards for such music.
—A. Heiller organ of the Franziskaner Church, Vienna); Vienna Symph. Orch., H. Gillesberger. HAYDN SOCIETY 1043 (with *Organ Concerto in C*, 1756). 11 min.

### KEYBOARD AND ORCHESTRA, IN C

It is pleasant to have someone of Mr. Veyron-Lacroix's stature consent to play a work like this, wherein there is no true solo but instead a keyboard (harpsichord here) prominent in a group. This sort of thing is poison to most professionals, who after all must dazzle to eat, and there is no dazzle in this perfect miniature as naïve as a Greuze *jeune fille*, as pure and simple in design as the hoop and stick of childhood. I do not think anyone before Mr. Veyron-Lacroix and myself has dared to admire it, and I do not think that Haydn wrote it. On the record (which with its four concertos is one of the most valuable

in the Haydn discography) the performance and
registration are delightful. It is called a concer-
tino, which fits, and also a divertimento, which
also fits.
—R. Veyron-Lacroix; Vienna Opera Orch., M.
Horvat. WESTMINSTER 18042 (with *3 Concertos*). 6 min.

## KEYBOARD AND ORCHESTRA, IN G

The three records utilize harpsichords, and by an
unusual concord of thought the three players are
subdued in force. Miss Heiller indeed is too weak
as we hear her, and that deficiency, combined
with uncertainty of orchestral direction, relegates
the Haydn Society record decidedly to the low-
est position of esteem. I cannot convince myself
that either of the others earns precedence, although they are different. The Veyron-Lacroix
effort is the most orderly and the most dynamic
too, with a highly polished accuracy in its sound
and a unified orchestral delivery by forces more
numerous than those of the other disks. I should
prefer Miss Elsner louder, but the Vox product
is one of warm intimacy, with the telling sweetness of strings that characterizes this company's
later registrations of small ensembles in Stuttgart.
Collectors will not err in choosing either or both.
—H. Elsner; "Pro Muscia" Ch. Orch., Stuttgart,
R. Reinhardt. Vox 9810 (with *Concerto in D*).
21 min.
—R. Veyron-Lacroix; Vienna Opera Orch., H.

Milan. WESTMINSTER 18042 (with *3 Concertos*).
20 min.

---

—E. Heiller; Vienna Collegium Musicum, A.
Heiller. HAYDN SOCIETY 1014 (with *Violin Concerto in G*). 22 min.

KEYBOARD AND ORCHESTRA, IN F
An odd little piece, with a wry Andante leading
into a pumping, bullying Finale of rare appeal,
played (on the harpsichord) with enjoyment,
and realistically recorded. The orchestra is of
strings and a pair of flutes only.
—R. Veyron-Lacroix; Vienna Opera Orch., M.
Horvat. WESTMINSTER 18042 (with *3 Concertos*). 12 min.

KEYBOARD AND ORCHESTRA, IN F ***
This is much more austere and refined in form
than the F major Concerto immediately above,
with a simple singing central Largo so much like
the slow movements of several of the later Mozart concertos as to incite doubt of its authorship.
Mme. Roesgen-Champion, an accomplished harpsichordist, plays the work—whose essential frailty
is the more apparent in the perspective of a
certain pretentiousness—on a piano in the only
recording, wherein all her delicate deftness can
prove no more than that aspiration outreached
realization in the composing. Save for some
spreading of chords the orchestra accounts well

for itself, and the engineers have contrived an accurate sound with unusually attractive string tone, when reproduction is kept at small or moderate volume. In a modest way it is a fine recording. As for the music—well, it has a minor charm after all.

—M. Roesgen-Champion; Paris Conservatory Orchs., A. Goldschmidt. PERIOD 556 (with *K. P. E. Bach: Concerto in C minor*). 21 min.

### KEYBOARD AND ORCHESTRA, IN D, OP. 21 ***

This marvel is an apotheosis of foam, and it is customary to sneer at it for not aspiring higher. It aspires to bubble; and, in an age more adept at the belch, anything mannerly, even effervescence, is immediately suspect to the dominant criticism. Then this great concerto is most ideally apt to the harpsichord, an instrument affected by ladies, who are moved to be coy about it: no doubt their preëmption of this music, as if it were a cosmetic, has been a repellent to manly men. Six of the seven recordings have a woman at the keyboard—without, thank God, any obvious emanation of womanliness—which is about the ratio observed in concerts where the concerto is offered. For in spite of the sneers, its impetuous *galanterie* wears like iron, and has won a wide public love duplicated only by the trumpet and cello concertos.

It is not easy to pick a champion from the recorded contestants. The music is nowhere bungled, and only on one disk the sound. That is unfortunately the only version using a piano, an ancient one whose wiry violins libel a good performance and which must go to the bottom of the list. An older record still is the Landowska, whose original dates from the '30s, but there is no bungling in the transference to LP, everything being smoothly agreeable, but weak and without vibrancy, vitiated by time. The trouble is that the record contains the best solo playing, no doubt of it, aided by a discerning partnership from the orchestra, both spirited and patrician. Very close to that performance in agile elegance, and superior to it in dynamic gaiety, is the Veyron-Lacroix demonstration for Westminster, matched by beautiful sound and the silkiest of these orchestras. This I am convinced gives the highest musical experience, considered in all the elements that form a record. I think the bolder sport of Mr. Litschauer's direction, its rougher vitality, driven home by the brilliant and thorough Vanguard sound—the most telling of all—has a strong special appeal, although Mme. Heiller's solo manner is not the same as the conductor's, and she gives signs of losing wind in the duel. Elsner-Reinhardt are cool and neat in the external festivities, the harpsichord too small, but their *poco adagio,* benefiting from close, suave reproduction, is mellow and melting. The very old Roesgen-Champion record had excellent sound when issued and still has, barring some excess of bass; and, forcing the tempos, this is the most vivacious romp of all. I have no fault to find with the solid sonics and straight play of the Nef-Colombo edition except that it has no distinguishing salients.

Among the seven, I have confidence in my choices for first and last. However, for reproduction on insensitive apparatus, I would choose the Landowska-Bigot record. In the list I have placed the contenders according to what I think to be their relative averages of merit. Collectors more influenced by sonic quality than anything else are offered this hierarchy: Vanguard, Westminster, Vox (Elsner-Reinhardt), Oiseau-Lyre, Vox (Roesgen-Champion), RCA, Mercury.

—R. Veyron-Lacroix; Vienna Opera Orch., M. Horvat. WESTMINSTER 18042 (with *3 Concertos*). 19 min.

—E. Heiller; Vienna Opera Orch., F. Litschauer. VANGUARD 454 (with *Trumpet Concerto*). 19 min.

—M. Roesgen-Champion; Lamoureux Ch. Orch., A. Goldschmidt. Vox 6320 (with *Oboe Concerto*), discontinued. 17 min.

—H. Elsner; "Pro Musica" Ch. Orch. Stuggart, R. Reinhardt. Vox 9810 (with *Keyboard Concerto in G*). 21 min.

—W. Landowska; Ch. Orch., E. Bigot. RCA LCT-1029 (with *Mozart: Concerto No. 26*). 20 min.

—I. Nef; Lamoureux Ch. Orch., P. Colombo.

OISEAU-LYRE 50007 (with *J. C. Bach: 2 Symphonies*). 19 min.

---

—R. Schmid (piano); Bavarian Radio Orch., A. Dressel. MERCURY 10047 (with *Beethoven: Concerto No. 1*), discontinued. 18 min.

KEYBOARD, VIOLIN AND ORCHESTRA, IN F

Composed in 1765, this double concerto is a transitional piece offering a hand to two epochs. The Decca musicians play with emphasis on its debt to the old concerto grosso, the soloists tending to extend the line of the orchestra, while the other version shows the solo effort to compete sharply with the group of strings and to insist on the difference between them. Which is the better way ought not to depend on the present recordings, for the old Concert Hall edition is burdened with an acrid sound that gives no pleasure and obviates the comparison. Not that the Decca is irresistible: sonics are competent and undistinguished, not inappropriate for a performance that conveys a tepid conviction.

—L. Salter (harpsichord), J. Pougnet; London Baroque Ensemble, K. Haas. DECCA DL-9561 (with *Symph. No. 22*), discontinued. 19 min.

---

—H. Andräe (harpsichord), P. Rybar; Ch. Orch., H. Swoboda. CONCERT HALL 1081 (with *Bach: Concerto for 2 Harpsichords, in C*). 22 min.

### Oboe and Orchestra, in C ***

No evidence, oral or historical, exists to show Haydn the composer of this glib and highly entertaining exercise consisting of alternating vehement ritornellos and stretches of oboe solo, all very tuneful and catchy. Regardless of its author, collectors should stretch an ear to the record, magnificently played by the solo and very competently engraved.

—P. Pierlot; Lamoureux Ch. Orch., A. Gold-schmidt. Vox 6320 (with *Keyboard Concerto in D*), discontinued. 17 min.

### Trumpet and Orchestra, in E-flat ***

Who tries to resist the bright contagion of cheerfulness in this heartiest of display-pieces, confected by a jovial thaumaturgist of sixty-four trying a new toy (keyed trumpet) for the first time? This is ideal bait for the neophyte in Haydn, and it is to be noted that the Vanguard version is back by a lure of equivalent value, the last harpsichord concerto. The phonograph's three editions are not far apart, and represent only two performances. Vanguard has some advantage in the splendid timbre of the solo trumpet and in the strength of the orchestral projection, but both soloists and conductor are more restrained—wrongly, I think—in matters of phrase and accent in this performance than the conductor—quite restrained enough—and soloist in the other. MMS and the Haydn Society have used the same tape, and the difference in their application is not great and seems to favor neither company, for although MMS is a little brighter, it is harder to adjust, and less smooth.

—G. Eskdale; Vienna Opera Orch., F. Litschauer. VANGUARD 454 (with *Keyboard Concerto in D*). 13 min.

—H. Wobitsch; Vienna Opera Orch., A. Heiller. HAYDN SOCIETY 1038 (with *Horn Concerto No. 1*). 14 min.

—H. Wobitsch; Vienna Opera Orch., A. Heiller. 10-in. MMS 55 (with *Flute Concerto*). 14 min.

VIOLIN AND ORCHESTRA, IN C***

Conventional baroque but fairly lively and with a fine chance for fiddlers to display their *cantabile* in the Adagio. Mr. Goldberg is particularly seductive there, and indeed I find that I prefer the Decca performance enough to offset some superiority in the Columbia sound, not a strong factor, since both disks are old and hardly striking although satisfactory. The Stern exhibition is not one to deplore: there is more dash to it, but I find the soft pliability of Mr. Goldberg more to my liking. The third record is in all respects inferior.

—S. Goldberg; Philharmonia Orch., W. Süsskind. DECCA DL-8504 (with *Handel: Violin Sonata No. 13*). 21 min.

—I. Stern; String Orch., A. Zakin. COLUMBIA

ML-4301 (with *Mozart: Po-Vn Sonata No. 36*).
20 min.

---

—A. Rüman; String Orch., K. Graunke. MER-
CURY 10056 (with *Mozart: Flute Concerto No.
1*), discontinued. 20 min.

VIOLIN AND ORCHESTRA, IN G

The performance here, from manuscript parts
assembled by the Haydn Society, is probably the
first in more than a century of a baroque concerto by Haydn other than the one in C (hardly
comparable to this one in originality and flavor).
The Finale, a cavorting duet with the spirit of
Handel, is a little revelation. Since the recording
is in effect a *première* for today's music-lovers,
they will forgive some uncertainties of solo intonation and murkiness in the orchestra during
the first two movements. The Finale apparently
insisted on a more thorough preparation. Call the
statement fair, but remember that it is unique.
There are no problems of reproduction.
—E. Bertschinger; Collegium Musicum, Vienna,
A. Heiller. HAYDN SOCIETY 1014 (with *Keyboard
Concerto in G*). 20 min.

VIOLIN AND ORCHESTRA, IN A, "MELK"

Here the record company rediscovered (at
Melk, in Lower Austria) most of the instrumental parts of a concerto vanished for nearly two
hundred years, corrected the abundant errors,
circumspectly wrote in the oboe parts indicated

but still lost, compounded a score, and proceeded to the registration of the first performance chronicled since Haydn's lifetime. It was the Haydn Society who did this, a record company like no other, in the integrity of its purpose, the breadth of its musical knowledge, and its (fatal) contempt for lucre when art is at issue.

The "Melk" Concerto leads the other Haydn violin concertos by an incalculable but vast distance, and ought to be given place, on its musical value, among the few representatives of real merit in this form, but it is to be feared that it is not encrusted with enough chrome to entice the virtuosos in vogue, still exclaiming about the discovery of another Paganini concerto. Haydn has given a fascinating account of escape from the baroque in this concerto half in, half out; a concerto grosso bedeviled in its sturdy soul by graceful felicities of shape that tease its counterpoint into complicity. I would not care to be without the record, which makes a fair plea for the music's great superiority to the other violin concertos. In a small, sweet and intimate way Miss Bertschinger delivers an unaffected and sympathetic line, the orchestra trailing along with a discretion that suggests timidity. Admittedly tame, but better than the assurance that manhandles. To be pleasant, the sound must be kept at moderate volume, which makes the solo very smooth, and saves the rest from coarseness.

—E. Bertschinger; Collegium Musicum, Vienna, A. Heiller. 10-in. HAYDN SOCIETY 1017. 27 min.

## VIOLIN, VIOLONCELLO, OBOE AND BASSOON (SINFONIA CONCERTANTE), IN B-FLAT

It is best not to tantalize ourselves by pausing to admire the artful combination of pomposity and piquancy in this big music which we can hear only on two inferior records. Mercury has a good performance terribly punished by metallic sound, and Vox's handful of performers are electronically distended to bring tears to a listener's eyes, or an oath to his lips.

—Soloists and Munich Philharmonia Orch., F. Rieger. MERCURY 10116 (with *Symph. No. 85*), discontinued. 23 min.

—Soloists and "Pro Musica" Orch., Stuttgart, R. Reinhardt. Vox 7390 (with *Cello Concerto in D*), discontinued. 22 min.

## VIOLONCELLO AND ORCHESTRA, IN D

There are occasions when one must be amazed and touched at the credulity of archaeologists, including those in music. Archaeologists like everyone else know that man is a lying animal; that he lies by instinct, by volition, and by perversity; but archaeologists differ from the rest of us in denying that talent for lying to men at least a hundred years dead. To archaeology, the words of a man gone have an inalienable truth that the words of no man present can possibly have, be the words spoken or written. This is not respect for the dead, but worship of paper.

For musical archaeology is principally the pursuit, study and comparison of paper. There are no quick witnesses, firsthand, for it to examine; and those at secondhand almost invariably take a quick, ferocious and efficient beating in their veracity, memory and integrity from the inquisitors of archaeology, who want a document to establish or substantiate a theory or a fact, and are most suspiciously hostile to living lips repeating what an ancestor said a long time ago. The browned or yellowed document is the passion of the profession, and I think we all admire the ingenuity, the methodism and the pertinacity devoted to its unearthing, the sagacity expended on its comparison with other papers, and the imagination given freedom for its interpretation. What perplexes and disturbs a layman is an archaeological inability to perceive that an indubitably genuine document may be false.

I do not think that this failure is in any degree allied to the vulgar adoration of mere print that induces people to believe advertisements, read editorials and give credence to political promises. Rather it is the very human disinclination to admit that the feet of the precious golden idol are made of clay. It is akin to the defense of his immeasurable wife by a man who after chasing, spending, struggling and agonizing to obtain her, glimpses the first bald evidence that she is a tramp.

Musicology has recently unearthed Haydn's holograph score of this cello concerto. The most acute musical opinion had previously favored

the belief that the real author was the famous
cellist Anton Kraft, who played under Haydn at
Esterház, and whose highest glory was his participation in the first performances of many of
the Beethoven quartets. The external testimony
promoting the Kraft authorship is pretty persuasive for this sort of matter, and the internal
testimony denying authorship to Haydn is inex-
orably convincing. The latter of course is an
infinitely more important kind of testimony. I
am not going to urge the case for Kraft, because
I was not there; but I cannot accept the case for
Haydn, because he never composed any other
music remotely like this dreary concerto, pre-
served only because his name has been attached
to it and because cellists need employment. Compared to Haydn the composer of this music was
a gelding.

The holograph? Presumably Haydn *wrote* it:
he did not *compose* it. It would not be the first
time that a man has acknowledged another's work
as his own. Why would Haydn have done a thing
like that? Well, the procedure was commonplace,
and he may have wished to do a favor for Kraft
(or another), or to have a cello piece at hand, or
to make fun of people, or for reasons of which
posterity could not possibly have an inkling. Conjecture gives life to history, and also murders
it, but it never proves it. Ruminate this one: that
a cellist—not improbably Kraft—needing a concerto to advertise his bow but not equipped to
compose a good one, took his ideas and sketches

to a benevolent man who was. The benevolent craftsman with habitual proficiency put the shabby material into conventional workmanlike order and at the further behest of his friend stretched his benignity far enough to permit the use of his name as composer, thus assuring the cellist's success, he alone with this work by the great Haydn in his repertory.

I do not insist on that solution, which is no more than plausible, but it is obvious to who will listen that Haydn could not have composed the concerto except under the influence of tranquillizers, for a man cannot be gelded temporarily. Two lullabies and a particularly noxious nursery tune in a row are inconceivable as the creation of a composer resistless to his lifelong bent for gusty contrasts. It is unbelievable that Haydn would have composed a solo part so dominant that the orchestra—of which he was music's first real master—is restricted to silence or to a mere strumming accompaniment during intolerably long stretches. It is inconceivable that against the gloom of the cello Haydn in 1783 would not have provided a more brightly glinting relief than can be provided by oboes, horns and strings. It is possible to concede that the well-built Adagio is Haydn's own, but its very merit forbids that he could have supplied it with two such dreadful bedfellows as the long-winded *allegro moderato* and the paltry Rondo. And who can believe the darting genius that created the wonderful keyboard Concerto in D, of the same putative year, capable of perpetrating so empty a repetitious piffle? It is Haydn's habit, when he seeks long service from material, to illumine it with the hundred devices at his disposal, so that each appearance is a change and every repetition a novelty.

Every age has its own morality, no more observed than that of ours; but every age acknowledges the morality of the white lie: the immoral act done for a moral purpose. I am fond enough of Haydn to hope that his deceit was in a kindly cause, and I know enough about him to believe it was. Still, that is what I want to believe, and after all, I wasn't there.

For two or three hearings the music exerts an elementary attraction but it has no stamina, and with time becomes repulsive.

Naturally, with my opinion of the concerto, my opinions of the records are offered with some constraint. London's registration is the best, and the performance carried by it is unlike any other in the nervous litheness of an orchestra conducted to make the most of every possibility of color and movement. This is certainly my favorite version, in the sense that it is less of a continuous sameness than the others. The nearest to it is the other, HMV, edition utilizing Mr. Fournier, who is less animated without the influence of the conductor Münchinger used by London. It goes without saying that all these cellists are professionally competent, and except the late Feuermann and Mr. Cassadó who seem to take the music with great seriousness, comfortable in the manufacture of smooth chunks of gunmetal sound. The Vox and Decca performances are particularly dull, the latter with dignity.

Late in the last century the Belgian composer F. A. Gevaert, pained by a defective edition, undertook to edit a new one. In the course of that work he added flutes, clarinets and bassoons to the orchestration (which of course so conscientious a musician would not have done to Haydn), thus brightening the fabric and raising interest. This orchestration is used in the RCA (HMV), Oceanic, Decca and Remington editions.

—P. Fournier; Stuttgart Ch. Orch., K. Münchinger. LONDON LL-1036 (with *Boccherini: Cello Concerto in B-flat*). 26 min.

—P. Fournier; Philharmonia Orch., R. Kubelik. RCA LHMV-1043 (with *6 "Encores"*), discontinued. 25 min.

—M. Gendron; Vienna Opera Orch., J. Sternberg. OCEANIC 23 (with *Saint-Saëns: Cello Concerto No. 1*). 24 min.

—A. Janigro; Vienna Opera Orch., F. Prohaska. WESTMINSTER 18406 (with *Boccherini: Cello Concerto in B-flat*). 24 min.

—E. Feuermann: Symph. Orch., M. Sargent. COLUMBIA ML-4677 (with *Schubert: Arpeggione Sonata*), discontinued. 25 min.

—E. Mainardi; Berlin Philharmonic Orch., F. Lehmann. 10-in. DECCA DL-7536. 27 min.

—L. Hölscher; Berlin Philharmonic Orch., C. Krauss. URANIA RS-731 (with *Bach: Concerto for*

*Violin and Oboe*), discontinued. 25 min.
—G. Cassadó; "Austrian" Symph. Orch., H. Wolf. REMINGTON 199-79 (with *Mozart: Symph. No. 35*). 26 min.
—W. Reichardt; "Pro Musica" Orch., Stuttgart, R. Reinhardt. Vox 7390 (with *Sinfonia Concertante*), discontinued. 31 min.


## DANCES

"DANCES FOR THE REDOUTENSAAL"

The record so called contains twenty-four dances for court use, "*Teutsche*" alternating with minuets in the full vigor of the old master's late prime. The richly imaginative orchestration of the German dances is a delight in itself, and the Haydn Society record is recommended although it is uneven in the quality of playing and in smoothness of registration, with the second side, in general, better than the first. Dr. Gillesberger's broad and jovial delivery of the bucolic German dances is quite pleasantly apt, but in stressing contrast he has made most of the minuets prim rather than gracious and lordly. The two minuets chosen by Decca are well played in a disappointing reduction for strings and badly recorded.
—Vienna Opera Orch., H. Gillesberger. HAYDN SOCIETY 1022. 41 min.

---

—London Baroque Ensemble, K. Haas (2 "*Hofball*" *Minuets only*). DECCA DL-9561 (with

*Symph. No. 22 and Concerto for Keyboard and Violin etc. in F*), discontinued. 4 min.

## OVERTURES

### No. 7, IN D

The richness of the material in this introduction to some stagework, now forgotten, induced Haydn to use it in at least two symphonies. The competent recorded performance lets us glimpse its spirited potential without making us feel that we have experienced its impact. Very clear sound, a little hard. A record good enough to have until there is another.
—Vienna Orch., F. Adler. Unicorn 1020 (with *M. Haydn: Symph. in C; K. Stamitz: Concerto for Clarinet and Bassoon*). 5 min.

### No. 13, IN G MINOR (L'ISOLA DISABITATA—THE DESERT ISLAND)

Suggests a miniature symphony, and suggests a medley. Thunder and sugar in a dramatic and entertaining union, sturdily delivered in a good MMS version of obvious professional competence and easy enjoyment. The withdrawn Allegro edition is one of the few disks I was unable to find for this discography.
—Winterthur Symph. Orch., W. Goehr. 10-in. MMS 6 (with *Symph. No. 96*). 7 min.
—Hastings Symph. Orch., J. Bath. 10-in. AL-

LEGRO 4053 (with works by Delius and Roussel), discontinued.

ITALIAN OVERTURE †

## SYMPHONIES

The ineradicable remains of a conjecture lazily hazarded and a million times abjectly repeated, that Haydn was the Father of the Symphony, owe their endurance to the attraction exerted by patent falsity on popular opinion. The legend has not the impudent inventiveness of the Betsy Ross story or of Marie Antoinette's less impossible *"Qu'ils mangent de la brioche, donc,"* but resembles with fair accuracy the credit allocated to two other of Haydn's contemporaries, Dr. Guillotin and Robert Fulton, for famous inventions which were not theirs. The latter pair improved on what they found, and so did Haydn, during his long, industrious life.

For even the most confident innovators in music, and Haydn was one of them, do not originate the great fruitful forms. They elaborate or transfigure an inheritance or a coeval tendency. When Haydn first applied the title of symphony to certain of his early orchestral works, he was imitating the structure of a hundred other composers, and utilizing, as they did, a convenient and ambiguous title for whose ambiguity he himself in his later symphonies was to be the principal agent of expulsion. After he had written thirty or forty his contemporaries imitated him, because he wrote best, and his successive innovations were quickly incorporated into a new orthodoxy.

Although he did not father the Symphony he fathered more than a hundred symphonies. In his maturity what he meant by the term is what we still apprehend from it primarily: sonata for orchestra. We do not know who was the first composer to write in rudimentary but indubitable sonata form, and we shall never be able to declare with assurance who was the first to employ the formula in orchestral music. It is not improbable that the earliest music, recognizable by today's ears as a symphony, was given another name by its composer.

In modern opinion the name fits best certain works of trim and positive architecture: Beethoven's Fourth, Haydn's No. 102, Dvořák's Fourth. These things are consummations of a form, but the name preceded the thing. The thing began to assume discernible shape about 1740, but a hundred years earlier the name was in wide and loose use to cover the instrumental portions of music predominantly vocal. For a long time it had that simplicity and breadth, of designating what was played and not sung, and did not get on the more definite track, which we are following, until it was used—by no means exclusively—to denote the instrumental introduction to a longer work. This is what we call nowadays an "overture," and it is in the formalization of that overture, when it was called *"sinfonia,"* into two or three sections of contrasting tempos, that we perceive the classical symphony sprouting. Pleasantly illustrative of the temporal vagaries of musical nomenclature is such a thing as the *"Sinfonia"* in a Bach "Overture," which we translate as the Overture to a Bach Suite.

For thirty-five years Haydn built symphonies on a framework in periodic transformation. He created related works in successive groups, in spurts of development. Beginning in emulation of the best of his predecessors, he soon led his contemporaries by the persuasion of his originality, and when he laid down his symphonic pen in 1795 he had become dictator in a form thenceforth in essence inviolable, whatever Beethoven was to do to its contents. His earliest symphonies, composed for the puny standard orchestra of strings supported by two oboes and two horns, are profuse in thematic material and perfunctory in development. Reliance on the characteristics of the moribund concerto grosso is very strong at the beginning, and a germ will persist until the last symphonies in the occasional interspersion of instrumental solos. He composes three, four, or five movements, but restricts himself to four in his full maturity. He essays a slow introduction early, discards it, reverts to it, and eventually decides that it is right: fourteen of the last fifteen symphonies have it.

His orchestra expands as he acquires confidence

and resources, and he experiments with novel combinations of instruments. All his life he composed for the forces available, knowing beforehand what they would be for the first performance, which would be under his control. A few of the very early works were played by a dozen musicians, some of the late ones by eighty. At the Salomon Concerts where the last twelve ("London") symphonies were first loosed on their ravishing flight, forty-odd were in the orchestra.

Such comparatively small forces have deluded modern concert managers and the producers of records into a continuance of inadequacy and indeed into an intensification of the difficulties confronting Haydn. What he had to accept they enforce when the necessity is gone; the small orchestra of a princely Hungarian country house is imitated in some vast warehouse of a concert hall; the restrictions on the composer are regarded as a virtue.

More than the concert managers, who after all do not promote much of Haydn, the manufacturers of records have flourished the banner of "authenticity" and skimped on the Haydn orchestra. Fortunately many conductors will not consent to do this, but a majority of the recorded symphonies numbered below eighty suffer from the thin sound of insufficient string sections.

The case here is not for the invariable use in Haydn of an orchestra of full modern symphonic strength, but for a proper application of forces to the music to be performed, from a minimum of twenty-five or thirty men for the symphonies of delicate or confiding mood, up to the maximum, for the grander works, appropriate to an acoustic enclosure that will not soften impact. If a large public hall is used, the maximum might properly be as great as two hundred, but in the modest dimensions of an enclosure designed for recording, without an empty expanse for an absent audience, an orchestra of from forty to sixty players would enable the Haydn symphonies to have the body and strength most of them require.

The case is presented to the supervisors of coming years. Few of the Haydn records have been made with such considerations in mind— few records by any composer, in truth. When large orchestras are used, they bring their customary auditorium with them to the disk. We do not hear Symphony No. 104 in its purity, but the recognizable Boston Symphony Orchestra in the recognizable Symphony Hall; and instead of the "Farewell" Symphony, we get on records the double dilution of the Philadelphia Orchestra's character and the character of the Academy of Music, infiltering the music with a new personality.

While waiting for the manufacturers to unshackle themselves from an invidious tradition, we can enjoy a recorded repertory of Haydn symphonies more extensive than one can hear in a lifetime of concertgoing. A hundred and four symphonies are numbered as genuine Haydn, and a few others are genuine although no editor has numbered them. Sixty-eight have been recorded on LP, most of these in satisfactory if not ideal versions, comprising a greater mass of purely orchestral music than that which has been allocated to any other composer. And one might add that in no other capacious block of music can one find such a preponderance of the devices of cheerfulness, for although Haydn wove gravity into his slow movements and on occasion nothing else into an entire symphony, for the most part he adhered to the taste of his age in stipulating the symphonic form fit rather for pattern and texture than for passion. For the most part.

Major keys, indelible tunes, positive meters and unstrained harmonies compound this music almost always immediately attractive. Never was learning, immense during the last thirty years of Haydn's life, less obtrusive in a composer than in the last dozen symphonies, where the teeming counterpoint is so natural in guise as to be inseparable apparently from the currents it embellishes. The last dozen are the ones to hear first, with perhaps Nos. 22, 49, 85, 88 and 92. In Haydn the best are the easiest, since the unfailing directness, the untormented simplicity, of his thought, increased in musical clarity as he acquired ever more elaborate resources for its expression. There is no more "profundity" in Symphony No. 103 than there is in No. 12, but the accumulation of art behind its creation gives to the later work an infinite superiority of point and authority, easy to assimilate and hard to forget.

### No. 1, IN D

The First is a minute fragrant canapé, a foretaste of much headier viands concocted during the thirty-six years following its first service. Its only recording, of a lively and unpolished performance, was appropriately the Haydn Society's first LP, and the 1949 sound betrays considerable distortion. Nevertheless the impression of proximity of the little orchestra has a certain raw effectiveness.

—Vienna Symph. Orch., J. Sternberg. HAYDN SOCIETY 1001 (with *Symphs. No. 13 and 28*). 7 min.

### No. 6, IN D, "LE MATIN"

Mr. Litschauer unfolds an affectionate if not dainty performance of the first important exercise in courtly music by Prince Esterházy's new *Kapellmeister*, the beginning of a trilogy ("Morning," "Noon," and "Evening") evocative of a day without trial. Bold sonics with surprisingly keen timbers for 1950, and noticeable, but tolerable, distortion at *fortes*. The other version, now retired, is afflicted with disagreeable sound.

—Vienna Ch. Orch., F. Litschauer. Haydn Society 1025 (with *Symph. No. 21*). 19 min.

---

—Bamberg Symph. Orch., H. Weisbach. Mercury 10079 (with *Symph. No. 13*), discontinued. 18 min.

## No. 7, in C, "Le Midi"

The five movements of "Noon" follow the four of "Morning" like a flutter of brave feathers. The mechanical skill of the Philadelphians and the unprecarious sound bestowed upon them by the Colombia engineers can lead to an initial illusion that theirs is the best record. On second hearing their bulldozing, rigid and unsympathetic style, devoid of both grace and dynamics, seems the worst of the three represented, for although the Randolf Orchestra play crudely, they are not by basic character inimical to Haydn. Mr. Litschauer has the idea, and conducts his band through the supple demands of the music with decency. The sonics of this old record are rather coarse, but are distinct in timbre and alone in presenting the horns in the strength hoped of them.

—Vienna Ch. Orch., F. Litschauer. Haydn Society 1016 (with *Symph. No. 8*). 24 min.

---

—Philadelphia Orch., E. Ormandy. Columbia ML-4673 (with *Symph. No. 45*). 24 min.

—"Austrian" Symph. Orch., K. Randolf. Rem-

162     THE COLLECTOR'S HAYDN

INGTON 199-71 (with *Mozart: Symph. No. 33*).
22 min.

## No. 8, IN G, "LE SOIR"

A lively and elegant celebration, "Evening" caps
the trilogy with a froth of shallow but exhilarating entertainment. It is surprising that there
is only one recorded version, and lucky that that
one is handled with spirit and discernment by all
the participants. The orchestra is a small one but
the engineers have contrived a full, if unglossy,
sound from it, good for its early era and satisfactory now, in its outright and unambiguous
projection a good deal smoother than that of the
first two parts of the trilogy in the same manufacturer's catalogue.
—Vienna Ch. Orch., F. Litschauer. HAYDN
SOCIETY 1016 (with *Symph. No. 7*). 18 min.

## No. 12, IN E

Is a superior example of the kind of short incipient symphony which a dozen of Haydn's
contemporaries in 1763 were turning out in in-
toxicated abundance. It is played with professional assurance without regard to subtleties (of
which there are not many) by an orchestra of
about twenty-five musicians guided by a tradition of style. The sound is good for its period
(1952) and still easygoing and still bright enough,
although articulation is not among its virtues.
—Ch. Orch., Vienna Academy of Music, W.

Loibner. LYRICHORD 36 (with *Symphs. No. 23, 29 and 30*). 10 min.

## No. 13, IN D, "JUPITER"

"Jupiter" because its Finale has a thematic prolepsis of Mozart's last symphony's Finale. It is an energetic, confident and assertive work premonitory of Haydn's symphonic leadership of a few years later. The Sternberg performance has the drive to make it interesting, and the reproduction, rough by present standards, is nevertheless alive and stimulating. The other version deserved, no doubt, its retirement by means of primitive sonics.

—Vienna Symph. Orch., J. Sternberg. HAYDN SOCIETY 1001 (with *Symphs. No. 1 and 28*). 17 min.

---

—Bamberg Symph. Orch., H. Weisbach. MERCURY 10079 (with *Symph. No. 6*), discontinued. 18 min.

## No. 19, IN D

Regretting that the brisk little symphony is no longer available, no one can regret the withdrawal of the only recording, atrocious in sound.
—Bamberg Symph. Orch., H. Weisbach. MERCURY 10077 (with *Mozart: Symph. No. 33*), discontinued. 12 min.

## No. 21, IN A

Experimenting all his life, Haydn makes the first

of the four movements an Adagio, and utilizes rhythmic patterns as thematic material in the even-numbered movements, a pronounced characteristic of many later symphonies of dramatic tenor. Here the modicum of drama is glib and superficial but interesting. The only recording is of a straightforward performance led by a conductor with a conscientious hand in these early symphonies, and played with precision but no beauty of tone by an orchestra of twenty-seven including the harpsichord continuo, here in admirable perspective. Despite its age the sound is by no means contemptible, and in bringing the orchestra near, the engineers have given natural force to the horns, which results in some blasting and a shorter life for the record.

—Vienna Ch. Orch., F. Litschauer. HAYDN SOCIETY 1025 (with *Symph. No. 6*). 18 min.

## No. 22, IN E-FLAT, "THE PHILOSOPHER"

The pungent and mysterious melancholy of the long first movement, *adagio*, a chorale for a pair of English horns and two horns backed by muted violins, followed by the peremptory fierceness of the *presto* second movement, arrests and holds attention fascinated as forcefully as by anything in Haydn. It is a great symphony, No. 22, but few are the readers of this who have ever heard it in a concert hall, although the late Felix Weingartner used to conduct it in Europe. The astounding indolence and timidity of star conductors and orchestral associations ignore old scores, however grand, if the parts have not already been purchased or if success is not guaranteed. The recorded versions are not good enough, and the attention of such leaders as Hermann Scherchen, Georg Solti and Sir Thomas Beecham, susceptive to this kind of music, is directed to Symphony No. 22.

Mr. Haas applies an abundance of professional skill and aplomb to an obliteration of the dramatic contrasts of the symphony, removing its viscera and denaturing its nerves, in the bland procedure of taking its *adagio* fast and its first *presto* slowly, this by a band of chamber-music dimensions. Competent sonics clarify all the details of the catastrophe.

With much less address in the elements of playing, the Sternberg version is far richer in musical discernment and satisfies the requirements of the score except in a clubfooted Minuet which is something of a Sternberg specialty. With the passage of time the sound of this disk, devoid of gloss and afflicted with some buzzing in the union of horns and English horns, is not very appealing although it has some rough strength; and until a new edition appears, by an orchestra of at least forty in good modern reproduction, it will be hard for Haydnists to deprive themselves of one of the master's greatest creations; and so the Sternberg record is imposed, the Haas being a travesty.

—Vienna Symph. Orch., J. Sternberg. HAYDN SOCIETY 1009 (with *Symph. No. 35*). 17 min.

---

—London Baroque Ensemble, Karl Haas. DECCA 9561 (with *Concerto for Harpsichord and Violin, and 2 Hofball Minuets*). 16 min.

## No. 23, IN G

Suggests practice for a longer work, in the variety of mood put into its short compass. It is worth having in its one recording, of a spirited performance not bothered with finesse, carried by satisfactory but far from compelling sound.
—Ch. Orch., Vienna Academy of Music, W. Loibner. LYTICHORD 36 (with *Symphs. No. 12, 29 and 30*). 12 min.

## No. 26, IN D MINOR, "LAMENTAZIONE"

This is fevered, violent and ungainly music of experimental rough strength, worth hearing in a more expert performance and cleaner sound. Gratification at having the symphony on records gives way with familiarity to impatience at the dowdy attack.
—Vienna Ch. Orch., A Heiller. HAYDN SOCIETY 1019 (with *Symph. No. 36*). 15 min.

## No. 28, IN A

If this symphony flirts overmuch with novelty to the detriment of form, it is the novelty which makes it attractive and which led to the great Haydn of the symphonies soon to come, and

the chopping Adagio has a neat and melting charm, seconded by a witty Minuet. The old record bears an intelligent performance and reproduces with a measure of authority in spite of its age and distortion.
—Vienna Symph. Orch., J. Sternberg. HAYDN SOCIETY 1001 (with *Symphs. No. 1 and 13*). 14 min.

### No. 29, IN E

After two and a half movements of perhaps overly sustained geniality, Haydn rewards us with a pungent and seizing little trio in his Minuet, and then dashes into a vehement and impatient Finale, as if to abash the spinelessness of the first half of his symphony. It is interesting to note that the principal theme of this Finale is the same as the leading subject in the first movement of Mozart's Violin Concerto in E-flat, that KV 268 whose authorship is in part indisputably Mozart's and in part indisputably not. Mr. Loibner gives a performance similar to that of the other symphonies on the same disk— knowing and assured in the broad lines, but sparing of the refinements whose realization requires arduous preparation. Pretty good sound, excellent for its date, with a more distinct bite than is apparent on the obverse of the same disk.
—Ch. Orch., Vienna Academy of Music, W. Loibner. LYRICHORD 36 (with *Symphs. No. 12, 23, and 30*). 13 min.

## No. 30, in C, "Alleluja"

Short, brilliant, festive and enlivening, this positive symphony receives the best performance and the best sound of any accorded to the four works on the disk, suggesting that more study was given to the prime than to the secondary pieces. The instrumental coloration is surprisingly accurate, and no instrument has been slighted.
—Ch. Orch., Vienna Academy of Music, W. Loibner. Lyrichord 36 (with *Symphs. No. 12, 23 and 39*). 10 min.

## No. 31, in D, "Horn-Signal"

Four horns are naturally allotted to a symphony singing the pleasures of the chase, and Haydn has taken good care to see that the players' virtuosity is thoroughly tested. Unfortunately he could not foresee that the subtle horn is the instrument most recalcitrant to imprisonment on records. Hoarse and throttled, without any of their characteristic mysterious bloom, the four horns, as distorted on this disk, carry their tonal infection to the rest of the orchestra—much too small for the music, incidentally—capping the despondency of an awkward performance whose participants show only one grace, that of being apologetic.
—Vienna Symph. Orch., J. Sternberg. Haydn Society 1002 (with *Symph. No. 34*). 21 min.

## No. 33, IN C

A little fellow lightly scored, but well built and easygoing, No. 33 has received a performance of decision and vigor, indifferent to ostentatious finesse but much of a neat piece, and smartly delivered by well-trained strings and full-bodied horns, with a pair of oboes for color. The sound is strong, unusually good in balance, and has a living vibrancy, but will be so realized only after careful adjustment of the control-unit, with particular attention to the subjugation of shrillness.
—"Philharmonia Orch. of Hamburg," A. Winograd. M-G-M 3436 (with *Symph. No. 46*). 16 min.

## No. 34, IN D MINOR

Emotionally pretentious music whose potentialities are nearly invisible in a drab and uncertain performance and sonics obscured by a muddy bass.
—Vienna Symph. Orch., J. Sternberg. HAYDN SOCIETY 1002 (with *Symph. No. 31*). 15 min.

## No. 35, IN B-FLAT

Nothing but sunlight, its beams diversified in a dozen directions by the commanding hand and inexhaustible invention of a composer now at thirty-five beginning to show himself as one of the most professionally adept of technicians ever, Symphony No. 35 is one of the most obvious

successes on records of these early symphonies. It is handled with understanding skill and good orchestral discipline, and its sturdy sonics are unusual in their clean articulation of the bass.
—Vienna Symph. Orch., J. Sternberg. HAYDN SOCIETY 1009 (with *Symph. No. 22*). 15 min.

### No. 36, IN E-FLAT

Elegant and ebullient both, No. 36 probably graced some festivity in the magnificent rustic court where Haydn had a free hand to compose what he wished so long as his prince wished it, too. The fast external movements are laudably animated and deft in the Heiller projection, a reduction of flexibility being noticeable in slow movement and Minuet. Reproduction is entirely acceptable although lacking sting, with the emphasis on a unified orchestral texture rather than on distinction of timbres.
—Vienna Ch. Orch., A. Heiller. HAYDN SOCIETY 1019 (with *Symph. No. 26*). 21 min.

### No. 38, IN C

The invigorating possibilities of a symphony not inappropriate for a military ceremony, hot with trumpets and drums, are on its only disk properly exploited for two movements before Mr. Sternberg stumbles over the Minuet, a form whose meter needs an airy flip which this conductor has not mastered. Depressed by his experience there, Mr. Sternberg moves glumly through a Finale crying for tautness and vitality. Thus half

the performance is good. The sound in a comfortable way is all pretty good.
—Vienna Symph. Orch. J. Sternberg. HAYDN SOCIETY 1010 (with *Symph. No. 39*). 14 min.

## No. 39, IN G MINOR, "THE FIST"

The contempt that reflective music-lovers entertain for the ignorance of publicized conductors and the poltroonery of fashionable orchestras in restricting repertory to what everyone knows by heart is intensified by the phonographic revelation of a symphony like this one. The revelation ought to have been made in the concert hall, but who in America has heard this first of the great dire symphonies except on this record? Sullen, vindictive and ominous, the G minor tirade cuts its indelible way into memory while it achieves an utmost felicity of art, growing as it lengthens; and nearly two hundred years ago its effect was as it is today, for the young Mozart used it as model for his own early G minor Symphony, No. 25, which musicologists have lauded as a trail-blazer while ignoring who did the blazing first.

It is strange that there is but one recording. It is fair to call this one fair and in places even excellent, for the conductor understands and respects the nature of the work he is leading, and the sound (of an orchestra too small for the boldness of the music) is meritorious as a whole although hardly as crisp and distinct as we should expect in 1957, the record dating from 1950. The playing faults result from insufficient rehearsal, and will not seem serious until a serious new edition has appeared. Until then the record is indispensable for lovers of Haydn.

—Vienna Symph. Orch., J. Sternberg. HAYDN SOCIETY 1010 (with *Symph. No. 38*). 15 min.

### No. 42, IN D

The glib and resourceful high proficiency of this musical construction, produced by the expert Haydn without help from the inventive Haydn, is more esteemed by professional musicians than by music-lovers less enamored of technique. To the latter the effect is of fruitless exhilaration, which after all is not wicked. Robust playing and sound, neither with superb virtues or grave defects, permit an honorable appraisal of the symphony as something cheerfully shallow but not dull.

—Vienna Ch. Orch., F. Litschauer. HAYDN SOCIETY 1026 (with *Symph. No. 47*). 25 min.

### No. 43, IN E-FLAT, "MERCURY"

The pliant adjectives bestowed on No. 42, above, would not be misplaced here were it not for certain subtleties in the "Mercury" which give it added distinction. The conductor, Mr. Wöldike, here leading a neat band of sure-handed musicians, is a classicist of renown, inclined to identify classicism with staidness, but not invariably. When he is ready to concede that precision on occasion must yield to higher but less calculable values, he is eminently a superior leader of music of the eighteenth century, but he does not make that concession here, and the quicksilver is elusive in the "Mercury." In extenuation of his reticences it ought to be understood that few conductors could lead with this assurance without study and rehearsals too costly for music which does not incite. Pretty good just the same, this half-hobbled "Mercury," crisp and easy in reproduction of the small orchestra.

—Ch. Orch., Danish National Radio, M. Wöldike. HAYDN SOCIETY 1041 (with *Symph. No. 50*). 22 min.

## No. 44, IN E MINOR, "TRAUER"

During three or four years, as he approached the drab age of forty, when a man is no longer young and has not yet acquired the measure of dignity conferred on his temerity in reaching fifty, Haydn made fitful forays into precincts alien to the musical boundaries of the time, hewing out a fistful of symphonies impassioned with troubled violence. These he set in minor keys and usually deviated far from the tonalities after setting them. Hard rhythms and staccato phrases are essential in his scheme, and a strong contrapuntal reënforcement (witness the canonic Minuet of this "Mourning" Symphony) leaves no doubt of the seriousness of his intentions.

Haydn declared that he wished the Adagio of the E minor Symphony to be played at his own funeral.

This Adagio, in the recorded editions, is twice (Fricsay and Wöldike) offered as the third movement and thrice traditionally as the second. There is good precedent for both positions, and neither form nor narrative seems adversely affected by either sequence.

Here for the first time appears Dr. Scherchen as a Haydn symphonist, although this was not his first Haydn record. For Symphony No. 44 the reader is not advised to look further. One hearing of the five versions corroborates the stunning impression made by the Scherchen edition alone. It is entirely clear that the Westminster conductor has studied the score with a thoroughness and insight amazing in view of the obscurity of the music, and has delivered his findings with a fervor of conviction that simply cannot fail to convince listeners. In sharpness of attack, decision of accent, and positiveness of shape, this startling interpretation—which the orchestra accepts with remarkable accord—dogmatizes the emotional asperity of the symphony to a degree approached by no other recorded essay. It is favored by the brightest and most compelling sound of the five recordings, exception made for shrill violins which may not be correctable on many reproducers.

The Decca sonics are the most euphonious, lacking the Westminster sting but avoiding trouble; and the Fricsay performance they carry is excellent although not an apocalypse. The Wöldike record is another good one, primarily crisp and clean in the unified stroke of the orchestra and the clarity, without great strength, of the reproduction. Mr. Sacher is less taut than these former, and the Epic sound has its virtues of force and good balance compromised by violin stridency impossible to subdue. The Haydn Society record is one of their poorest.

—Vienna Opera Orch., H. Scherchen. WEST-MINSTER XWN 18613 (with *Symph. No. 49*). 24 min.

—Rias Orch., Berlin, F. Fricsay. DECCA 9614 (with *Mozart: Symph. No. 35*). 20 min.

—Danish National Radio Orch., M. Wöldike LONDON LL-844 (with *Symph. No. 48*). 20 min.

---

—Vienna Symph. Orch., P. Sacher. EPIC 3059 (with *Symph. No. 85*). 20 min.

—Vienna Symph. Orch., J. Sternberg. HAYDN SOCIETY 1003 (with *Symph. No. 48*). 20 min.

No. 45, IN F-SHARP MINOR, "FAREWELL" ***

The "Farewell" receives an occasional public performance because of the allure exerted by the charming anecdote associated with its nickname. It is even possible that the anecdote is true, although this is more than one asks. It is enough that it is credible, and it is certainly a delightful illustration, fact or fancy, of the amiable spoofing we know Haydn liked to perpetrate. In the

Finale, pair by pair of musicians snuff their candles and slip away from view and further participation, until at last a couple of violinists alone remain to play the expiring measures. Supposedly this was the composer's hint to his patron that the Esterházy orchestra had been retained too long away from their families.

Anecdotes aside, one must accept this final Adagio—an epilogue really to a symphony already complete in four movements—as a culmination more by its beauty than its novelty of preponderant importance in the scheme, in spite of the vigorous inventiveness of the preceding movements. The epilogue cannot be conceived as other than a gentle and direct, lovely, disarming appeal, no matter what it appeals for.

That is much too simple for the Philadelphians. After the hearer has shaken off the beguilement bestowed by the succulence of their orchestral tone, he realizes that they are above this sort of thing and eager to be done with it quickly. Mr. Leinsdorf, influenced by his apprenticeship with Mr. Toscanini, a baneful influence in this kind of music, rips through the "Farewell" in a sort of insensate bravado painful to listeners who know the conductor's true ability. In reproduction this performance shimmers with intrusive metal. The Seegelken browse lacks lilt and lift.

Remain two finely tempered performances compromised, one grievously, by sonic faults. The responsive, felicitous playing in the Melichar version suffers from vaguely wiry sound, and the sensitive, expert statement of the Stuttgarters—easily the best playing here—is produced by a band too small and with a deficiency in the bass which may be because the bass was not there or because the engineers subtracted too much. Withal, this London version is decidedly attractive, and the only one worth having.

—Stuttgart Ch. Orch. and Members of the Suisse Romande Orch., Geneva, K. Münchinger. LONDON LL-525 (with *Wagner: Siegfried Idyll*). 25 min.

---

—Munich Philharmonic Orch., A. Melichar. 10-in. MERCURY 15028, discontinued. 29 min.
—Philadelphia Orch., E. Ormandy. COLUMBIA ML-4673 (with *Symph. No. 7*). 23 min.
—"Pro Musica" Orch., Stuttgart, W. Seegelken. Vox 7310 (with *Symph. No. 96*), discontinued. 25 min.
—"American Artists' Symph. Orch.," E. Leinsdorf. GA 319 (with *Beethoven: Symph. No. 5*). 18 min.
—Same performance on GA 301 (with *Mozart: 4 Overture*).

No. 46, IN B
A rare key and an obscure symphony albeit good-humored, animated and entertaining, in two commendable editions. It will be noted at once that the Goehr performance is more deftly styled, but the excellence of the Hamburg strings and their warm blend with the oboes and horns

may balance that virtue sufficiently. MMS has registered with a long reverberation that blunts articulation but gives a symphonic billowing, while the more outward thrust of the M-G-M sound is cleaner but hard to adjust whereas its rival's is easy. My preference is the Goehr.
—Netherlands Philharmonic Orch., W. Goehr. 10-in. MMS 129 (with *Symph. No. 96*). 19 min.
—"Philharmonia Orch. of Hamburg," A. Winograd. M-G-M 3436 (with *Symph. No. 33*). 18 min.

## No. 47, IN G

With playing and recording as good as this we do not have to deplore the lack of a competitive edition in a symphony as temperate as this. Actually, the weakness of the music is confined to the first two movements, ingenious in an aimless and unsatisfactory way. The clever Minuet and precipitate Finale are capital and captivating. Sinewy and urbane in performance and solid in bold sound which belies its origin in 1950, the symphony may well wait a long time before it is accorded a better edition.
—Vienna Ch. Orch., F. Litschauer. HAYDN SOCIETY 1026 (with *Symph. No. 42*). 21 min.

## No. 48, IN C, "MARIA THERESA"

A visit of Maria Theresa, Holy Roman Empress and King of Hungary, an immensity of maternalism, the ruler of a thousand princes and the victim of a dozen spoliations which she emulated where she dared ("*Elle prenait toujours en pleurant*," said Frederick II)—a visit of this formidable creature to Esterház was not to be taken lightly. Haydn's part in the splendid festivities was of course of intimidating importance, of which the ceremonial flattery of the symphony he composed for the visit is a cheerful segment. To the more-or-less standard orchestra, oboes, horns and strings, he had used in most of his symphonies until then, he adds trumpets and drums and gives license for them to be forceful. He alternates brilliant pomp with easy reflection for twenty minutes, and it is hard to be displeased with the parade. The empress was not.

The Danish conductor Wöldike has a sure hand in dispensing the splendors of pageantry, and his very skillful orchestra displays a fine unity of calculated enthusiasm. The sound is bright and full, strong and deep, commanding from the beginning and never troublesome. Not much more can be wanted.

The other record is distressingly inferior in every respect and ought to be repealed.
—Danish National Radio Orch., M. Wöldike. LONDON LL-844 (with *Symph. No. 44*). 20 min.

---

—Vienna Symph. Orch., J. Sternberg. HAYDN SOCIETY 1003 (with *Symph. No. 44*). 20 min.

No. 49, IN F MINOR, "LA PASSIONE"
The Passion is that of the Saviour Jesus. Haydn with the becoming reticence of his epoch did not

provide a scenario of his emotions to accompany this music, whose turbulent torment, however, can hardly be mistaken for anything else. Although composed earlier than its present number would suggest, and in fact one of the first of his impassioned exercises in a minor key, in the directness of its narrative and the tautness of its form No. 49 is probably the greatest of them. The four movements allow no moment of holiday from tragedy, and the symphony culminates in a Finale all breathless terror at the contemplation of an onrushing happening infinitely dreadful.

All three recorded editions are the opposite of lax in projecting the sinister energy of this music. Very few Haydn symphonies have been presented on records with an average of merit comparable to that accorded to No. 49. The principal currents are strikingly similar in every version, and only in lesser details do points of superiority become apparent. The Blech attack has not the relentlessness of savagery displayed by the others, and a rich, glowing orchestral texture contrived by the engineers, attractive in itself, is less suitable than the lean and crisp sound of the Newstone players. However, it is Dr. Scherchen who exacts the greatest intensity, which, when combined with the superior unanimity of his orchestra and the most distinguished sound of all, imposes the Westminster disk as the one to be preferred. The domineering bass of this recording, deep and smooth but sharp in bite, and the positiveness of oboes and horns, are eminent and difficult accomplishments. It might be added that the Scherchen disk is one of those very rare ones with a leader on each of its sides.

—Vienna Opera Orch., H. Scherchen. Westminster XWN 18613 (with *Symph. No. 44*). 20 min.

—Haydn Orch., London, H. Newstone. Haydn Society 1052 (with *Symph. No. 73*). 22 min.

—London Mozart Players, H. Blech. London LL-586 (with *Mozart: Divertimento No. 2*). 21 min.

## No. 50, in C

Is amenable to the general description applied to Symphony No. 48, "Maria Theresa." Fanfares and lyricism, broad opposition of extremes of strength, a jubilation composed for a showy event. The one recording, sonically clear and sturdy, excellent, carries a comfortable performance forthright in pomp and a little measured in vivacity.

—Ch. Orch., Danish National Radio, M. Wöldike. Haydn Society 1041 (with *Symph. No. 43*). 19 min.

## No. 52, in C minor

This is a symphony of severe but not grim essence, organized with a confident *expertise* which from now (1773) on is always at the command of the composer. Not so attractive at first hearing as many of Haydn's symphonies of this period, its tough fiber wins greater admiration with greater familiarity. The performance is adequate, but familiarity reveals some shortage of alertness in making point. Similarly the strong recording suffers with time from a growing awareness from its hearers of a persistent minor harshness; and good apparatus are required to subdue the stridency from the violins at *fortes*. —Vienna Opera Orch., A. Heiller. HAYDN SOCIETY 1039 (with *Symph. No. 56*). 19 min.

## No. 53, IN D, "IMPERIAL"

Associated like No. 48 with a visit of Maria Theresa, the "Imperial" Symphony is furnished with little pomp for a justification of the nickname. Indeed the middle movements are notable for a tidy homespun style in rebuke to ceremony if not necessarily to the empress. The naïve and beguiling Andante is the work of an accomplished courtier and an enormously proficient composer.

Neither recording is first class although both are better than ordinary. Dr. Stokowski does some of the delicate tracing in tenuous tones for which he is noted, admirable and very pretty but overscented for this healthy music. The rather ancient sonics are sweet but lack the acuity of modern reproduction. Mr. Sacher gives a frank and hearty exposition with an orchestra less supple, and despite harshness in reproduction the modern engineering does have a telling effect

of real strings, vibrating reeds and glinting brasses.
—Vienna Symph. Orch., P. Sacher. Epic 3038 (with *Symph. No. 67*). 21 min.
—Symph. Orch., L. Stokowski. RCA LM-1073 (with *Liszt: Les Préludes*). 17 min.

## No. 54, in G

Is another requiring time to make its right impression. Antithesis in the first movement flirts with buffoonery and is initially perplexing, as in the vapory instrumentation of the long Adagio. Unfortunately, with understanding of the symphony comes realization that the record is dated. The orchestra is penurious with both grace and gloss, and the recorded sound of the small force of strings inclines to scrawniness, while the winds fail to show the urgency of their timbres.
—Ch. Orch., Vienna Academy of Music, H. Swarowsky. Lyrichord 32 (with *Symph. No. 70 and Mozart: "Paris" Overture KV 311a*). 28 min.

## No. 55, in E-flat, "Schoolmaster" ***

The amusing didacticism of the second movement dictated the nickname. Neat, prepossessing, demure and suave; and so played, with continuous finesse and punctuations of gusto. The responsive stroke and affable tone extorted by Dr. Scherchen and the Westminster engineers from the Vienna Symphony Orchestra as long ago as 1950 were marvels for their time and have not begun to diminish in appeal in spite of the steady advances in the science of recording since their first dazzling appearance. It is not likely that the only version of the "Schoolmaster" ever made will soon be superseded by a better. —Vienna Symph. Orch., H. Scherchen. WEST-MINSTER XWN 18614 (with *Symph. No. 80*). 20 min.

## No. 56, IN C

C major in Haydn means trumpets and drums, and in this symphony as the Haydn Society has recorded it the trumpets are supported by specially constructed high horns in C, sounding an octave above our expectation, in a giddy, rather hysterical and compulsive cry. In this case authenticity, by supplying the salt of novelty, injects a strong interest of its own, counterbalancing the authenticity that prescribed too small a group of strings for the music, with the resultant strain at *fortes*. Notwithstanding this fault and a paucity of refinement, the record may have to serve for a long time until new enterprise is found for a new production more thoroughly rehearsed and provided with contemporary sonics. It is more arduous to prepare and record the cool niceties of a symphony of this period than to rely on the "1812" Overture, certain to be more arresting in a mediocre projection than the symphony in a perfect one. Conductors and orchestras in vogue are still try-

ing to maintain the pretense that Haydn's first
symphony was No. 88.
—Vienna Symph. Orch., A. Heiller. HAYDN
SOCIETY 1039 (with *Symph. No. 52*). 24 min.

No. 60, IN C, "LE DISTRAIT"
Haydn wrote incidental music for a French
comedy, whose title was appropriated as nickname for the symphony drawn from the incidental music. Nothing is absent-minded in the
gay hodgepodge of blandishments united under
cover of the austere designation "symphony":
six movements in disparagement of dignity, three
of them brazen with tomfoolery, and all staying
close to the C major tonality, enlivened by drums
and trumpets, customarily assigned by the composer to stately or at least courtly celebrations.
Its highly diverting values are permitted in the
one recording a relaxed and genial expression
in which we are never allowed to misapprehend
its basic flippancy. The orchestral depth is more
satisfying than that of most of the records heard
so far, and the sound is expansive and pleasant.
—Glyndebourne Festival Orch., V. Gui. RCA
LHMV-1064 (with *Mozart: Symph. No. 38*),
discontinued. 26 min.

No. 61, IN D
The restraint of the urbanity clothing the unpretentious subjects is capable of obscuring the
charm of this artful music wherein nothing in

particular is salient but where everything fits in snug logic. The Wöldike disk is the opposite of obscurity, transparent and cohesive in both playing and sound, one of the most successful of the Haydn Society's presentations of a Haydn symphony. (A large proportion of the disks of Scandinavian origin that reach America are technically excellent.)
—Ch. Orch., Danish National Radio, M. Wöldike. HAYDN SOCIETY 1047 (with *Mozart: Clarinet Concerto*). 25 min.

## No. 64, IN A

Understood that the depressing sound necessarily conceals features of the interpretation, a good deal of what is not concealed is disappointing. The conductor seems to be trying to obtain what the orchestra cannot or will not: never was fluency more elusive or phrasing less compact. Westminster, who made the record back in their green first year—1950, phonographically remote —know a bad one when they hear it, and they tampered with the tape's output to create a new disk minus the defects of the old. They did not fail; but in replacing shrill distortion by turgidity they did not effect a satisfactory substitute.
—Vienna Symph. Orch., H. Swoboda. WEST-MINSTER XWN 18615 (with *Symph. No. 91*). 20 min.

## No. 67, IN F

Under the best conditions of reproduction the

sonics here are singularly convincing. A lifelike,
throaty bubbling distinguishes the woodwinds,
the string texture is pretty good, and at the
optimum point of adjustment the balance between bass and treble lines will be impressive.
The response seems to be best at moderate volume. Furthermore, we have a performance based
on knowledge and sympathy in the conductor
backed by fluent response from the orchestra
save in a few irregular chords. The symphony,
not strikingly attractive at first, has the invalu-
able Haydn capacity for holding more than first
meets the ear, and the record is strongly recommended to those music-lovers who will have
patience with it.
—Vienna Symph. Orch., P. Sacher. Epic 3038
(with *Symph. No. 53*). 22 min.

## No. 70, in D

Short, but flaunting a canonic Andante and a big
double fugue in the Finale, Symphony No. 70
receives a much better exposition than No. 54
on the obverse of the same record. The more
difficult work has induced a more careful preparation. There are little felicities of subtle expression here, whereas overside the players merely
tried to keep their places. The musicians' confidence endows the instruments with a zip of
new life, and the sound of this side, especially for
the winds, is brighter and sturdier than that
achieved for No. 54. Not that a sound as hard
as this is commendable, but it does suffice as an

acceptable conveyance for the symphony. —Ch. Orch., Vienna Academy of Music, H. Swarowsky. LYRICHORD 32 (with *Symph. No. 54 and Mozart: "Paris" Overture KV 311a*). 15 min.

### No. 73, IN D, "HUNT"

After the very successful reception evoked by a brilliant descriptive overture, *"La Chasse,"* garnished with fat horns lustily saluting St. Hubert with those irresistible rhythmic tunes still used for the chase, Haydn could see—nor can we after him—no disadvantage in assuring greater longevity to the sure-fire by establishing it as the Finale of a symphony. This is it, three appealing movements, two tidy and one tipsy, preceding the pursuit of the stag or the boar. The Newstone version is excellent in nearly all respects of playing and reproduction, while the old Sevitsky recording is furred although agreeable in sound and its stylization is not persuasive. —Haydn Orch., London, H. Newstone. HAYDN SOCIETY 1052 (with *Symph. No. 49*). 23 min. —Indianapolis Symph. Orch., F. Sevitsky. RCA LBC-1062 (with *Glazounow: From the Middle Ages*), discontinued. 18 min. —Same performance on RCA LM-31, 10-in., discontinued.

### No. 77, IN B-FLAT, "DON OTTAVIO"

Now nearly fifty, Haydn writes symphonies whose anticipated technical sophistication is warmed by a curious, individual and mellow good-fellowship that will seldom be absent from his work in the future. Everyone has sensed this benignity in those later works that are really familiar, and the deprecation most frequently made of the composer is that he exploited cheerfulness to unwarranted lengths. Musical intellectuals commonly esteem the more brutal emotions more highly than amiability, and uncultivated music-lovers reverse the preference, but both judgments impose in fact a limitation of musical enjoyment on the judges. It is not the good humor of the later Haydn symphonies that ought to excite the admiration of listeners, since many imbeciles have a far greater abundance of it, but the ten thousand resourceful contrivances that make the innumerable aspects of good humor sparkle their way into immortality.

No. 77 begins the parade, to be interrupted briefly only once or twice, of the artful abstract pleasantries on which Haydn's greatest renown reposes. It is one of the few major works by Haydn where the adjective "Mozartian" would not be grossly misapplied: this means that it must have had a considerable influence on the younger composer. The great similarity of the Adagio to "*Il mio tesoro*" is less significant than the shape of both subjects in the first movement and the shaded variations given to the Minuet. Mozart knew what was worth emulation, and we to whom the phonograph has given an acquaintanceship with three times as many symphonies as

Mozart ever heard will not easily designate any short symphony by anybody as more continuous in interest than No. 77.

An old recording, and rather musty in sound, but remarkable for the bold force and true timbre permitted to the horns, the performance intelligent and even gracious except in the fast and messy Adagio wherein conductor and players are in disaccord.
—Symph. Orch., H. Swoboda. CONCERT HALL 30 (with *Symph. No. 78*). 15 min.

## No. 78, IN C MINOR

Not often is the mordant key of C minor used as it is here without implications of conflict. Serious and dogmatic, its vindictive interpellations serving only as punctuation, this music stimulates by patterns and tones separate from sentiment, and ought to satisfy the requirements of the most austere classicists. Phonographically it is better served than its overside No. 77, cleaner and more substantial in the sound and more confident in the playing. The Adagio is patently fast, but the other movements are both powerful and orderly.
—Symph. Orch., H. Swoboda. CONCERT HALL 30 (with *Symph. No. 77*). 16 min.

## No. 80, IN D MINOR

A beautiful and unstable symphony, mixing bubbles and forebodings, suavity and prankishness, in a performance of knowing style and polished projection (the Vienna Symphony Orchestra is

always transfigured for this conductor) kept
vivid by sonics still serenely excellent after nearly
seven years.
—Vienna Symph. Orch., H. Scherchen. Westminster XWN 18614 (with *Symph. No. 55*).

"Paris" Symphonies: Nos. 82-87

These six symphonies were composed in 1785-
1786 for production at Paris, and three of them
were accorded French nicknames—"*L'Ours*" to
No. 82, "*La Poule*" to No. 83, and "*La Reine de
France*" to No. 85. Haydn was now recognized
to be a perfect practitioner of his craft by musicians and music-lovers all over Europe, and he
rewarded their attention by a succession of
masterpieces of which not one is tentative, each
is homogeneous and all, as a matter of course,
are fresh and stimulating in the new guises of
an ever-changing invention. The parts no longer
tend to dominate the whole, elegance is supplanted by a lustier grace: good humor slips
spontaneously into every symphony.

No. 82, in C, "The Bear" ***

"*The Bear*" moves with the self-propelled facility
that makes the notes of all the Paris symphonies
seem dictated by an impregnable logic. The title
is earned by the gruff but cheerful growls of bass
pedal-points in the Finale: the rest belongs to a
lither zoology, and it is too bad that the records
do not give enough air to its airiness. The Rosbaud performance has more life and authority

than the Sternberg, but the old Mercury sound is uncomfortably plated with metal, while the old Haydn Society sound, admittedly lacking distinction, is acceptable as a whole and commendable in the woodwinds. Coarseness in the string tone probably is an honest reflection of the strings, which show roughnesses elsewhere that cannot be attributed to the engineers.
—Vienna Symph. Orch., J. Sternberg. HAYDN SOCIETY 1008 (with *Symph. No. 85*). 21 min.

---

—Bavarian Radio Orch., H. Rosbaud. MERCURY 10050 (with *Symph. No. 104*), discontinued. 23 min.

## No. 83, IN G MINOR, "THE HEN"

The sobriquet (derived from the tranquil cackling of upper strings and oboes in the subsidiary subject of the opening movement) has the convenience, for purposes of identification, of a name rather than a number, but it tends to belittle the virile drive of a symphony complex in mood but not jocular anywhere for long. In the six symphonies of the Paris group the composer is patently trying to balance the savory with the substantial, and the epithet does not exist with enough pliability to suggest the gist of any.

In affection for the Haydn Society, which did more for the music of Haydn than any other agency, this century, has dared to try, the blemishes of sound and performance of the Heiller record will not be specified here. Suffice it that they are many and mortal. Fortunately the Malko statement is crisp and lively, its sound better than acceptable.

—Danish Royal Orch., N. Malko. RCA LBC-1060 (with *Symph. No. 100*), discontinued. 23 min.

---

—Collegium Musicum, Vienna, A. Heiller. HAYDN SOCIETY 1015 (with *Symph. No. 84*). 25 min.

No. 84, IN E-FLAT

Opposing a big aggressiveness to restless uncertainty, defying the anticipated, this symphony requires particular care in analysis and preparation if its startling qualities are to be manifest. Unfortunately the only recording reveals a minimum of virtues in direction, playing and sound.

—Collegium Musicum, Vienna, A. Heiller. HAYDN SOCIETY 1015 (with *Symph. No. 83*). 28 min.

No. 85, IN B-FLAT, "LA REINE"

The queen whose presumed liking for the symphony gave it its sobriquet was the feckless, reckless and hapless consort of Louis XVI; Maria Theresa's daughter, "*l'Autrichienne*," who expiated her birth and her marriage under the triangular knife in what was not then called the Place de la Concorde. Her musical taste, which championed Gluck and admired Haydn, was far sounder than her discretion.

"*La Reine*" is a symphony without any auster-

ity at all, whose continuous natural charm is compounded of melodious, earthy materials and astute manipulation. Its pleasure is so gently absorbed that its resourceful devices are not apprehended and sensibilities are not blunted after many repetitions. Luckily one of the four recordings is good. Of the bad ones the well-paced and well-shaped Baltzer performance is gravely injured by piercing violins and a noisy background. Brusquely directed and absurdly short-handed, the M-G-M group render the symphony both naked and emaciated. The sonics of the ancient Mercury disk are repulsive. Epic with pretty accurate if a rather overbright reproduction of playing responsive to sensitive leadership occupies the only post of glory.
—Vienna Symph. Orch., P. Sacher. Epic 3059 (with *Symph. No. 44*). 21 min.

---

—Vienna Opera Orch., E. Baltzer. HAYDN SOCIETY 1008 (with *Symph. No. 82*). 18 min.
—M-G-M Ch. Orch., I. Solomon. M-G-M 3109 (with *K. P. E. Bach: Concerto for Orchestra*). 23 min.
—Munich Philharmonic Orch., F. Rieger. MERCURY 10116 (with *Sinfonia Concertante in B-flat*), discontinued. 27 min.

No. 86, IN D ***
Music-lovers not familiar with this beautiful work, the crown of the Paris set of symphonies, are begged not to make its acquaintance through

either of its atrocious recordings. Both have a
supreme high-frequency distortion conferring
eligibility to compete in a tourney of dreadful
sound. The ways of the phonograph are mysterious, and there is no use hunting the cause of the
relegation of No. 86 to disks like these while sur-
pluses of acceptable versions of No. 88, the "Surprise" and the "Clock" continue to accumulate.
However, the two calamitous records having
been retired, the catalogue shows a void that
names like Beecham, Münchinger, Scherchen and
Walter would fill capitally. Dr. Walter did in
fact record the symphony on 78 rpm's for Victor
about twenty years ago, and that old album emits
an infinitely better sound than the two LP's. Dr.
Walter is still happily available.
—Mozarteum Orch., Salzburg, Z. Fekete. Mercury 10071 (with *Symph. No. 88*), discontinued.
24 min.
—Same orchestra, P. Walter. Period 516 (with
*Symph. No. 95*), discontinued. 24 min.

## No. 87, in A

87 is the highest number given to any of the
"Paris" Symphonies, but Symphony No. 87 was
actually the second of the six to be composed.
That it is seldom played in public, and only once
has been recorded, are facts to heat one's impatience of impresarios, for the symphony is ravishing and as well built, save for a slimmer orchestration, as its celebrated followers in the two London series. Not that one has a fair right to

complain of the one record, a good one except in some sonic aspects related to its age. Above *mf* the orchestra is harsh, and the bass is consistently dry. Not until 1952 did these defects cease to be commonplace in recording, and even now we are always prepared, in listening to a disk for the first time, to wince a little at edgy violins, as often present as not. The 1950 recording of Symphony No. 87 was not bad for the time, and is still acceptable although not attractive in its sound. The performance is limpid and gracious, far above the mere efficiency of so many Haydn presentations; and arresting in discernment, alertness and delicacy of adjustment. A record far from perfect, but one intolerable not to have until a better supersedes it.
—Vienna Opera Orch., H. Swarowsky. Haydn Society 1018 (with *Symph. No. 89*). 22 min.

## No. 88, in G

Each of its four movements a small perfection and a great blessing, its whole a benevolence of smiles (wide smiles, and grave); suggestive and flip, courtly and bucolic; shadowy, downcast and tremulous) bestowed in every direction, No. 88 is the very essence of the great composer on his mettle to captivate everyone. It is immediately lovable and forever meaningless. It is the only Haydn symphony before the twelve composed for London to have honeyed a permanent place for itself in the international repertory. (Declared with full consciousness of the "Oxford"

Symphony, No. 92, never established in the American repertory, and of the "Farewell," No. 45, famous but infrequently played.)

The Haydn discography appearing in *High Fidelity* late in 1952 and early in 1953, of which this book is an expansion, listed six versions of Symphony No. 88, all so disappointing in performance or sound that readers were advised to select the cheapest if they selected any. It is interesting and encouraging to note that all the subsequent editions have been of much higher quality. That is the principal justification of duplications, that they are sometimes improvements. Alas, often they are the contrary.

On a careful counting of points coolly estimated, as at a dog show, the Münchinger version accumulates the biggest total. This is a sunny and natural performance played by one of the warmest orchestras in the world, recorded to reproduce with easy, well-detailed accuracy. It is one of those records with which one finds no outstanding fault; and this is not intended as cold praise, although it is true that its high excellence is devoid of the exceptional eloquence of the Scherchen, Furtwängler and Busch records which display a higher total of faults. Considering the last first, its wonder is in the way a feeling of relaxation is maintained in a projection of innate delicacy fortified by manly strength. Of the others only the Münchinger has this ease of naturalness, a little less of it. The HMV sound procured for the Busch record is by no means

as bad as this writer once thought it after reproduction through equipment less flexible than
that he enjoys now, but it has neither the smoothness of the Münchinger, the discrimination of the
Scherchen, nor the crisp realism of the Szell; and
it is blemished by violins too prominent and
always a little acrid. In stout compensation, the
winds are clear and true, the tuttis symphonic.

Naturally Dr. Scherchen, now the foremost
exponent of Haydn, lets nothing evade his sharp
eye in this score at once disarming and challeng-
ing, and we hear in his record a delineation of
episode not found elsewhere, a slower Largo,
and a Minuet of more alacrity, than anyone else
presents, with a calculated expanse of dynamics
surpassing all the others; without, it must be
stated, making contrasts for their own sake, such
as we hear in the Ormandy record. The Westminster sound is the most seizing of all, sharpest
in timbre and cleanest in the bass, but the violins
—in the first movement especially—are cutting
and uncomfortable. Reproducers equipped to
banish such shrillness may convince collectors
that this is the most effective edition of the dozen.

The Furtwängler performance is remarkable
for the appeal exercised by its comparative gravity, obtained not by a slowness of pace but by
a smoothness of texture and subjection of episode
to the principal line. Proportion comes first, in
a place unexpected, and with unexpectedly impressive results. The general effect of orderly
sport, of composure in delight, is aided by sturdy

but rather dark sonics without bite or distinctness of timbre.

Whereas the Szell version is provided with notably clean and arresting definition in all the choirs. It is as easy to reproduce as the Münchinger, and although cooler its sound is as accurate as London's. Furthermore, the playing, in the expert conciseness in which this conductor excels, is hardly to be faulted anywhere. But to the writer the conductor errs by his impatience in the solemnity of the Largo; for although the solemnity is not to be taken seriously, the conductor ought not to show that he knows it.

The remaining versions are markedly inferior in one respect or another: Toscanini—overwrought first movement and rather wooden sound; P. Walter—not bad, but nowhere distinguished; Ormandy—display of the orchestra obscures display of the music; Molinari—sweet performance, crude sound; Fekete—dreadful sound.

Note that both Furtwängler editions are of the same performance and are tied in unusual fashion to other music. One edition is the fourth side of a beautiful set devoted primarily to Schubert's last symphony, and the other follows the Finale of a woeful performance of Schumann's Fourth Symphony on the second side of a disk whose obverse is occupied by the rest of the Schumann. The latter edition is a very little brighter in sound.

—Vienna Philharmonic Orch., K. Münchinger.

LONDON LL-1199 (with *Symph. No. 101*). 20 min.

—Vienna Symph. Orch., H. Scherchen. WEST-MINSTER XWN 18616 (with *Sym. No. 92*). 22 min.

—Berlin Philharmonic Orch., W. Furtwängler. DECCA 9767 (attached to *Schumann: Symph. No. 4*). 21 min.

—Danish National Radio Orch., F. Busch. RCA LHMV-1019 (with *Mozart: Symph. No. 36*), discontinued. 22 min.

—Berlin Philharmonic Orch., W. Furtwängler. Two 12-in. DECCA DX-119 (appended to *Schubert: Symph. No. 9*). 21 min.

—Cleveland Orch., G. Szell. EPIC 3196 (with *Symph. No. 104*). 20 min.

---

—Salzburg Festival Orch., P. Walter. 10-in. REMINGTON 149-29, discontinued. 19 min.

—Same performance, REMINGTON 199-89 (with *Symph. No. 100*).

—NBC Orch., A. Toscanini. 10-in. RCA LCT-7, discontinued. 21 min.

—Philadelphia Orch., E. Ormandy. COLUMBIA 4109 (with *Mozart: Symph. No. 39*). 21 min.

—Orch. of St. Cecilia Academy, Rome, B. Molinari. TEMPO 2036 (with *Mozart: Seranade No. 6; Strauss: Rosenkavalier Waltz*).

—Mozarteum Orch., Salzburg, Z. Fekete. MERCURY 10071 (with *Symph. No. 86*), discontinued. 20 min.

No. 89, in F

A bland and inviting symphony, built on miniature lines with Mozartean traits, in a capable,
somewhat hesitant performance less winning than
the overside's. The sound is small, but pleasant
enough although not orchestral, when volume at
the amplifier is low. With increased volume
comes a tonal hardness accompanied by background noise.
—Vienna Opera Orch., H. Swarowsky. Haydn
Society 1018 (with *Symph. No. 87*). 20 min.

No. 90, in C

There has been no LP, perhaps because this
wispy, erratic music does not sound like Haydn.
Since the void is the only one in the list from
No. 82 to the end, No. 104, fervent collectors
may be interested to know that a six-sided 78
rpm version (Deutsche Grammaphon 69377-9)
was made during the 1940's and must be available
somewhere. The sound of this is laudable, but the
performance, by a chamber orchestra from the
Leipsic Gewandhaus conducted by Paul Schmitz,
is of chamber music style and proportions.

No. 91, in E-flat

Like its overside, the recording in fact represents
two attempts from one tape. The first disk
emitted a scrawny sound carefully mellowed in
the second, to pretty fair effect in No. 91 which
is orchestrally clearer than No. 64. Not a great

symphony but an agreeable one with an Andante superbly varied—a pause for breath before the final take-off for the supreme accomplishment of the culminating thirteen—No. 91 receives honorable treatment from conductor and orchestra after they have shaken off uncertainties in the first half of the first movement. The second, improved guise of this recording can be distinguished from the first by the letters "XTV" on the label under "Side B" (or "Side A" in the case of Symphony No. 64), which do not appear on the label of the earlier version.

—Vienna Symph. Orch., H. Swoboda. Westminster XWN 18615 (with *Symph. No. 64*). 23 min.

### No. 92, in G, "Oxford" ***

When Oxford conferred a degree on Haydn, July 8, 1791, his acknowledgement was naturally to have been one that no one else could have made: a new Haydn symphony. Haydn had it ready, but the orchestra had not had time to rehearse it, and Symphony No. 92, composed two or three years earlier, was played as a substitute. Thus the nickname "Oxford" is appropriate although it has misled many people into a belief that the symphony was written specially for Haydn's first London journey. No shame is such an error, except possibly to musicologists, and some suggestive value in the fact that it could have been made, for it shows Haydn complete and ready for the twelve "London" Symphonies two years before he composed the first of them.

The three quick movements of the "Oxford" Symphony are an exhilaration of vivacity, fortified in the first and last by cunning counterpoint; but it is the Adagio which remains unforgettable in a sequence of unparalleled naïveté, when the placid sentimentality of the rather ordinary song, introduced in the dominant, D, and established by slightly varied repetitions, is suddenly torn apart by the invasion of a violent, peremptory, tramping and resentful but pompous raid in D minor, quickly evicted by the beautiful rebuke of a gracious long gliding phrase in F, come from nowhere. In a listener's sensibilities only memory refuses to be upset by this giddying instability.

Of the seven recorded editions three are variously outstanding albeit one of these disappoints in the Adagio. That is the Koussevitsky record, a big and suave representation of the Boston Symphony Orchestra at its most mellifluous, a tonal joy throughout and excellent in gait and contours wherever vigor is essential; irresistible in the Finale. But the easy song of the Adagio lumbers in a concentration of attention on the euphony of its vertical structure, a mischance impossible to ignore, and which drops this version definitely below two others.

The smooth logic of Dr. Szell deftly weaving refinements in and out of a smooth but powerful fabric and alert to all the little opportunities to make point without being ostentatious about it, seems to this writer more winning than the more foursquare and stronger logic of Dr. Scherchen. Both orchestras are excellent and bent to the will of their chiefs, but the Clevelanders have a cleaner unity of stroke. The Columbia sound may with decency be called wondrous in view of its birth in 1949, for it is telling in 1957, particularly in its sturdy and steady bass giving backbone to the crisp decisiveness of the lightweights.

It ought not to be inferred that the Scherchen projection is short of finesse because the Szell has more of it. Certain Scherchen delicacies pass unnoticed in the forcefulness of the whole, and the imposing Westminster sound, although equally expert with delicacy and force, makes its strongest impression naturally with the latter. There is a physical excitement contagious from the vitality of this sound that adds a sting to the Scherchen record, whereas the Columbia sound, for all its good realism, conveys a smaller portion of immediacy. Between the two editions the writer's choice wavers and has for four years. The reader will not err in choosing either.

Of the rest, the Malko production is commendable but not distinguished by the high qualities of the first three. London has given juicy sound to Mr. Krips's exposition, consistently prosy until the Finale. Injections of sonic digitalis into the dull old sound of the Walter have not made it alive, and the retirement of the Rieger will not be regretted.

—Cleveland Orch., G. Szell. COLUMBIA 4268 (with *Symph. No. 101*). 23 min.

—Vienna Opera Orch., H. Scherchen. WEST-
MINSTER XWN 18616 (with *Symph. No. 88*).
24 min.
—Boston Symph. Orch., S. Koussevitsky. RCA
LM-1102 (with *Mozart: Seranade No. 13*). 27
min.

---

—Danish National Orch., V. Malko. RCA LBC-
1087 (with *Beethoven: 3 Overtures*). 24 min.
—London Symph. Orch., J. Krips. LONDON LL-
780 (with *Mozart: Symph. No. 40*). 24 min.
—Paris Conservatory Orch., B. Walter. CAMDEN
257 (with *Symph. No. 100*). 22 min.
—Munich Philharmonic Orch., F. Rieger. 10-in.
MERCURY 15040, discontinued. 24 min.

"LONDON" SYMPHONIES: Nos. 93-104 ***
These are the twelve "London" Symphonies,
Haydn's last, composed during his two sojourns
in England, 1791-1792 and 1794-1795. The dazzling success of British imperial policy—intrepid
and obstinate piracy justified by a practical, sinu-
ous morality and supported by God—was bringing the world's finest fruits to London to nourish
the grand surges of vitality that would extirpate
French hegemony forever, after France would
first have obligingly reduced Haydn's own Holy
Roman Empire to a sprawling evaporation. England had a German king, a little mad but more
dogged even than the British; and what more
natural that among the fruits purchased for the
kingdom there should be German music, England then as now making none?—none that is in

the sense that the great Germans have given to the word.

Haydn at sixty, the foremost musical reputation of the day and after thirty years freed from the bucolic bondage of Esterház and the loathesome intrigues of Vienna's musical coteries, was in London a first citizen of the world. He was respected there, and in potent quarters revered. Accustomed to admiration and esteem, he had never experienced adulation, and his initiation into this delightful bath in London had the effect, on his rare character, of stimulating his determination to do the best he could. He would not let these Londoners down, the most appreciative folk he had known; and never did gratitude materialize so admirably.

He composed other excellent things in England, but the twelve symphonies are the crown of his work there and the crown of his symphonic work. In his long career—and an artist's creation is usually over by the time he is sixty—he had written perhaps eight or ten symphonies made of stuff not inferior to those composed for London. But those were punctuations, not a procession. Thirty years had gone into their making, not thirty months. They are jewels in the sceptre, not the intact crowning chaplet.

New resources in London assisted Haydn's gratitude in the culminating expression of Haydn's genius. There were more instruments available for him; for although his Paris symphonies had been played by an orchestra large even by modern standards, the strength of this orchestra had been mainly in the string section. At London for the first time Haydn found the winds of what we call the pre-Beethoven classical orchestra, the orchestra that Beethoven inherited from Haydn and used in his First, Second, Fourth and Seventh Symphonies. In London Haydn does not have to choose between flutes and oboes: he uses both. In earlier symphonies he had specified trumpets *or* horns: both are in the London scores, with drums as a matter of course. Clarinets appear for the first time in the London work, and increasingly independent writing is done for the bassoons, at Esterház normally blown to back up the bass. In Symphony No. 100, the "Turkish" battery of big drum, cymbals and triangle is introduced to confirm the kettledrums. It is a pity that trombones nowhere add their subtle stentor to the color of a Haydn symphony, but even Beethoven only used them three times, and Schubert (dead before he could hear his own mastery of them) was the first great man to give them continuous symphonic hard work (to Mendelssohn's constraint and distaste).

With the heart overflowing and the machinery at hand, the head, full of sixty years, went freshly to work. An endless suppleness of resourceful invention was slipped into twelve symphonies for an England that had no native symphony worth playing, not one; and backing the coruscation of ideas, the sweetness, the might, the bravado and the jocosity of the invention, a profound learning of the art and science of music as the most professional of her practical practitioners had absorbed it in a lifetime already long was most sedulously employed to make the invention indestructible. A hundred and sixty years after the *Laus Deo* was inscribed on the autograph of Symphony No. 104, the music has the life and force it had in 1795, and the beneficence of the venerable composer's gratitude to England has enriched a world in which England is no longer very rich.

Few people will agree which are the best, which the least, of these symphonies. Some are more quickly assimilable than others, and five with accepted nicknames have acquired more prominence, and receive more public performances, than the other seven; but the nicknames are the persuasive element. If we called No. 99 "The Frigate," or No. 93 more ripely, "The Kiss," the number of their performances would treble. Over a span of ten years the usual American orchestral association presents four of the London symphonies—"Clock," "Surprise," "London" and one other. The phonograph does better.

The phonograph has worthy editions of all, and striking editions of most. One company—one company in the history of recording—has recorded all twelve, by an unlikely tour de force the work of one conductor; and all twelve, by a most improbable continuity of musical and electronic success, excellent. The twelve symphonies conducted by Hermann Scherchen were originally issued by Westminster over a span of three years and encountered considerable success in their distribution over eight records with four other symphonies by Haydn filling out the complement of sides. They have since been collected in an album of six disks with a symphony to a side, presented in numerical order. For this Westminster album 6601 the tapes have been edited to give records conforming to the RIAA curve, with the concomitant result for several of the symphonies of a smoother response; for although in general provided with imposing sonics, the dozen in their first appearance included two or three with a too-enterprising treble. Rid of that defect, the records in the corrected edition comprise one of the serenely best achievements in phonographic history.

For the reproduction of the weakest of the lot is on a level of excellence equal, or nearly, to that of the best of any of the records in competition, a consistency of expert accomplishment not matched by any extensive homogeneous orchestral edition of anything. More important, the leadership maintains an extraordinary authority of imagination and knowledge. Throughout twelve symphonies, forty-eight movements, Dr. Scherchen is in effect opposing a field of two dozen conductors leading only those works in which they are reputed to be particularly adroit. No more than anyone else could be is he successful in leading the field in forty-eight heats or twelve sweepstakes, but wherever it is necessary to judge him beaten he is never found distanced.

Complete editions offer the convenience of easy and rational filing. The one under consideration offers the immeasurably greater advantage of a five hours' delight of music beautifully played and recorded. Nevertheless it is not recommended without reserve, nor any complete edition. To collectors for whom convenience in filing is a first necessity, and to those whose wealth permits and whose thrift does not deny an accumulation of duplications, a complete edition can bring undiluted solace; but a thousand times as many collectors, coveting the absolute best wherever it can be determined, will find too many of the best outside the limited editions for the latter to satisfy both their musical and economic requirements. And fortunately the records of the Westminster Complete Edition are available separately.

## No. 93, in D

One will not find an absolute best here, for the Beecham record excels in performance and the Scherchen in sonics. Since the Beecham sound is eminently satisfactory and the Scherchen performance is admirably eloquent, collectors face the impossible task of weighing disparate values against each other. The withdrawn Cantelli disk, not bad but harder in all respects, cannot offer, in its drier sound and less supple interpretation, a serious rivalry. There are some virtues in the Singer record, but its quality is notably lower than that of all the others.

It is in the matter of finesse that Sir Thomas evinces a clear superiority. Leading an orchestra collected by his own hand and bent to his will and ways, he is able to draw a transparent and undulant line in *cantilenas* that is more delicate and more pliant than anything revealed in the preceding Haydn symphonies as they have been recorded. The disk is not new, but the engineers gave clean and solid substance to it, so that although it lacks the brightness and keen articulation accorded to Dr. Scherchen it is able to make its points with authority, and with very little missing.

The German's slower pace in the first movement seems less valid than that taken by Sir Thomas, in that it offers an insufficient foil to the following Largo, but Scherchen regains ground in the hearty tramp of a Minuet wherein the poised tread of the other is less convincing. Call the Finale a toss-up: in both cases the sparkle is exhilarating.

In fact call the whole rivalry a toss-up, Beecham-Columbia and Scherchen-Westminster. Both are outstanding, but which stands more firmly this umpire, although willing, is unable to decide.

—Royal Philharmonic Orch., T. Beecham. Co-
lumbia 4374 (with *Handel: Faithful Shepherd Suite*). 22 min.

—Vienna Opera Orch., H. Scherchen. Westminster 18322 (with *Symph. No. 94*). 26 min.

—Same performance on Westminster 5178 (with *Symph. No. 88*).

—NBC Orch., G. Cantelli. RCA LM-1089 (with *Hindemith: Mathis der Maler*), discontinued. 21 min.

—"Austrian" Symph. Orch., G. Singer. REMING-TON 199-110 (with *Schubert: Symph. No. 3*), discontinued. 20 min.

### No. 94, IN G, "SURPRISE" ***

There are twenty editions if four are counted that were not heard. Informed correspondents have advised the writer that hearing them would be a bleak adventure. The "Surprise" was the first Haydn symphony to be recorded, and in multiplicity of versions from the beginning has not been pressed closely. This favoritism is not implicit in the gay and sunny music, for Haydn wrote other symphonies as attractive and gay and sunny, but in the nickname, which helps the appetite and helps the memory. The "surprise" itself always evokes a smile but is of minimal importance: a full *fortissimo* chord crashing into the *pianissimo* repetition of the simple staccato theme that introduces the second movement and then is embellished in variations. Haydn is supposed to have said of this sudden bang—and indeed must have said it, since it had to be said— that it would wake up the ladies in the audience.

In other respects the "Surprise" is one of the least surprising of the "London" Symphonies. It has no cares, and some jocular heroics in the Andante are paralleled in half a dozen others. No doubt at all that its imperturbable cheerfulness, given a currency far exceeding that of any other Haydn symphony, is in large measure responsible for the persistence of the repellent image of the composer as a man who never thought deeply about anything.

The recorded performance of greatest distinction is Sir Thomas Beecham's, whose few liberties with tempo are so moderate as not to matter. The lines here are finely drawn within a solid frame, the ripples of a firm muscularity nowhere distended; and the pleasant sound is of the satisfactory sort that calls no attention to itself in impressive plus or serious minus. The best sonics have been accorded to the Schmidt-Isserstedt (Hamburg), Leinsdorf, Scherchen and Swoboda records. The full, imposing tone of the Concertgebouw is marred by occasional distortion too apparent for complaisance, although very little injurious at low volume; and the general mellowness of the Lehmann version suffers from a distortion more persistent. Of the latter pair of disks the first carries a spirited and expert interpretation, the second a more relaxed statement, excellent except in the Minuet whose slowness palls with familiarity.

The remainder are acoustically of a lower order, and only the old Schmidt-Isserstedt (Berlin) performance, ripe and strong, a little deliberate, seems worth qualified commendation. This and the Sargent have indistinct sound. The unlikely whiz of the Toscanini has been engineered with bright wood but woody strings. Unlovely sound in the Furtwängler does not help its excess of conducting. And so on.

Dr. Scherchen's slow pace in the *vivace assai* first movement seems detractive although the rest is splendid and the orchestral bite in reproduction splendid too. The newer pressing of this, in the complete edition of the "London" Symphonies, is better than the older in its erasure of shrillness. Dr. Schmidt-Isserstedt's new version has the richest sonic substance of all, but is a little inferior to the Scherchen and the Leinsdorf in crispness of detail. The performance is very similar to the same conductor's excellent earlier one. The bright strong sound bestowed on Mr. Leinsdorf adds persuasiveness to his quick and nervous leadership, and it surely is worth noticing that this record and the MMS are available at singularly modest prices; not that price is ever a factor in determining these judgments. The Swoboda effort is short of glory but has a curiously effective sound in which a long reverberation gives orchestral sweep and a certain benignity to the string tone, while the bold winds resound with authority.

—Royal Philharmonic Orch., T. Beecham. Columbia 4453 (with *Symph. No. 103*). 23 min.

—Northwest German Radio Orch., Hamburg, H. Schmidt-Isserstedt. Capitol P-18022 (with *Mozart: Serenade 13*). 22 min.

—Rochester Philharmonic Orch., E. Leinsdorf. Columbia RL-6621 (with *Symph. No. 101*). 20 min.

—Concertgebouw Orch., Amsterdam, E. van Beinum. LONDON LL-491 (with *Mozart: Symph. No. 33*). 22 min.
—Netherlands Philharmonic Orch., H. Swoboda. 10-in. MMS 59 (with *Symph. No. 100*). 20 min.
—Vienna Opera Orch., H. Scherchen. WESTMINSTER 18322 (with *Symph. No. 93*). 25 min.

---

—Boston Symph. Orch., S. Koussevitsky. RCA LM-9034 (with *Symph. No. 104*), discontinued. 23 min.
—Berlin Philharmonic Orch., H. Schmidt-Isserstedt. CAPITOL P-8038 (with *Mozart: Serenade 13*), discontinued. 25 min.
—Berlin Philharmonic Orch., F. Lehmann. DECCA 9617 (with *Symph. No. 101*). 27 min.
—Liverpool Philharmonic Orch., M. Sargent. COLUMBIA 4276 (with *Symph. No. 100*), discontinued. 21 min.
—Boston Symph. Orch., S. Koussevitsky. 10-in. RCA LM-28, discontinued. 23 min.
—NBC Orch., A. Toscanini. RCA LM-1789 (with *Mozart: Symph. No. 40*). 19 min.
—Vienna Philharmonic Orch., W. Furtwängler. RCA LHMV-1018 (with *Mozart: Serenade 13*), discontinued. 23 min.
—Boston Symph. Orch., S. Koussevitsky (very old version). CAMDEN 146 (with *Mendelssohn: Symph. No. 4*). 22 min.
—Munich Philharmonic Orch., A. Melichar. 10-in. MERCURY 15023, discontinued. 26 min.

## No. 95, in C minor

The only "London" Symphony in a minor key, and the only one to forego a slow introduction, No. 95 flourishes an impudent variety of moods resistant to easy classification, and perhaps responsible for the hostility and indifference entertained by conductors for a wonderful, albeit disheveled, work. Blandness and vehemence have an inconclusive struggle in the first movement which opens with menace and subsides, for a while, to cajolery; and the variations in the Andante take delight in flirting with the advance guard of a tragedy that never arrives. The sneaking, whining Minuet, gravely chided by a compact little Trio, is one of Haydn's best.

It is worth remarking, since good sense is not a customary aspect of phonographic procedure, that the two recorded editions removed from circulation are the least attractive of four. The Period reels under a burden of injurious sound, and the Gui, an honorable effort, is patently less successful in all the important elements than the impressive records of Westminster and Decca. Between that pair it is justifiable to choose either: my preference is for Dr. Scherchen because his preponderance of eloquence in the central movements is for me more decisive than Mr. Fricsay's preponderance in the outer movements. The latter has a hotter fire, the former a warmer glow. In both editions the orchestra is orderly and the reproduction realistic, brighter in the Decca, rounder for Westminster.

—Vienna Symph. Orch., H. Scherchen. Westminster 18323 (with *Symph. No. 96*). 21 min.
—Rias Orch., Berlin, F. Fricsay. Decca DL-9745 (with *Mozart: Symph. No. 41*). 20 min.

---

—Glyndebourne Festival Orch., V. Gui. RCA LHMV-11 (with *Mozart: Symph. No. 39*), discontinued. 20 min.
—Mozarteum Orch., Salzburg, P. Walter. Period 516 (with *Symph. No. 86*), discontinued. 19 min.

No. 96, in D, "miracle" ***
The London audience at the first performance of one of the Haydn symphonies composed for them left their seats to applaud the master, and immediately a vast chandelier dropped from the ceiling to the vacated seats. Thus Haydn's symphony had lured away from death enough people to multiply the cry of "Miracle! Miracle!" and establish a nickname for No. 96 that will last long after it has been shown that another symphony was the magician, a task to which musicology is now devoting itself.

I find less inner glory than external splendor in the "Miracle," and agree with its author that the Finale is meager. Still it is good if not best Haydn, and the twelve "London" Symphonies do have to have a least one.

Phonographically it has been treated as a great one, with five of the seven editions laudable and two outstanding. With no concern for my readers' pocket I should like to recommend the purchase of both the Scherchen and van Beinum

versions, which when compared provide as pretty
an illustration as one could wish of two gifted
conductors showing that opposite directions can
sometimes both be right. My preference is for
the supple, sensitive, ever-variable delineation of
Dr. Scherchen, who gives the most delicate, and
the most forceful, of all these statements. Every
measure of his work is defined by *volition* and
by a searching care against any lapse into routine: there seems to be no repetition. Contrarily
Mr. van Beinum takes an absolute course of the
most positive directness in an exposition that
would be severe without the beautiful blending
of his orchestral choirs. The crisp unity of his
phalanx is not challenged by Dr. Scherchen's
orchestra, where in fact it probably would have
been intrusive for such a willowy performance.
Dr. Walter's work is neither so supple as Dr.
Scherchen's nor so incisive as Mr. van Beinum's,
but it has insinuating merits, not least the seductive curving of the New York Philharmonic
strings succulent as peaches.

Those three versions have been granted excellent reproduction, with the London technically the best and very fine, in its noble balance
and whiplash smartness, with a minimum of distortion and imposing definition. Westminster,
closer and warmer, featuring individuality of
timbres, and expressing the conductor's more demanding dynamics, is technically perhaps less
admirable, but musically quite as effective. The
hall-influence is too pronounced in the Columbia

for it to have the clean impact of the first two.

MMS has issued a good product, strong and animated in the leadership but rather offhand in the shading of dynamics and with an Andante a good deal less fluent than the best. Its sound is of decent standard, enveloping and decidedly bright, leaning to hardness in the violins. The two editions by this company are from the same tape and show no great sonic difference, but the pitch of MMS 129 is a little lower in consequence of the master's having been speeded to include the whole work on one ten-inch side. The older Walter recording and the Reinhardt are sonically outdated.

—Vienna Opera Orch., H. Scherchen. Westminster 18323 (with *Symph. No. 95*). 22 min.

—Concertgebouw Orch., E. van Beinum. London LL-854 (with *Symph. No. 97*). 22 min.

—New York Philharmonic-Symph. Orch., B. Walter. Columbia ML-5059 (with *Symph. No. 102*). 21 min.

—Winterthur Symph. Orch., W. Goehr. 10-in. MMS 129 (with *Symph. No. 46*). 21 min.

—Winterthur Symph. Orch., W. Goehr. 10-in. MMS 6 (with *Desert Island Overture*). 23 min.

---

—"Pro Musica" Orch., Stuttgart, R. Reinhardt. Vox 7310 (with *Symph. No. 45*), discontinued. 23 min.

—Vienna Philharmonic Orch., B. Walter. Two 12-in. RCA LCT-6015 (with *Mahler: Symph. No. 9*), discontinued. 20 min.

No. 97, in C***

People who go faithfully to hear the symphony orchestras have a right to hear the procession of felicities in this C major Symphony, but conductors will never recognize the right until the music receives a nickname. I have accordingly dubbed it "Janus," perhaps because its Minuet looks at tramping troops and the Trio looks at dalliance; but I thought of "Porpoise," "Steenkirk" and "Cynthia" first, not because they are apposite, but because they are sharp in color and easy to remember. If music-lovers will call No. 97, please, the "Janus" Symphony, there will soon be many more than a paltry three recordings.

Not that we need any more, in view of the high quality of two. These are, again, the versions of Westminster and London directed by Hermann Scherchen and Eduard van Beinum, respectively, the former mellow and heated with human sentiment, the latter exact, regimented, in the cleanest of geometric patterns. It would be entirely correct to repeat here the comparison made between the same conductors' work in Symphony No. 96 above, with the observation that the qualities signaled there are even more strongly in evidence in No. 97, the stronger music. Again we find the Concertgebouw without a rough projection, fine in detail and blended to a rare homogeneity, and again the Vienna orchestra is superior in its timbres and its juices to its unity. The respective sounds are as noted

for No. 96, with the London more admirable,
Westminster in more personal contact with its
auditor. My preference is for the more undulant
classicism of Dr. Scherchen, but I think many
tastes will incline to Mr. van Beinum, and I urge
readers to compare for themselves. They need
have no thought for the third version.
—Vienna Symph. Orch., H. Scherchen. WEST-
MINSTER 18324 (with *Symph. No. 98*). 25 min.
—Concertgebouw Orch., E. van Beinum. LONDON
LL-854 (with *Symph. No. 96*). 22 min.

---

—Homburg Symph. Orch., P. Schubert. 10-in.
REGENT 5014, discontinued. 26 min.

## No. 98, IN B-FLAT

Readers may be surprised at the paucity of editions. They will not be after hearing the heroic
Scherchen enterprise. At any rate, everyone
ought to be assured that the symphony is one
of Haydn's best and a favorite of a man who also
knew symphonies: Beethoven. It is an eye-opener
for music-lovers who have not heard it, as indeed
they have had little opportunity to. Few expect
a Haydn domineering and infuriated, but here he
is; and as may easily be expected, Dr. Scherchen
drives the strong sentiments to the hilt, without
neglecting, between the tempestuous outer movements, to coax an utmost sympathy from the
astonishing polyphony of the chorale *Adagio
cantabile*. The Westminster reproduction is remarkable—huge but well defined, timbre-true

and honeyed in the strings—and caps one of the most completely successful recordings of a Haydn symphony. In such a competition all we can grant to the other record is pity.
—Vienna Opera Orch., H. Scherchen. WEST-MINSTER 18324 (with *Symph. No. 97*). 29 min.

---

—Munich Philharmonic Orch., F. Rieger. 10-in. MERCURY 15039, discontinued. 31 min.

### No. 99, IN E-FLAT ***

Another supreme achievement neglected for lack of a name, Symphony No. 99 bears so rich a freight of consummate and assimilable Haydn that it is amazing that any other of his symphonies could be played more often. All the things we have learned to expect are abundantly there—the incontrovertible tune, the inherent counterpoint, the unguent grace, the sudden joke—with some in transformation, plus a very sensitive orchestration and an extraordinary compactness of distribution. Surely the Adagio, in its heavenly resignation, is the most beautiful slow movement in a Haydn symphony.

I do not believe that anyone will hear No. 99 better played than it is on the best of its records until Dr. Scherchen re-records it with the Adagio very slightly quickened. Haydn symphonies have the pulse to conduct themselves, and many conductors let them do that, knowing that they sound good; but Dr. Scherchen is at the rudder every second, enforcing a thousand tiny modifi-

cations of the course. The leadership is robust
and the sound vast; and both are exceptional in
their delicacy. Here we have the perfectly expiring *diminuendo* and the *crescendo* in conical
symmetry, the phrase in dynamic inflection as it
progresses, a continuous plasticity that seems
immanent. We seldom hear *pianos* like this,
dwarf but immaculate and complete; and
throughout this unfolding of finesse I can detect
nothing that seems a mere contrivance. Equipped
with sonics of an outstanding order, solid and
deep but fine in bite and definition, the Scherchen
edition is a foremost treasure in the Haydn repertory.

Although in sound the Vanguard disk may be
as laudable in its different, brighter, more insistent way. The company have obviously taken
great pains with their presentation of the last
six symphonies directed by the proficient Danish
classicist Mogens Wöldike, and it is a pity that
the series must begin with No. 99, whose ineffable
Adagio the conductor takes at such a rare clip
that its haunting beauty dies. The Royalton-
Kisch record is much better and in fact is estimable except for being split in the Adagio, but
it is no challenge to the champion. Professor
Keilberth's abilities have been traduced by the
engineers.

—Vienna Opera Orch., H. Scherchen. WEST-
MINSTER 18325 (with *Symph. No. 100*). 27 min.

—London Symph. Orch., A. Royalton-Kisch.
10-in. LONDON LS-171, discontinued. 25 min.

—Volksoper Orch., Vienna, M. Wöldike. VAN-
GUARD 491 (with *Symph. No. 102*). 25 min.
—Bamberg Symph. Orch., J. Keilberth. MER-
CURY 10051 (with *Symph. No. 100*), discon-
tinued. 26 min.

## No. 100, IN G, "MILITARY"

The military bearing is not restricted to the
second and fourth movements in which a battery
consisting of big drum, cymbals and triangle
supplements the kettledrums, but those movements are the only ones to bloody the sabre and
stain the uniform with war. I think that the
Allegretto must be considered a sad farewell to
scores of gallant friends* of Haydn hacked and
cannonaded at Jemappes, Hondschoote, Wattig-
nies and Neerwinden to manure the soil of
Flanders, a soldier's elegy whose grief must not
weep. To be this the Allegretto must be played
*andante*, but many conductors will not permit
themselves the seeming liberty, and expunge the
sentiment from the movement.

Many collectors will remember the thunderous
impact of the original Scherchen record (then
coupled with Symphony No. 95) late in 1950,
projecting the conductor known previously
mainly to scholars into a sudden, loud and con-
troversial celebrity, and fixing respectful atten-

---

* Let us hope that he had no friends among the
Croatian battalions whose filthiness and vile behavior are
to this day an execrable souvenir in the vicinity of
Mauberge.

tion upon the freshman Westminster Company
as a dictator of new standards in the recording
of a symphony orchestra. Dr. Scherchen, in addition to the conference of a supple long line on
the music in general and retarding the Allegretto
perhaps overmuch, had his battery of percussion
smite with a vehemence unheard-of since some
of the London critics complained of Haydn's
having supervised a similar clamor at the first
performances. That was the first record to hit
out with a whole heart, but since its great success
—nourished by an outburst of denunciation—
other conductors have smote as hard, without
necessarily an equivalent eloquence when the
percussion is resting.

The old record is still very good although it
no longer dazzles, and its sound may even appear
a little thick by today's standards. The performance has been excelled by the same conductor in
a better recording of a better orchestra, with the
Allegretto quickened to its proper pace of slowish, not slow; but the "Laboratory" disk containing it bears an exalted price, and I invite the
attention of those who do not care to pay it to
the brilliantly recorded and naturally shaped
version on Vanguard, in which Mr. Wöldike
shows how well a colloquial interpretation can
sound when delivered with energy and conviction.

The three most desirable records are Scherchen
II, Wöldike and Scherchen I, very closely followed by the Swoboda, surprising in the

226 THE COLLECTOR'S HAYDN

ingratiation of a sound so reverberant and compelling in its vivid contours; less closely by the Solti, a sharply rhythmic performance strong in the military virtues and persuasively registered; and at a growing distance by the others, all either furnished with outstanding faults or devoid of outstanding merits.

—Royal Philharmonic Orch., H. Scherchen. WESTMINSTER LAB-7024. 23 min.

—Volksoper Orch., Vienna, M. Wöldike. VANGUARD 492 (with *Symph. No. 101*). 22 min.

—Vienna Symph. Orch., H. Scherchen. WESTMINSTER 18325 (with *Symph. No. 99*). 25 min. Also on 18579 with *Beethoven: Symph. No. 5.*

—Netherlands Philharmonic Orch., H. Swoboda. 10-in. MMS 59 (with *Symph. No. 94*). 23 min.

—London Philharmonic Orch., G. Solti. LONDON LL-1043 (with *Symph. No. 102*). 20 min.

—Danish Royal Orch., N. Malko. RCA LBC-1060 (with *Symph. No. 83*), discontinued. 23 min.

—Concertgebouw Orch., C. Zecchi. EPIC 3258 (with *Schubert: Symph. No. 5*). 25 min.

—London Philharmonic Orch., E. van Beinum. LONDON LL-339 (with *Symph. No. 104*), discontinued. 19 min.

—Liverpool Philharmonic Orch., H. Rignold. COLUMBIA ML-4276 (with *Symph. No. 94*), discontinued. 20 min.

—"Orchestral Society of Boston," W. Page. 10-in. COOK 1069. 21 min.

—Vienna Philharmonic Orch., B. Walter. Camden 257 (with *Symph. No. 92*). 22 min.
—Mozarteum Orch., Salzburg, F. Weidlich.
Remington 199-89 (with *Symph. No. 88*). 23
min.
—Bavarian Radio Orch., H. Priegnitz. Mercury
10051 (with *Symph. No. 99*), discontinued. 24
min.

### No. 101, in D, "Clock" ***

The "Clock" is one of those Haydn symphonies,
like "*La Poule*" and the "Surprise," to which a
great affection is applied along with a discernible
scoffing. This has been caused by its title, and
by the plain fact that its second half is of less
memorable stuff than the bold inventiveness of
the first movement and the tranquil lyricism of
the tick-tocking Andante. The Minuet is very
long and the Rondo cannot quite escape from
frivolity.

The Münchinger performance, relaxed and
natural, all easy grace even when the music is
most proclamatory, seems to me to be rivaled
only by the rich and glowing gaiety of the
Ormandy, a surprising apparition in a position
so high, for the Philadelphia is a textural not a
patternal orchestra, and the great eighteen century composers are a reproach to it. Still the
evidence is there not to be missed, sparkle and
substance, and a spontaneity of very happy
phrasing. That the Münchinger edition prevails
is a normal victory of new over old sonics, but

the Philadelphia sound, after cautious adjustment, is by no means bad, although it lacks the distinction and differentiation of the Vienna. The best sound has been accorded to Mr. Wöldike's steady interpretation, a plain and prudent demonstration that side-steps every opportunity to give special enlightenment, but never errs in honest delivery of the fundamental theses. Dr. Scherchen, whose record is a highly successful reworking from the same tape that fathered an earlier and sonically inferior issue, frets over the barrenness of the Finale and does not improve it by a coating of refinement that really makes the barrenness more apparent. Otherwise this is, in its refurbished sound and vital performance, an excellent edition.

The rest are less commanding, although the beautifully mellow exposition directed by the late Fritz Busch would be placed with the highest if its reproduction were less vitiated by age; and the Fricsay version is appealing in spite of its briskness, in a sound with stretches of leanness that lower its good average. The Leinsdorf sounds at first better than it is: that bright unyielding energy inevitably begets a stupor of fatigue. The sound of the Toscanini is wooden, of the Reinwald coarse. So little can be said for the Ansermet that it is best forgotten; and I suppose it is necessary to pretend to believe that Mr. Markevitch's foul ball was intended as a joke. Hard, hurried, offhand and uncomfortable, it is a fulsome effort whatever its intent.

—Vienna Philharmonic Orch., K. Münchinger. London LL-1199 (with *Symph. No. 88*). 25 min.
—Philadelphia Orch., E. Ormandy. Columbia ML-4268 (with *Symph. No. 92*). 26 min.
—Volksoper Orch., Vienna, M. Wöldike. Vanguard 492 (with *Symph. No. 100*). 27 min.
—Vienna Opera Orch., H. Scherchen. Westminster 18326 (with *Symph. No. 102*). 29 min.

---

—Rias Orch., Berlin, F. Fricsay. Decca DL-9617 (with *Symph. No. 94*). 25 min.
—"Austrian" Symph. Orch., F. Busch. Remington 199-149 (with *Beethoven: Symph. No. 8*), discontinued. 28 min. Has also appeared as Masterseal 39 and Remington 149-32, 10-in.
—Rochester Philharmonic Orch., E. Leinsdorf. Columbia RL-6621 (with *Symph. No. 94*). 27 min.
—NBC Orch., A. Toscanini. RCA LM-1038 (with *Mozart: Symph. No. 35*). 27 min.
—Munich Philharmonic Orch., G. Reinwald. 10-in. Mercury 15018, discontinued. 30 min.
—Suisse Romande Orch., E. Ansermet. 10-in. London LS-54, discontinued. 23 min.
—French National Radio Orch., I. Markevitch. Angel 35312 (with *Symph. No. 102*). 23 min.

No. 102, IN B-FLAT

Haydn composed nothing more virile, and no symphony more admired by the advanced classes of his devotees. The conductors who have undertaken an engraving of its tempests and puckish-

ness, its solemnity and brilliance, its splendor of
instrumentation and transparency of thought, are
not neophytes in the late music of the man who
immortalized the name of Esterházy. The records
of this symphony prove it. Every one is a display of knowledge, ability and sympathy, and
the least fortunate of the six conductors do not
undergo disgrace. Only one version suffers from
bad sonics, the Reinwald; and the poorest of the
others, the Markevitch, is capable of imposing, if
not silky, sound when its volume is kept low.

Awkwardness in the Adagio and a Minuet slow
to dreariness compromise the pointed strength of
the other movements in the Solti projection; and
the Scherchen deliberation in the first movement,
an uncertain fluency in the second, and in truth
a vague general unwieldiness as of a thoughtful
man whose mind is not made up, make the great
Haydnist's essay here his least convincing among
the twelve "London" Symphonies. The sharp decisive vigor of Mr. Markevitch, in spite of some
orchestral coarseness, is in its surety plainly more
estimable.

Two versions remain, a stunning positive mani-
festation from the venerable Bruno Walter fired
with an inextinguishable romanticism, and a
strong, undeviating acquiescence in classical rec-
titude from Mr. Wöldike in an immaculate registration whose absence of strain and fuzz permits
a bright, facile reproduction through almost any
good apparatus. The Walter, contrarily, presents
a challenge in place of facility, and brandishes

edged violins in most of their *fortes* when they are reproduced through most assemblages of sensitive electronic components. The sonics here utilize a long reverberation that gives a majestic billowing surge to the tuttis and the bass, an unrelenting push of power ideal for the forcefulness of Dr. Walter's projection, but isolating the violins in their special shrillness. Utilizing patience and half a dozen pickups, and modifying the output of each of four speakers devoted to different heights of the cyclic climb, I was able to get finally a magnificent response from this record, but I do not believe that many phonographs have the flexibility to duplicate it. I cannot advise collectors to obtain a disk whose eloquence may remain latent, but I must point out that the eloquence is there, latent or manifest, and that collectors ought to try out the record on their own reproducers. It contains in any event a great performance, and under optimum conditions of reproduction is a great record. Since the Vanguard sonics are safer and invariably first class, I do recommend the Vanguard disk wholeheartedly, with the understanding that when its conditions are met the Columbia is better than any and by far.

—New York Philharmonic Symph. Orch., B. Walter. COLUMBIA ML-5059 (with *Symph. No. 96*). 24 min.

—Volksoper Orch., Vienna, M. Wöldike. VANGUARD 491 (with *Symph. No. 99*). 23 min.

—French National Radio Orch., I. Markevitch.
ANGEL 35312 (with *Symph. No. 101*). 22 min.
—Vienna Symph. Orch., H. Scherchen. WEST-
MINSTER 18326 (with *Symph. No. 101*). 26 min.
—London Philharmonic Orch., G. Solti. LONDON
LL-1043 (with *Symph. No. 100*). 26 min.
—Munich Philharmonic Orch., G. Reinwald.
MERCURY 10084 (with *Symph. No. 103*), discon-
tinued. 25 min.

### No. 103, IN E-FLAT, "DRUMROLL" ***

Opens with a long mutter from the kettles solo,
thus the sobriquet inadequate for the tireless and
captivating ingenuities of No. 103. Both the first
and the last movements complicate a swift ju-
venile sport by interspersions of portent and
mysticism. The beautiful Andante is one of
Haydn's most compelling excursions into the
double-theme, double-variation form he controlled with ever-growing mastery. The symphony as a whole is particularly resistant to the
snobbery of either the vulgar or the learned,
bearing as much beneath as above its surface.

My favorite among six good performances
(five good records) is Sir Thomas Beecham's, for
reasons hard to convey, since they are based on
a reaction to the projection over-all rather than
to any particular saliencies of style or sound.
Professor Heger's knowing work must be relegated to the depths because of the inferior sound
it cannot escape. Between this pair of disks are

four editions impossible to arrange in a fair hierarchy, so disparate are their merits and defects.
It is a comfort to lean on the reliable Mogens
Wöldike, strong and upright, not brilliant but
authoritative, and aided by the most incisive of
these registrations. Dr. Scherchen has viewed the
music with far more serious eyes than his rivals
and has held back the pace of all four movements,
which I find does not wear well in spite of the
loving finesse with which he has executed his
concept. Sir Thomas bestows quite as much refinement of detail within a course of more even
procedure, in gait, dynamics and phrase; and his
orchestra excels in the finer nuances. Mr. Solti's
performance is spry and able except in the latter
part of the Andante (split into two parts on the
ten-inch disk), where control of pace escapes
him. This conductor has an exciting, urgent hand
for classical finales, and in Symphony No. 103's
no one equals his breathless dash. Mr. Munch too
realizes a true climax in his Finale, as the result
of a plan in which strength is reserved until the
Finale demands it, making a performance of
inexorable growth, formally apt. The Bostonians
are the blandest orchestra here, with a performance seemingly unconducted; for except the Finale there are no peripeties and the sound flows
like melted butter seeking a level. The mellow,
undramatic and polished reproduction matches
perfectly. The version is unique in its oneness
and its slighting of point in favor of demeanor.

To many collectors it will seem the best, to some perhaps the worst. To one it is a vexation to assess.

—Royal Philharmonic Orch., T. Beecham. Co-LUMBIA ML-4453 (with *Symph. No. 94*). 25 min.
—Volksoper Orch., Vienna, M. Wöldike. VAN-GUARD 493 (with *Symph. No. 104*). 29 min.
—Boston Symph. Orch., C. Munch. RCA LM-1200 (with *Beethoven: Symph. No. 1*), discontinued. 27 min.
—Vienna Symph. Orch., H. Scherchen. WEST-MINSTER 18327 (with *Symph. No. 104*). 31 min.
—London Philharmonic Orch., G. Solti. 10-in. LONDON LS-124, discontinued. 25 min.

---

—Bamberg Symph. Orch., R. Heger. MERCURY 10084 (with *Symph. No. 102*), discontinued. 29 min.

### No. 104, IN D, "LONDON" ***

So ends the beguiling procession of Haydn's symphonies, in healthy, full-throated glory. The last of twelve *London* Symphonies, No. 104 is everywhere known as "The London Symphony," with a comfortable indifference to good sense. I wish I could describe it, but good music is not acquiescent to description. Its notes are made for translation into tones, not words, and the prudent auditor confines himself to a confession of his impressions. "The London Symphony" gives out tumult, grace, majesty, regret, struggle, determination, recklessness, etc., and so do half of the other

"London" Symphonies. The final impression is of exhilaration, as it nearly always is in a Haydn symphony not specifically exploring darkness. I do not find, as so many Haydnists feel that they must find, the last symphony the greatest. I find it in keeping with the lofty creative spirit of the last thirteen, and among Nos. 92, 93, 95, 97, 98, 99, 100, 102, 103 and 104 I am unable to choose a favorite. With No. 104 Haydn did not reach a culmination because he had already reached one with the "Oxford" Symphony composed before his first English visit. I think he intended *The Creation* to be the definitive culmination, and in several senses it was. No subsequent oratorio by anyone has disturbed the lonely eminence of *The Creation*, but Beethoven's First appeared with little delay to continue in expansion the marvelous symphonic route along which Haydn had posed a hundred and four milestones.

Only three of the recordings of the last of Haydn's symphonies are blessed with sound altogether acceptable by the most recent standards. The five others are very old, and three among them carry performances of distinction, particularly the Beecham and Dressel, whose sonic inadequacies are to be lamented. Vanguard and Epic have the clearest and cleanest etching, with Westminster less outward but presenting a sensuous blend of tones in a softer type of recording. After the sonically faulted Beecham the most seizing statement is the Szell for three movements, alert, energetic and limpid, with a very attractive interfusion of the orchestral choirs. The trouble here is that the conductor affects a quick Andante, and unless this difficult movement is taken slowly it sounds rushed and its sentiment is thwarted. Dr. Scherchen, who takes the movement perhaps too slowly, makes it a song of deep regret, ominous with shadowed tragedy. This conductor's leadership is one of refined forcefulness throughout, deliberate and individual, unconventional in many phases and stimulating to both thought and query. I think most collectors will prefer the even tempos, the strong stroke and the bright urgency of the Wöldike display, indifferent to polish and full of life in a brilliant, peremptory reproduction.

—Volksoper Orch., Vienna, M. Wöldike. VANGUARD 493 (with *Symph. No. 103*). 28 min.

—Vienna Symph. Orch., H. Scherchen. WESTMINSTER 18327 (with *Symph. No. 103*). 28 min.

—Cleveland Orch., G. Szell. EPIC LC-3196 (with *Symph. No. 88*). 23 min.

---

—London Philharmonic Orch., T. Beecham. COLUMBIA ML-4771 (with *Schubert: Symph. No. 5*), discontinued. 25 min.

—Boston Symph. Orch., C. Munch. RCA LM-9034 (with *Symph. No. 94*). 25 min.

—"Austrian" Symph. Orch., N. Annovazzi. REMINGTON 199-56 (with *Mozart: Symph. No. 28*). 27 min.

—London Philharmonic Orch., J. Krips. LON-

DON LL-339 (with *Symph. No. 100*), discontinued. 24 min.
—Bavarian Radio Orch., A. Dressel. MERCURY 10050 (with *Symph. No. 82*), discontinued. 27 min.

## SYMPHONY (CALLED QUARTET) IN B-FLAT

This terribly tenuous little thing underwent from a publisher theft of its oboe and horn parts and was printed as Op. 1, No. 5, in the second edition of that opus number. It is very early and not much. Haydnists are grateful to the enterprise that salvages obscurities and puts them on records, but their gratitude will be temperate for the performance here, minimal in alacrity and expression, in a clear but colorless registration of a handful of dazed instruments.
—"Vienna Orchestral Society," F. Adler. UNICORN 1019 (with *M. Haydn: Concerto for Viola, Keyboard, etc.*). 17 min.

## SYMPHONY (DOUBTFUL) IN C

Calling this pleasantry "doubtful" is giving the benefit of the doubt to the record. The Haydnish features are in small measure, no more than we should naturally expect from any of his talented contemporaries, and the features discordant with Haydn's habits are strong and multiple. The three-movement piece has been edited by Mr. Zoltan Fekete who conducted the recording, and who makes no categorical deposition on who wrote it. The sound of the recording is of an obscurity to hide what values may lie in the playing.

—Mozarteum Orch., Salzburg, Z. Fekete. Mercury 10066 (with *Handel: "Jepthta" Suite*). 18 min.

### Toy Symphony ***

"One day Papa Haydn's trusted musicians—his *Kinder*, he called them—rebelled. '*Nein, nein!*' they shouted, pointing to some bars in Symphony No. 82, which tells in lovely tones how the kindly composer saved a *Mädel* from a ferocious bear, 'Dot iss too hardt'; and nothing the saddened old master could say would mollify them.

"To tell the trtuh, Papa Haydn was himself no little vexed that his lads—his very own hand-trained *Buben*—seemed, on reflection, to be no better than a pack of lazy slobs.

"But the kindly old man was not one to bear a grudge. Passing through a street where toys of all kinds were displayed to delight the hearts of children, he espied hanging in a booth gaily festooned with colored ribbons a tiny trumpet, a sturdy rattle, and a miniature metal drum. His eyes began to twinkle at an alarming rate, and leveling at the booth's proprietor the long, ancient forefinger the high-born Esterházys so much dreaded, he demanded:

" '*Wieviel macht's?*'

" '*Zwei Thaler* the lot, Pop,' responded the rotund and ruddy toymaker, who like everybody

else, of high or low degree, worshiped the totter-
ing composer of so much music he had never
heard.

" 'You take *mich* for a sucker, no?' demanded
the venerable chapelmaster; and they fell to bar-
gaining merrily.

"But the vendor was no match for the shrewd
business brain behind the ancient twinkling eyes,
and Papa was able to get the tiny instruments for
a fraction of their value. While he bargained he
carelessly composed the immortal masterpiece
children from six to sixty cherish as the "Toy"
Symphony; for the old rascal wrote for Hänsl,
his dignified trumpet-virtuoso, a part for the toy
bugle just bought; for Fränzl, his superb tim-
panist, some waggish tapping for the tiny tin
drum; and for his great oboists Fritzl and Poldl
dramatic ejaculations for cuckoo-call and other
bird lures. With a warning to the baffled toymaker, 'Watch *deine* mannerss next time, *mein
guter* man,' he skipped back to rehearsal, where
the vivacity of his twinkle did not fail to arouse
dire apprehension.

"But you can be sure that fear was changed to
hilarity when he showed what he had wrought.
With right good will his *Buben* fell into the spirit
of the delicious joke. Amidst a guttural chorus of
approval, that favorite (of children from seven
to seventy) known as the "Toy" or "Children's"
Symphony had its first rehearsal. Never again
would a member of Papa Haydn's musical family
dare '*nein-nein*' him; and at the next performance

of Symphony No. 82 the growling of the bear
was so realistically expounded that the poor old
composer received a reprimand from his patron,
Prince Nicholas, for frightening all '*die Damen*'
from the auditorium."

I have ventured above to put into proper form
for television the tale of the "Toy" Symphony
more or less as it has been circulated these last
hundred years. Usually the account is more cir-
cumstantial than I have given it, with dates,
names, places, costumes, weather, etc., abundantly offered. Writers on music plume themselves on the thoroughness of their data. I believe
that the chronicle of the Toy Symphony has been
more influential in providing a picture of Franz
Josef Haydn than any other information published about this great man.

The "Toy" Symphony was composed by Leopold Mozart, and its amusing charm does not
belong in a Haydn discography. However, lest
collectors curse me for leading them this far to
barrenness, I am pleased to say that the best
recording is on Vox 9780, by a Stuttgart orchestra conducted by Rolf Reinhardt, the record containing also Mozart's *Musical Joke* and one of
the twenty-odd versions of *Eine kleine Nachtmusik*. As Mozart's father wrote the music, it
was a seven-movement cassation in G, from
which someone, perhaps Haydn's brother Michael, extracted three movements for employment as a "Toy" Symphony in C. The cassation
can be found in its entirety on Unicorn 1016.

# VOCAL MUSIC*

## ARIAS

"Ein' Magd, ein' Dienerin"
"Son pietosa, son bonina"
"Chi vive amante"
"Berenice, che fai?"
"Solo e pensoso"

The best of these remarkable arias is the long
scena "Berenice," daring and impassioned, with
the deep, regretful "Solo e pensoso" less affecting
only because of its narrower scope. These, capably sung by the soprano and fairly well delivered
by the orchestra, occupy the second side of a record most of whose first side ("Son pietosa" ex-
cepted) is miserable in the singing, slovenly in
the accompaniment and precarious in the sonics.
"Ein' Magd" in this version is a severe trial for
both singer and audience, but since the three
successful arias are not likely to be attempted
again in the predictable future and Haydnists

* All categories, including music for the church and
the stage.

ought not to be without them, I recommend that
collectors give the disk a hearing.
—G. Hopf, soprano; Vienna Symph. Orch. M.
von Zallinger. HAYDN SOCIETY 2045, discontinued.
11, 4, 6, 15, 8 min.


## CANTATAS AND ORATORIOS

### ARIANNA A NASSO

Ariadne, abandoned on Naxos by Theseus, flings
out her bewilderment, despair, love, hope and
rage in an extraordinary record of a superb solo
cantata. In recitative broken by song, and song
interspersed with recitative, with every line set
to its emotional essence without recourse to orna-
mentation or other musical cosmetics, Haydn,
not for the first time, in this late work forces us,
the hearers, to accept as indisputably Grecian
the musical bearing of a German composer of
the classical part of the eighteenth century, as
Gluck had done before anyone else, and as
*Idomeneo*, the great Gluck of Mozart, had done
too, and as Haydn would do again in his *Orfeo*.
Officially withdrawn, the record will no doubt
be restored to circulation after the little eulogy
here, for what music-lovers have avoided is not
this performance or this music, but the form. The
solo cantata with piano accompaniment does not
seduce our epoch. This one should. Miss Tourel
has managed a little miracle in sustaining a notable purity of vocal line throughout its dramatic

vicissitudes, so telling in the sepia tints of her soprano; while Mr. Kirkpatrick's commentary, in the mellow voice of a piano built to eighteenth century plans, has the authority of knowledge directed by taste, and betrays no vulnerability to criticism. Reproduction is easy and natural.
—J. Tourel, mezzo-soprano; Ralph Kirkpatrick, piano. HAYDN SOCIETY 2051 (with *6 English Songs*), discontinued. 16 min.

## THE CREATION (DIE SCHOEPFUNG)

In London Haydn learned what could be done with choral glorifications of Scripture. Handel, perpetual king of English music, was a revelation to the viceroy, whose previous knowledge of oratorio was almost entirely limited to the moribund Italian form, ornate and superficial. At sixty-four he went to work on a German text, originally English, from *Genesis* and *Paradise Lost*, with the announced intention of composing a work that would make his name remembered. To such a believer as he, the Word was literal; under the holy obligation of setting It perfectly, he began and ended his days of intense concentration, on his knees in prayer, elated but humble in the blessing of his powers.

Everyone who has ever crept into a church knows the result. *The Creation* is the greatest splendor that innocence has ever worn. The deepest resources of a profound musical mind have been lavished to prove an absence of guile. This music has the obviousness of the very earth, the sweetness of the south wind, the happiness of sunlight, the exultation of completeness. It is the lyrical imagery of eyes that find nothing to question. It is cherubic, and it cannot be doubted. It makes one believe in God, and even for a while in man: that its author has never been beatified or canonized or sanctified or otherwise officially anointed makes one despair of churches.

Two of the five phonographic versions are unqualified blessings, and something favorable may be said for the other three. The noble elements of the pioneer essay by the Haydn Society are obscured behind musty and messy sonics, and the reëditing by the Musical Masterpiece Society of the tape that produced that first effort has effected remarkable improvement but has not been able to challenge the sound of the two best or to erase certain deficiencies in some of the solo singing. The Urania version gives reproduction of strong impact, good clarity and fair tone to a leaner performance than the rest, and the soloists of this one are better than they sound, since the disproportionately close recording allotted to them—the major fault in these sonics—sharpens the soprano and coarsens the bass.

The control exercised by the Danish conductor Wöldike over his Viennese forces is direct, forceful and steady, very effective in clarifying the polyphony and displaying the rich hues of the orchestra. There is a greater dignity of classicism here than in the very intense Markevitch leadership, in which each number is presented in separate treatment, without reference to that whole that the Dane keeps always apparent. Hence in the Decca a greater scope of dynamics and of coloristic shadings, a much greater employment of hush and hesitation, of burst and impetuous drive. *The Creation* is not a dramatic work but a commentary with dramatic illustration, and it seems unreasonable to complain when the illustration is vivid.

If there is uncertainty on the relative merits of the two interpretations, there can be very little on the execution. The Berlin Philharmonic Orchestra of these disks is obviously, in most of the ways in which orchestral ability is measured, superior to the Viennese orchestra employed by Vanguard, and in vocal quality the St. Hedwig Choir can hold head to any chorus in the world. In reproduction both versions are outstanding in their difficult type, with Vanguard brighter, more decisive in timbre; Decca smoother and darker; the first with some advantage to trumpets and trombones, and the second preserving remarkable articulation in offering velvet strings, rare in recording.

The soloists are without exception so imposing that their comparative virtues do not influence choice except with collectors who judge *The Creation* on the basis of a favorite aria or two.

All these editions are sung in German, and all are equipped with album, notes, text and translation.

—I. Seefried (s), (Gabriel, Eve); R. Holm (t),

(Uriel); K. Borg (bs), (Raphael, Adam); Choir of St. Hedwig's, Berlin, and Berlin Philharmonic Orch., I. Markevitch. Two 12-in. DECCA DX-138. 1 hr. 46 min.

—T. Stich-Randall (s), (Gabriel); A. Felbermayer (s), (Eve); A. Dermota (t), (Uriel); F. Guthrie (bs), (Raphael); P. Schoeffler (bne), (Adam); Vienna Opera Chorus and Orch., M. Wöldike. Two 12-in. VANGUARD 471-2. 1 hr. 49 min.

---

—S. Korch (s), (Gabriel, Eve); G. Unger (t), (Uriel); T. Adam (bs), (Raphael, Adam); Chorus and Orch. of Radio Berlin, H. Koch. Two 12-in. URANIA 235. 1 hr. 50 min.

—T. Eipperle (s), (Gabriel); F. Riegler (s), (Eve); J. Patzak (t), (Uriel); G. Hann (bs), (Raphael); A. Pernerstorfer (bs), (Adam); Chorus of the Vienna National Opera and the Vienna Philharmonic Orch., C. Krauss. Two 12-in. MMS 2015. 1 hr. 49 min.

—Same performance as that immediately above. Three 12-in. HAYDN SOCIETY 2005.

### THE SEASONS (DIE JAHRESZEITEN)

*The Seasons* was finished three years after *The Creation*, and beautiful as it is neither Haydn nor we could possibly find in our hearts for it the love the earlier work commands. The cause of our failure is in the libretto: Haydn rose to his subject in appropriate spirit, but it was not the spirit that animates *The Creation*, a chronicle of

Archangels, of Life from Naught, of Man and
Woman. The inexorable succession of Spring,
Summer, Fall and Winter certainly promises
grandeur in music by a man like Haydn, but
when this inescapable majesty is complicated by
the life of a Styrian Darby and Joan sharing joys
and pain as imagined by the condescension of a
chilly, transplanted Flemish noble, we have to
face the fact of vaudeville. Haydn transfigured
this spurious stuff, and *The Seasons* is wonderful
in the appeal of any part of it, but never convincing as an epic. Initially a great success, the
oratorio has had some difficulty in keeping in
repertory against the disadvantages of its long
length and the ill ease of audiences on guard
against being taken in by spoofing. In compensation, the phonograph offers the great advantage
of making available the seasons one by one, each
entire as a magnificent tableau and an involved
culmination of light music.

The brave early effort by the Haydn Society
is sonically unacceptable by today's standards.
The gross faults of balance diminish the chorus
and magnify the soloists, at the same time libel-
ing the latters' voices. In the long reverberation
finesse is swallowed and the details of what seems
to be a fine performance vanish. The verdict
must be to Decca, adequate if a little disappointing. Again the soloists are too forward to the
detriment of their quality, particularly the soprano's; and the direction of Ferenc Fricsay
mixes curiously fire and water. But the chorus is

superb, and the orchestra satisfactory, with the sound of steadily good value except for the distension of the soloists.

Cetra has or had a shrunken version of *The Seasons* in Italian, one season to each of four sides, an old and dusky recording of curious, intimate and Mediterranean charm, too crude in sound to be recommended, but hard to forget, and endowed with Gabriella Gatti's voice at its loveliest. For collectors who care to investigate, this is catalogued as Cetra 1202.

—E. Trötschel (s), (Hanne); W. Ludwig (t), (Lukas); J. Greindl (bs), (Simon); RIAS Ch. Choir, Choir of St. Hedwig's, Berlin, and RIAS Orch., F. Fricsay. Three 12-in. Decca DX-123. 2 hr. 20 min.

---

—T. Eipperle (s), (Hanne); J. Patzak (t), (Lukas); G. Hann (bs), (Simon); Chorus of the Vienna National Opera and the Vienna Philharmonic Orch., C. Krauss. Three 12-in. Haydn Society 2027. 2 hr. 26 min.

The Seven Words of the Saviour on the Cross (Die sieben Worte des Erlösers am Kreuze)

The sublime pity of this music is most ethereal in the quartet version, most human in its final form, oratorio. The emotional imprint left by the one is so different from the stamp of the other that listeners easily fancy other changes than the interludes inserted for the oratorio, when in fact the later form follows as faithfully as possible the notes of the quartet. The recording is an old one made at a public performance and has many crudities (overweighted bass, indistinct enunciation, audience noises) but has an undeniable force of persuasive impact. The well-trained chorus is the principal positive element, for the orchestra shows raw patches and the soloists are opaque in the sound transmitted to us. Add a leadership of knowing affection, very eloquent in the phrase, and the tragedy emerges much as it does in any cathedral equipped with good musicians, fairly low in sonic fidelity but darkly compelling in its invasion of every recess. It is not a recording to be lauded, but it is a hardship to be without it. —H. Gueden (s), C. Oschlager (a), J. Patzak (t), H. Braun (bne); Cathedral Choir and Salzburg Mozarteum Orch., J. Messner. Two 12-in. REMINGTON 199-66. 62 min.

## MASSES

No. 1, IN F (MISSA BREVIS FOR TWO SOPRANOS) A touching innocence characterizes this sweet little devotion (scored for soprano duo, chorus, organ and strings) by a boy of seventeen who was teaching himself the way to immortality. It is probably the earliest piece of music we have from him. The performance is unpretentious but spirited, conforming to the gentle requirements of the score; and the sound, healthy in a fresh outwardness, does not betray its age and is better than commendable.

—H. Heusser, A. Berger, sopranos; Akademie Choir and Vienna Ch. Orch., H. Gillesberger. LYRICHORD LL-30 (with *Mass No. 5*). 13 min.

### No. 4, IN E-FLAT (MISSA IN HONORAM BEATISSIMAE VIRGINIS MARIAE; "GREAT ORGAN MASS)

"Great Organ" Mass because the organ has considerable lively play and the Mass is extensive and must be distinguished from No. 5, a short work with a long prominent passage for organ in one movement. No. 5 is the "Little Organ" Mass. The "Great" is an early composition with none of the majesty that signals the last six, written thirty and more years later, but it is delicate and fragrant and joyful except during a few wistful moments. The recording is a good production, and with a more animated beat the performance would have been exemplary, with its gifted solo quartet and small chorus in high form. The sound is assimilable and pleasant but short of orchestral detail; unusual in that particular, choral recordings being generally more satisfactory in the instruments than in the voices.

—E. Roon (s), H. Rössl-Majdan (a), W. Kementt (t), W. Berry (bs); Akademie Ch. Choir and Vienna Symph. Orch., F. Grossmann. Vox 7020. 41 min.

## No. 5, in B-flat (Missa Brevis Sancti Joannis de Deo; "Little Organ" Mass)

This is the most immediately lovely and the most obviously devout of Haydn's Masses, small-scaled and touching, a gentle avowal of humility. The Austrian version is to be preferred to the Danish in spite of some felicities in the latter, being as a whole more liquid and mellower, with a bright and sufficiently spacious sound against the thicker Danish sound a little over-reverberant and consequently mottled with soprano hoot.

—H. Heusser, soprano; Akademie Ch. Choir and Vienna Ch. Orch., H. Gillesberger. LYRICHORD LL-30 (with *Mass No. 1*). 19 min.

—K. Frederiksen, boy soprano; Copenhagen Boys' and Men's Choir and Ch. Orch. of the Copenhagen Palace Chapel, M. Wöldike. HAYDN SOCIETY 2064 (with *Songs for Mixed Voices*). 17 min.

## No. 7, in C (Missa Sanctae Caeciliae)

The Gloria in Haydn's longest Mass lasts about half an hour, and I think we must accept this spanking music as an intentional glorification of the joy of faith. No other Mass has such a bravado of energetic sport, in which the few interludes of reflection seem to have been devised to allow the participants to regain their wind for a new excursion into operatic polyphony, trumpets in the van. The archaic construction is that of J. S. Bach, the dramatic effect that of *Aïda*, Act I. I do not know why anyone should deplore it, but it has been deplored by many of the eminent faithful, frightened of their own unseemly exhilaration, and by some of the cultivated heathen, angered that their domain be invaded in the interests of sanctity.

Dr. Gillesberger has an experienced and sympathetic hand for the ecclesiastical aberrations of an epoch when cardinals dismissed their mistresses for a solecism and reprimanded them for appearing in church unrouged; note in the gusty spirits of his strong control a dogged adherence to steady tempo and regular accent in the accepted baroque manner, manifest as an undercurrent even when the proclamations of pure sport are most vociferous. The choral delivery is strong and vivid, the orchestra lively, the soloists able or better. The latter, far from being too prominent, are for once a little reticent, not unrealistically, and the balance of the three divisions is unusually right. Close, with little echo, the sound gives a concentrated impact. There are some evidences of clumsiness, such as the premature stifling of closing cadences, and some buckling of the chorus, but roughness is a venial fault in a projection of such forceful and exciting gusto.

—R. Schwaiger (s), S. Wagner (a), H. Handt (t), W. Berry (bs); Akademie Chorus and Vienna Symph. Orch., H. Gillesberger. Two 12-in. HAYDN SOCIETY 2028. 1 hr. 15 min.

## No. 8, IN C (MISSA CELLENSIS; MARIAZELLER-MESSE)

Composed ten years later than the latest of the preceding masses, and almost fifteen years before the final six incited by Haydn's submission to English choral practices, the *"Mariazell"* Mass belongs more to the past than to the future, relying on the baroque devices cherished by the preceding musical generation and in 1782 dying. It is a brilliant and peremptory entertainment in the main, festive; but with far more time for reflection than we can find in the ripsnorting "St. Cecilia" Mass in the same key. The recorded performance is not dissimilar in its principal lines from that of the "St. Cecilia," but the sound is much less attractive, with an irritating shudder as invariable accompaniment for the solo quartet and a less regular intruder with the chorus. In other respects reproduction is satisfactory.

—G. Rathauscher (s), A. Janacek (a), K. Equilus (t), W. Berry (bs); Akademie Chorus and Vienna Symph. Orch. H. Gillesberger. HAYDN SOCIETY 2011. 40 min.

## No. 9, IN C (MISSA IN TEMPORE BELLI; "KETTLE-DRUM" MASS) ***

There is no persuasive testimony that one great Haydn Mass is greater than another, but the ones called great are the last six, composed from 1796 to 1802, beginning with this "Mass in Wartime." Haydn's long life knew many wars, but none more terrible, none more humiliating for his empire, than the series undertaken against the infant French Republic to seize its territory under the cloak of restoring the dynasty that the republic had expelled. While Haydn worked on his Mass in the summer of 1796 the Imperial armies in Italy were collapsing under the uninterrupted mauling dealt them by a new French general twenty-seven years old, but this had not yet become a habit, and contrasting with the defiance in Haydn's Mass it is rather lament for the dead than resignation we hear when the drums and trumpets are not sounding their command to arms. Liturgical forms, and the Mass particularly, droop from the fatigue of repetition, and the composer who writes a dozen Masses needs an outer stimulus to inflame his inner belief and supplement his professional competence. In the contrary emotions stirred by disastrous but always hopeful war Haydn found a human exaltation that made his last six Masses creations of a fervor that will not die.

In the recording of the "Mass in Wartime" note a soprano of a vocal purity made for the music, and other capable singers, well placed for clear projection without absorption by the chorus or domination of it; a strong beat from the orchestral and choral forces, and a constant glow of confidence in the broad sound that presents no problems and seems right.

—J. Topitz-Feiler (s), G. Milinkovic (a), H. Handt (t), H. Braun (bs); Akademie Chorus and

Vienna Opera Orch., H. Gillesberger. Haydn Society 2021. 48 min.

## No. 10, in B-flat (Missa Sancti Bernardi de Offida; Heiligmesse)

The conductor is an accomplished classical technician who has worked the involved counterpoint of this "Holy" Mass (so called from the inclusion of the tune of an old hymn, "*Heilig, heilig*" in the Sanctus) into an opulent texture. The performance is big but refined in its proportions and smoothly disciplined. It is not Viennese: emotional acuity is secondary to musical nicety, slow passages proceed without lingering, and brilliance is more apparent than mellowness. Brilliant it is indeed, in sound and performance, the sound a bit brittle for the sexless sopranos but clean and solid everywhere else and especially for the smart, positive orchestra. My own taste does not savor boy sopranos in a passionate work, but I have no other strong antipathy to this record, and no doubt the majority of collectors will not share my prejudice.
—Copenhagen Boys' and Men's Choir and Danish Royal Opera Orch., M. Wöldike. Haydn Society 2048. 40 min.

## No. 11, in D minor (Missa Solemnis, 1798; "Lord Nelson" Mass; "Imperial" Mass)

After Haydn had started this Mass Nelson annihilated the French fleet in the Bay of Aboukir, and the second event supposedly is responsible for much of the martial demeanor of the music. The over-victorious admiral, who disapproved of gun-sights, later had some intercourse with the composer at Esterház and Vienna; and the electrifying woman who owned him, Emma Hamilton, both patronized and snubbed the great man to whom her lover's victory was a clear act of God.

The "Nelson" Mass has a continuity of interest equal to that of any extended musical work for church, and not only because of its exciting military reflection. Even its contemplations are heated, as if the entire concept were dictated by an urgency to be intense before the occasion faded. The old recording by the Haydn Society was a remarkable success during the first years of its existence, doubly remarkable in view of the crudeness of its sonics, no longer tolerable. Now that there is another version we can forget that old one, not without regret for the singing of Miss della Casa giving an example to the angels. The Vanguard edition of seven years later has a taut, fiery performance in trouble-free, dramatic reproduction and simply must prevail in anyone's judgment.

—T. Stich-Randall (s), E. Höngen (a), A. Dermota (t), F. Guthrie (bs); Akademie Ch. Choir and Vienna Opera Orch., M. Rossi. VANGUARD 470. 37 min.

---

—L. della Casa (s), E. Höngen (a), H. Taubmann (t), G. London (bs); Akademie Chorus

and Vienna Symph. Orch., J. Sternberg. HAYDN
SOCIETY 2004. 44 min.

## No. 12, IN B-FLAT (MISSA SOLEMNIS, 1799; THE-
### RESIENMESSE)

Lacking accessory interests like Bonaparte and
Nelson, the "Theresa" Mass is unable to stimulate
that curiosity before being heard that has so
greatly promoted the popularity of other Masses.
It is, however, deeply admired by musicians, and
is more obviously a churchly exercise than the
others in the final series. From its sobriquet we
deduce that the consort of Franz II, a less con-
spicuous Maria Theresa devoted to Haydn, admired it or sang in it. This is a more courtly Mass
than Haydn had been writing, bountiful with
grace. It is also rich in complicated counterpoint,
an observation one must make about each of the
final Masses, unilluminating as it is. As in so
many Masses of the day the stage is frequently
sensed below the altar: a grubbier age was required before such realism was denounced as
impropriety.

Grace and fluency are notable in the recording
under the limpid organization of the late Clemens
Krauss. This is a flexible performance, supple and
benevolent beyond our experience with most of
the Haydn Mass recordings, and less dramatic in
contours kept generally cool and symmetrical.
The sound is pretty good as a whole, although the
orchestral winds are not bright and there is some
slight occasional flutter in the voices. The chorus

Masses are strong and reasonably distinct. In
sum not perfect but worth having.
—A. Felbermayer (s), D. Hermann (a), J. Patzak (t), A. Poell (bs); Vienna Opera Chorus and
Vienna Symph. Orch., C. Krauss. Vox 6740. 43
min.

### No. 14, IN B-FLAT (MISSA SOLEMNIS (1802); HAR-MONIEMESSE; "WINDBAND" MASS)

Let me forgo discussion of Haydn's magnificent
last Mass until the phonograph has a good edition.
—Soloists, Viennese Chorus and Orch., A. Larsen
(pseudonym). RENAISSANCE 57, formerly PERIOD
541. 50 min.


## OPERAS

The twenty-odd works composed by Haydn for
the stage are not standard in the repertory of any
theatre. Many music-lovers will be surprised to
learn that he fancied himself as a composer of
operas; but having learned that will hardly be
astonished that he was a good one. A good composer of operas, that is; not a composer of good
operas. In his time every composer worth the
name tried his hand at stage works, and it is
amazing to realize how much really splendid
music was wasted on paltry, stereotyped librettos.
There were of course good librettos as well as
bad, but no law dictated then or now that the
good ones should be at the disposal of the good
composers. Haydn had both kinds, but the rejec-
tion of his operas by the twentieth century is a

result not of their merit or lack of it in the libretto, but of librettos unacceptable in form, structure and subject to the conventions of the modern stage. The libretto of *Il Trovatore* has universal recognition as the very perfection of badness, but we can hear its lively music whenever we wish, since the public finds nothing unexpected or improper for opera in this kind of literary claptrap. Germane but opposite is the sensational success of Puccini, than whose no nose was ever keener for the essential oils of slick melodrama, dominating the opera house with a trio of librettos baited with every sure-fire device of the theatre, for which the music is interchangeable and almost identical. If the genius of Haydn had been given promising titles like "Raped on the Subway" to work on, no doubt that his operas would be everywhere mounted.

The record companies have shown no disposition to restore the Haydn operas to circulation. In fact, of the four recorded essays, two are attempts to degrade the original concepts. Yet this is a promising province for the phonograph in collaboration with a small and conscientious opera company, especially that part of the province devoted to comedy, for which stylists exist and whose expenses would not be large. Perhaps someone will have the enterprise to survey it after the tenth *Butterfly* (only two more to go).

## THE APOTHECARY (LO SPEZIALE)

The libretto of this early *opera buffa* is a rather routine effort by Goldoni, but a supernal flower of verbal refinement compared to the lamentable doggerel of the truncation and translation, purportedly English, that it has suffered for the one appalling recording. This effrontery employs an "orchestra" of piano, violin and cello to support, if that is the word, some young voices in a projection without style or finesse, in sonics pretty clear, pretty dry and pretty hard. Recommended for oblivion.

—Singers and piano trio, F. Kramer. MAGIC TONE 1007. 32 min.

## THE MAN IN THE MOON

Haydn wrote no opera with this title. He did compose a *drama giocoso* to Goldoni's *Il mondo della luna,* which serves as the basis of the present recording. To adorn the Haydn Bicentennial in 1932 two Germans "updated" the agreeable little comedy into a German travesty. Nevertheless, they did not spoil the music although they altered its sense and introduced incongruous items from other Haydn music, notably *Orfeo.* It is easy to find entertainment in the record, particularly for those who do not understand German, since the music is tuneful and animated, the performance competent if not polished (why should it be?) and the reproduction satisfactory. Several of the singers conduct themselves very well, especially the tenor Gassner, in spite of the absence of any celebrity. (Neither German nor English text is supplied.)

—F. Schneider (s), H. Muench (m-s), A. Gassner (t), W. Lindner (t), K. Schwert (bne), W.
Hagner (bs); Munich Ch. Opera Orch., J. Weis-
enbach. PERIOD 703. 57 min.

ORFEO ED EURIDICE

The album full of Haydn's last opera set, at its
issuance in 1951, an amazing precedent: the album was the first performance. The records
created the *première*, a hundred and sixty years
after composition. Haydn had not been able to
produce it in London as he hoped, and only fragments were publicly presented until the Haydn
Society, in their most spectacular feat, assembled
a true score for the first time and put ORFEO into
disks. The gallant temerity and rare importance
of the enterprise have not received adequate recognition. Here is a case of a record company
acting as entrepreneur of an unknown, unper-
formed and uncommercial opera, beautiful indeed
but sick in its libretto and exalted in sentiment,
dreadfully unfit to compete with the bangaway
theatrics no first performance in the flesh would
nowadays dare not to have. No matter how we
examine the fantastic undertaking, it seems like
damned poor business, precisely what the world
most needs.

*Orfeo* is a ripe example of eighteenth century
*opera seria* on a classical subject, and its remarkably beautiful music transcends without illumi-
nating a text quite hopeless in its verbal im-
poverishment, its absence of characterization and

its ludicrous proportions of event. It is certainly
better on records, where it can be regarded as
a dramatic cantata of interest exclusively musical,
than it would be on the stage, where credulity
for its situations and sympathy for its personages
are required. Haydn has put a wonderful pun-
gency of expression into the rich scoring of the
clothed recitative that shakes with naked recitative the burden of the action, and as cantata this
vigor of statement is welcomed for its pure eloquence, contaminated on the stage by the visible
evidence that it leads to nothing. The choruses,
into which Haydn gave out a knowing art hardly
equaled in any other opera, and which are sung
by active participants in the drama, never seem
more than elevated commentaries, so artificially
their entrances and exits have been contrived.
There is little left for the exquisitely formed
arias to do except provide a lyrical punctuation.

The success of the Haydn Society, in giving
voice to the great cantata for the first time, is
naturally a qualified one. Inexperience is revealed
in the singing of every principal including the
experienced Alfred Poell, not at ease in the part
of Creonte, and particularly in the two young
sopranos, fresh-voiced and earnest, but not yet
qualified for floral coloratura. The Orfeo, with
a good Italianate tenor and a feeling for style,
is promising but incomplete. Chorus and orchestra are better and show that there was some
preparation for the recording, while the direc-

tion is alive and supple, surprisingly confident for an exposition of maiden music. Although there is an accumulation of the sonic faults of six years ago—background noise, changes of volume, instability of vocal projection—the reproduction is in sum sturdy and gives a strong effect of proximity to a stage, while the faults noted are intermittent and by no means crippling.

Most of those have been corrected in a Musical Masterpiece Society (M2030-OP18) from the same tapes, which is also superior in brightness to the Haydn Society's complete edition. But the MMS record, a generous fifty-eight minutes, gives less than half the opera, omitting not only all the naked recitative but much of the recitative clothed, and a number of other items. It is true that what remains has been sagely selected and presents a continuous flow of excitement or lyricism. Collectors without strong objections to abridgement might profit by examining the MMS epitome.

Printed with the text and translation supplied with the Haydn Society album are historical notes, a musical analysis and an account of the procedure in assembling a score, nearly a hundred illustrated pages.

—J. Helwig (s), (*Euridice*); H. Heusser (s), (*Guardian Spirit*); H. Handt (t), (*Orfeo*); A. Poell (bs), (*Creonte*); W. Berry (bs), (*Pluto*); Vienna Opera Chorus and Orch., H. Swarowsky. Three 12-in. HAYDN SOCIETY 2029. 2 hr. 5 min.

### PHILEMON UND BAUCIS

This is one of several marionette-operas composed by Haydn for the well-equipped theatre at Esterház. Until a few years ago it was believed lost, but an old manuscript copy unearthed in Paris by Dr. Jens Peter Larsen seems to be complete except for the prologue. It is a slender pastoral charmer very skilfully turned and scored, with a soprano aria of singularly beautiful simplicity, "*Dir de Unschuld.*" Of the recorded stage works of Haydn the disk is the most successful we have been granted, with singers well chosen and in form, a spirited direction and a satisfactory although rather overbright sound. The largest objection will be taken to a non-musical element: the spoken dialogue (for this is a *singspiel*) given too much volume and reverberation to fit into the progress of the opera without repeated adjustment at the control-unit. This is an annoyance, not a disablement, and I recommend the record as very beguiling and in little danger of supersession.

—E. Roon (s), (*Narcissa*); S. Naidic (s), (*Baucis*); E. Majkut (t), (*Philemon*); W. Kmentt (t), (*Aret*); Vienna Opera Chorus and Vienna Symph. Orch., M. von Zallinger. Vox 7660. 58 min.

### SONGS

It is protocol to speak patronizingly of the songs of Haydn, Mozart and Beethoven, which is

simply an awkward and offensive way of saying
that there is only one Schubert. Unfortunately
the observance of the protocol has kept most of
the Haydn songs off records. The ones recorded
are among the most familiar, the majority distinguished by an easy vocal line to match a simple
sentiment. I have not tried to ordinate according
to relative quality the records listed below, because they do not cover the same music exactly
and because the multiplicity of titles naturally
includes very uneven displays, impossible to
average sensibly. The only one I am inclined to
recommend strongly is the highly professional
effort of Miss Tourel aided by excellent accompaniments and good sound in the six *English
Songs* issued by the Haydn Society; and even
this outstanding one suffers from obscurity of
enunciation. The tenor Earl Rogers, essaying
some of the same songs in German translation,
in addition to one sung in the original language,
has a convincing, suave warmth of delivery but
is less eloquently seconded by his pianist and the
sound is difficult to adjust. The Niemela record
has the virtues of sensitivity and knowledge in
control of a well-mannered voice a little inclined
to overdo vibrato, but I find the accompaniments
weak and prosy. The *Four-Part Songs* of the
composer's full maturity are handled coolly with
very patent skill and organization by the Copenhagen Choir in a recording excellent except for
the sopranos, always on the verge of hoot.

The ten *Scotch Songs*, traditional or popular

melodies for which Haydn, like Beethoven later, composed introductions and codas, provided harmony and created an accompaniment for piano trio, represent an intelligent venture into a field ripe for the phonograph; but the dry sound accorded to singers and instruments is a constraint and a falsification. I detect a becoming simplicity in the vocal delivery, but the electronically-vexed tones impart a compromised pleasure.

—E. Rogers, tenor; E. Mitrani, piano. *She Never Told; Piercing Eyes; Das Leben ist ein Traum; Sailor's Song.* 10-in. ALLEGRO 13 (with *Mozart: 4 Songs*), discontinued. 13 min. (all).

—J. Tourel, mezzo-soprano; R. Kirkpatrick, piano. *Mermaid's Song; She Never Told; The Spirit's Song; Fidelity; My Mother Bids Me; Sailor's Song.* HAYDN SOCIETY 2051 (with *Arianna a Nasso*), discontinued. 23 min. (all).

—Ch. Choir of the Danish National Radio; B. Linderud, piano. (*6 Four-Part Songs in German*). HAYDN SOCIETY 2064 (with *Mass No. 5*). 26 min. (all).

—M. Bleiberg, soprano; E. Charney, mezzo-soprano; anonymous piano, violin and cello. (*10 Scotch Songs*). MAGIC TONE 1014. 28 min. (all).

—T. Niemela, soprano; P. Koskimies, piano. *Das Leben ist ein Traum; Mermaid's Song; She Never Told; My Mother Bids Me; The Spirit's Song.* WCFM 10 (with *Schubert: 7 Songs*), discontinued. 21 min. (all).

STABAT MATER

Haydn's contemporaries admired this music, composed in 1773, in a way that we cannot duplicate. For them it was a renovation, a modernization of the baroque church music a thousand composers had been writing throughout the century, and for us it is baroque primarily, spiced with authentic Haydn it is true, but circumspect, imitative and much too long. I think the only recording available is worth having in a collection, once the Masses, have been acquired. The one serious reservation in approving it concerns the thin tone of the small string body employed. Regardless of the number of string players Haydn might have had available to perform this work, he was always ready to use a large band when there was one, knowing as all cultivated ears do that the string body gathers unction with numbers.

—A. Felbermayer (s), S. Wagner (a), W. Kmentt (t), O. Wiener (bs); Akademie Ch. Chorus and Vienna Ch. Orch., H. Gillesberger. Two 12-in. Vox 7410. 1 hr. 21 min.

# ADDENDUM

# ADDENDUM

THE MANUSCRIPT for *The Collector's Haydn* was
finished more than a year ago. Delays in the
publication world are inevitable and understand-
able. Since recordings of Haydn's music had
progressed steadily since Mr. Burke had completed his study, the publishers requested that I
bring the compendium of recorded Haydn information up-to-date—Mr. Burke being unavail-
able for this task.

The notes that follow cover all recordings
issued in the period between early 1957 to date.
In addition, a few records are discussed that were
not covered by the author. The possible disadvantage of an addendum has been minimized, it
is hoped, by the simple device of indicating all
additional recordings of a work by asterisks
(\*\*\*). These are found in both the main part as
well as the addenda. New titles, recorded for the
first time, will be found in their proper order,
indicated by a dagger (†). No cross-reference
is given to these, naturally, in the addenda.

Discussing the recorded performance after

another critic has had his say poses a delicate task. Regardless of different performers, the selective analysis is concerned with the same topic. All things being equal, critics differ. What Mr. Burke has said, he has said exceedingly well. The only time I have added to his remarks is in the case of a reissue of a recording, or when a new coupling of works has appeared. But, we have mentioned the common denominator of critical decision. I have applied this yardstick—first, the judgment of a recording singly; second, when there has been more than one issue to consider, comparisons have been made and comment has been registered as to preference. It follows that this must be compared to Mr. Burke's viewpoint, so that the definitive selection is as though the work of one, not two men. The "rightness" of any critic is an elusive game. If he bears in mind that his opinions are less important because he happens to have them, and much more important because they will be read and considered, then perhaps he is worth reading. In the case of this book (specifically, when a work is discussed in the main body and addendum) a type of twofold, "democratic" estimate is given the reader. It should make the judgments more convincing.

The listing of timings has not been continued here. I have, whatever my opinions, retained the numbering utilized by the author in regard to the quartets, piano sonatas, and the like.

With the re-entrance of the Haydn Society the future of Haydn recordings can well be termed of bull-market indication. A new label, Washington Records, plans to issue a large corpus of Haydn music, especially filling the gaps still prevailing in the quartets. Haydn's music is a means of economic return to the recording companies. Its musical proceeds are a parallel to the record-purchaser.

I would like to express my grateful thanks to the following for making it possible to obtain recordings for this survey: Jean-Pierre Marty of Angel; Clair W. Van Ausdall of Mercury; Charles Schicke of Epic; Madaline Ciccolela of RCA Victor; Ernest Werner of Vox; Deborah Ishlon of Columbia; Israel Horowitz of Decca; Jack Roman of Capitol as well as other officials connected with the recording industry. Named or un-named, their tolerant coöperation was unstinting. Especially, I wish to thank James Lyons, editor of *The American Record Guide*, for permission to use material which originally appeared in that publication.

ARTHUR COHN

*September 10, 1958*

# CHAMBER MUSIC

## QUARTETS FOR STRINGS

### Opus 9

One need not belabor the fact that each new opus of Haydn's brought advance. This set of six quartets shows more progress in relation to the Opus 3 group than that half-dozen did in relation to the dozen works represented by Opus 1 and 2. Haydn was very nearly at the half-way mark of his life. These quartets were composed in 1769, when he was thirty-seven. Forty years of activity remained—and what years they were to be! The four-movement plan was now set securely; the first violin remains dominating, but the other voices are enriched with more liberties permitted them. A purer net quality hovers over the six works. Haydn himself was quite conscious of this. He even requested his publisher to discard the previous "eighteen" works and list these as his first quartets.

### No. 20, in C, Op. 9, No. 1

A double recording debut marks this disk. For

some unexplained reason the Schneider Quartet bypassed the Opus 3 and Opus 9 sets of quartets during their project of recording the entire Haydn corpus. Although this admirable plan was interrupted, the various *opera* preceding and succeeding these twelve quartets were recorded in their chronological order until the series was suspended. The initial recording of Opus 9 makes a very auspicious curtain-raiser to usher in the Beaux-Arts group. Tempting as the prospect may be, some critics do not agree that the complete works of even a master composer should be recorded. Their considered opinion is that some of the music is nothing more than warmed-up cabbage, and not worthy fare. Well, the best portions become tastier, and all the juicy morsels are not found in the main course.

Save for one section which is bald accompaniment pinned to a melody, the entire opening movement is free of primitive writing. The last movement is impetuous, but the first violin, contrary to conditions in the earlier quartets is not greedy. The best skills of the Beaux-Arts gentlemen are displayed in the fast, end movements. If the other portions are not as beautiful, style is not given secondary position. The sound is good, but the "chronorama" that occupies part of the liner copy is the opposite (*see* remarks at the conclusion of the notes for Op. 9, No. 6).

—Beaux-Arts Qt. Washington WR-450 (with *Qt. No. 21*)

## No. 21, IN E-FLAT, OP. 9, No. 2

Proper tempo must be chosen to project the more-than-average ornate style Haydn used in the opening movement. In this respect, as well as in realizing that pace must be regulated for the final movement, so that all the spicy syncopations are clearly exposed, the performance by this group is distinctive. Haydn left a place in the *adagio* for a cadenza insertion. Sensibility (and sensitivity) rules—it is hardly stylistically fitting to employ the artifice of a twentieth-century cadenza in a Haydn work, regardless of its correctness in the eighteenth century. Good sound, save the occasional metallic edge to the first violin's upper gamut. Since this is not apparent on the reverse side of the record, the finger of accusation is toward the engineer's headquarters. —Beaux-Arts Qt. WASHINGTON WR-450 (with *Qt. No. 20*)

## No. 22, IN G, OP. 9, No. 3

Brilliance surrounds the opening of this quartet. The first violin uses double-string work, ornate trills, grace-noted leaps, scales, and arpeggios. The violinists of Haydn's day must have been good technicians. Mr. Tarack needs no advice on how to get about a fiddle. His colleague, Mr. Tekula, does as well in the one try Haydn assigns to the cello. But the Beaux-Arts foursome does not have a sufficiently blended quartet sonority. They play acceptably, but need seasoning. The

inner voices are too obstinately restrained, whereas the cello has a heaviness that it would lose if the second violin and viola gave more response. The skills of these young men become best pronounced in the speedy movements. Their recognition of the Haydn brand of fun is displayed in the final portion of the work. This is musical sly wit. And new coinage in quartet literature. But Haydn's joke book never repeated any stale stories.
—Beaux-Arts Qt. WASHINGTON WR-451 (with *Qt. No. 23*).

## No. 23, IN D MINOR, OP. 9, No. 4

By far, the most pertinent work in the set. It marks Haydn's initial employment of a minor key in the quartets. And with a decided vengeance. The later gradational shift so that minor-based pieces shifted into more-optimistically concerned major keys is not present as yet. The D minor tonality is used for every movement save the slow one. Only the bald change to D major in the minuet's trio deviates from this norm. Tonality inspiration carries over to the performers; their playing is richer here than in any of the other five works in the opus. Some more intensity is required, however. Even in the frugally scored minuet—where the sum is greater than the parts (three-part writing for the pair of violins; an honest-to-goodness minuet trio), one wishes for more urgency. The record is worth owning because of Haydn's dynamic creativity. More years of work are required before this quartet's playing becomes large-scaled. —Beaux-Arts Qt. WASHINGTON WR-451 (with *Qt. No. 22*).

### No. 24, IN B-FLAT, OP. 9, No. 5

Further evidence of Haydn's growing concern for total equality in his string-quartet instrumentation is shown in the set of variations which ushers in the work. In the second of the four variants the assignment is given to the three lower instruments. Both the slow and final movements are usual middle-road Haydn, with the latter ending in surprise *piano* quality. Mozart was not looking the other way when such plans were exposed—note his use of this very subtle dramatic method. The Beaux-Arts gentlemen play this quartet with nicety of detail. A richer sound of the inner voices would aid the total performance. It is quite straightforward. Thereby, the subtle method of obtaining weight by grouped sounds, rather than by accent, is overlooked. A pioneer performance, but by no means the definitive one.

—Beaux-Arts Qt. WASHINGTON WR-452 (with *Qt. No. 25*)

### No. 25, IN A, OP. 9, No. 6

Good reading of a lightweight work. The first movement marks a move toward mature sonata design, with distinctness of themes related yet opposed, to form the necessary drama and requisite contrast. A subsidiary theme will be recognized by its barcarolle-like contour. To this, a third—pyrotechnical elaboration of the initial theme—adds further contrast. Dancing about on the prongs of a scale line, the whole last movement is a tossed-off musical bonbon with little to chew on. One merely relaxes.

—Beaux-Arts Qt. WASHINGTON WR-452 (with *Qt. No. 24*)

### Postscript

The album note of the Opus 9 quartets, issued by Washington, contains a "Chronorama" showing the number of string quartets written by important composers, relating these totals to their life span. This is an excellent idea, but executed with some astonishing boners. Schoenberg is listed as having composed three quartets. Four are acknowledged (actually five, since a "lost" early quartet has turned up). Schubert is given a total of three! Reger and Glazunov both are cheated of one quartet apiece; Grieg's "unfinished" (two-movement opus) is just as much a quartet as Schubert's B minor Symphony—thus his total should be two. Last, Beethoven's quartet total is traditionally indicated as seventeen; the amount of sixteen indicated seems to consider the *Grosse Fuge* as still belonging to the Opus 130 quartet.

No. 38, in B minor, Op. 33, No. 1 ***
No. 39, in E-flat, "The Joke," Op. 33, No. 2 ***

No. 40, IN C, "THE BIRD," OP. 33, No. 3 ***
No. 41, IN B-FLAT, OP. 33, No. 4 ***
No. 42, IN G, OP. 33, No. 5 ***
No. 43, IN D, OP. 33, No. 6 ***

The original Haydn Society releases of these works offered a pair of quartets per record, or all the quartets in one album. Now, with the reissuing of these fine records, the buyer is given a real bargain. Three quartets per disk is a real chamber-music bounty, and there is no loss of quality by this more compact issue. The third quartet of the set is available in a triple assortment with the Opus 50, No. 6 and Opus 76, No. 2. Those that prefer this C major quartet, with its chirping violins, and the heady-with-laughter finale will not lose by choosing the miscellany rather than the Opus 33 combination. Since nicknames are mentioned throughout this book, it is well to indicate that the fifth quartet also bears a name: "How Do You Do?" The first four tones of this quartet are a short scale, with the lengths greatest at the extremes. These therefore match quite nicely the phrase "How—do-you-do—" (if one can picture the rhythm in speech). Since the phrase rises, the questioning of the polite query is manifested as well. European musicians know this nickname much better than their American colleagues.

—Schneider Qt. HAYDN SOCIETY 9017 (*Qts. No. 38, 39 and 40*)
—Schneider Qt. HAYDN SOCIETY 9021 (*Qts. No. 41, 42 and 43*)

—Schneider Qt. HAYDN SOCIETY 9015 (*Qts. No. 40, 50 and 70*)

## No. 51, IN G, OP. 54, No. 1

Haydn's set of three quartets under this opus opens with brilliance and a very alive theme. The ideas are sprightly. Both this portion and the following movement are played with beauty of finish by this one-quarter British; three-quarters Austrian team. Especially compelling is their realization that the "slow" movement is in quickened state: an *allegretto* taking its place. The first violin delivers the melodic statement with exquisite taste. Both the minuet and finale are beautiful music, the former mixing the mode of key skilfully and changing the dance form into a miniature of larger-canvased concepts. Semicontrapuntalistic style is on view in the last division of the quartet. The Amadeus Quartet plays with decision; the sound is a gem; only a pinched tone, now and then, from the first violin, can be criticized.

—Amadeus Qt. ANGEL 45024 (with *Qt. No. 52*)

## No. 52, IN C, OP. 54, No. 2 ***

If the absence of reverberation cramped the performance of the Kroll Quartet, the recording of the Amadeus tends to be opposite, but the voicing is not always in balance. This results from a more romanticized Haydn than one generally hears. Haydn shades the fluorescence of his quartet writing in this work. The finale consists of

an *adagio* which incloses a short *presto* in between its extremes. Having had a previous *adagio*, the effect becomes almost stultified; one wishes for the graced gentility and springboarded drive of the usual Haydn finale. Only the *presto* section gives it. This, then, is a moment that can be termed of architectural mishap, but not of musical content. Performers can be expected to be concerned with the proper style of a work cut from a different pattern than usual. This concern shows in the playing of the Amadeus, though their performance is to be preferred.
—Amadeus Qt. ANGEL 45024 (with *Qt. No. 51*)

### No. 61, IN D, "LARK," OP. 64, No. 5 ***
The "thoroughly satisfactory" recording that Mr. Burke has been awaiting still has not appeared. The recording noted below is the second time the Hungarians have recorded this work (see last entry in initial discussion of Quartet No. 61). Since their previous effort has been withdrawn they do not compete with themselves. Though the quality of the disk is beyond reproach, the Hungarians do not achieve the proper mood of relaxation in the *allegro*, are too percussive in the minuet, and commit tempo murder in the last movement. The objective here is speed, speed, speed, beyond anything else. What price the kinetic formation of this *perpetuum mobile?* Musical exhibitionism is no special talent and the ability to play faster than the next quartet team is small coin these days.

Haydn's bombardment of peppered sixteenth notes almost skims off the disk—so hurried is the playing. Breathlessness results in place of the lightfooted mercurial significance indicated by the music.

—Hungarian Qt. ANGEL 45018 (with *Qt. No. 70*)

## No. 66, IN C, OP. 74, No. 1

In the thirties the comforts of LP listening were not available, but those who wanted their Haydn quartets served up handsomely had only to shuffle the Pro Arte Quartet recordings. Or else be fortunate enough to live in a city where this magnificent foursome would present quantities of the latest contemporary music and then end with the credo of a Haydn quartet (supreme program making!). There have been many recordings of Haydn string quartets since that day. But none other has the sound dicta and classical wisdom that these Juilliard gentlemen display. We are grateful for the relish with which this quartet team performs Bartók *et al.* It is just as rewarding to have their viewpoint on one of the great masterworks of the classical period.

As constantly as Haydn added to his quartet catalogue he added new features and these are to be heard clearly in the Juilliard performance. The opening theme is in *legato*, smooth as silk in the *mezzo forte* indicated. When development takes place in the more excited states of syncopation and polyphonic sport, the theme returns

in *staccato*. The development has made its effect on the thematic material. Some musicians might (many do) interpret the music in their own manner. The Juilliard Quartet re-creates—a maxim that might be used by many other chamber ensembles. Every movement of the work is touched by cognate and full knowledge of Haydn's wisdom.
—Juilliard Qt. RCA LM-2168 (with *Qt. No. 75*)

### No. 70, in D minor, "Quinten," Op. 76, No. 2 ***

The latest version of this exhilarating work is given a rather restrained reading at the start, then the gloves are taken off. In the variations the playing is superb. After this, however, there is no ecstatic portrayal of sound definition. The strict *canon* of the minuet is performed with stiffness and the last movement is given a workaday run through. The Hungarians are far better than the Vienna Konzerthaus, the Schneider, the Pascal, and the Galimir aggregations. They stand in third place in the "Quinten" league; the Quartetto Italiano and the Budapest hold first and second places, respectively.
—Hungarian Qt. Angel 45018 (with *Qt. No. 61*).

### No. 75, in G, Op. 77, No. 1 ***

By far the best performance available (strangely enough very few are available). Only the be-

ginning is not properly proportioned. The
Juilliard group plays with palpable percussiveness
at that point. After that their reading is totally
true to the score and also to all stylistic demands.
They realize that the "menuetto" is actually a
virile and wild scherzo. Further, they probe the
finale with amazing understanding. Everything—
themes, development, and subsidiary material—
all stem from the opening theme. It is cut apart
and splintered for use in a formal movement, but
the rondo design is shadowed by music built on
a motive. The Juilliard performance realizes the
creativity that makes this one of the most inform-
ative and exciting movements in all quartet literature. The sound is beyond reproach and Victor
should be proud of this release.
—Juilliard Qt. RCA LM-2168 (with *Qt. No. 66*).

### No. 77 (Unfinished), in B-flat and D minor, Op. 103 ***

The Amadeus Quartet's version has been reissued
on a single record, with the early-period "Serenade" Quartet and the string trios.
—Amadeus Qt. Westminster XWN-18609
(with *Qt. No. 18 and String Trios, Op. 53, Nos. 1, 2 and 3*)

### The Seven Last Words of the Saviour on the Cross (Quartet Version), Op. 51 ***

Another example of the rebirth of the Haydn
Society recordings. The same performance with

excellent sound and a consideration of the music
that is satisfactory in all respects. The moving
power and profound intensity of the music cannot be denied. The final picture of a supposed
earthquake does not improve with age. It is a
little naïve, not in quartet style, and mainly in
unisons and block chords. The Schneiders do
whatever any four-string instrument group can
accomplish with this cursory picture-painting
section.

—Schneider Qt. HAYDN SOCIETY 9041

## TRIOS FOR KEYBOARD AND OTHER INSTRUMENTS

### No. 1, IN G ***

Some people tell the news, other make it. The
two latest recordings of this work are so opposite that it would be a shame not to own both.
This is not meant to signify the odiousness that
relates to comparisons. The newsworthy performance is the 1926-27 recording of that team
of master musicians: Cortot, Thibaud, and
Casals. Rescued from the vaults and transferred
onto LP, this original 78 rpm performance is
startling in its freshness—not of sound, which
is not to be compared to presentday quotients,
no matter how expert the transfer—but, of insight into this, quite simple music. If greatness
can be communicated, it is illustrated in this
instance. The playing is acute, perceptive, and

the intonation is miraculous. Casals has little to do, since the Haydn trios are tentative, timid in their longing to lose the tyranny of the *basso continuo* hangover. But he has his innings with the companion work of the record.

The other recording has the shine and vibrancy of high-fidelity, but only partial fidelity of translating the notes into sound. Mr. Guilet's slurpy slides do not fit the music at all. Greenhouse, however, shows what can be done with the primitive doubling of the piano's bass line. Don't worry about the label copy for the Haydn. A printer's gremlin changed the tonality to G minor —it's still major.

—Alfred Cortot, Jacques Thibaud, Pablo Casals. ANGEL COLH 12 (with *Schubert: Trio No. 1, Op. 99*).

—Beaux-Arts Trio. M-G-M E-3420 (with *Mendelssohn: Trio No. 1, Op. 49*)

## TRIOS WITHOUT KEYBOARD

FLUTES (OR FLUTE AND VIOLIN) AND VIOLONCELLO
No. 1, IN D ***
No. 2, IN G ***
No. 3, IN C ***
No. 4, IN G ***
No. 5, IN A ***
No. 6, IN D ***

Of the ten listed, these six (indicated as Opus 38) represent an initial recording. The three

Danish gentlemen play cleanly, clearly, and with pristine intonation. But, despite the light course of Haydn's trio formations, their emotional range is narrow. Though the composer's wishes must be respected, his dynamic scale should not be short-weighted. And why do the liner and cover indicate "trios" when these half-dozen works are in fact "divertimenti"? The writer of the notes (excellent ones, by Joseph Braunstein) refers to the generic title correctly throughout his essay. The sound, a Vanguard reliablity, is all that one could ask.

—Poul Birkelund, Arne Karecki, Alf Petersen. VANGUARD VRS-1008

### HORN, VIOLIN AND VIOLONCELLO, IN E-FLAT ***

Eger is the most eager (one must forgive the obvious pun) hornist on the scene today and must be given credit for a great deal of missionary work. With the lamented death of Dennis Brain, he is in the front-rank of solo players of this warm, brass instrument. His performance of the rarely-heard trio is much better than the older version listed. The horn part is crucifying in its difficulty, especially of range. Eger has superb control and his colleagues support him well—support, due to the imbalance of the instrumental parts as Haydn conceived the work. Victor has done wonders with the sound.

—Joseph Eger, Isidore Cohen, Sterling Hunkins. RCA LM-2146 (*Around the Horn*)

## LUTE, VIOLIN AND VIOLONCELLO

A delightful combination of instruments makes this record appealing. While at best the "Cassationa per il Liuto Obligato, Violino, e Violoncello" is Haydn's contribution to *Gebrauchsmusik*, there is more than mere note-making. The lute adds color to the simplicity of the music. The violinist poses a problem. Her tone is so rarified that it sounds like a flute for the greater part of the record. Sometimes this is an asset, but otherwise it annoys. The solidity of fatty, string sonority would be more integral to the combination. One doubts another version of this work will make its appearance. One must be satisfied with the smaller conception.
—Janine Tryssesoone, Michel Podolski, Fernand Terby. PERIOD SPL-587 (*18th Century Lute Trios*)

## VIOLIN, VIOLA AND VIOLONCELLO:
G, OP. 53, No. 1 ***
B-FLAT, OP. 53, No. 2 ***
D, OP. 53, No. 3 ***

These trios are now companioned by the early Opus 3, Number 5 string quartet, and the last, "unfinished" (two-movement) quartet, Opus 103. The Wilton trios that formerly were coupled with the Haydn are now partnered with Hummel's *Septet*. The checker-board moves of record releases is a mystery to most of us.

—J. Pougnet, F. Riddle, A. Pini. WESTMINSTER XWN-18609 (with *Qts. No. 18 and* 77)

# INSTRUMENTAL MUSIC

## SONATAS FOR KEYBOARD (Piano or Harpsichord)

### No. 34, IN E MINOR

The ill-conditioned realization of a composer's work stems so often from an overbearance on the personal views (thus, sympathies) of the performer, rather than his stylistic translation of the music. This does not signify that the performer be cool, impersonally detached, but it does demand a warm kind of communication. Miss Reisenberg is somewhat inconstant in her playing. She prefers a rubato within otherwise carefully proposed playing. The sound of the recording is excellent, without any explosiveness or echo. I prefer this to that which makes the piano a semi-electrical disguise.

—Nadia Reisenberg. WESTMINSTER XWN-18358 (with *Sonatas No. 43 and 52*)

### No. 35, IN C ***

Balsam's positive playing gives him top consideration in the performance of this work. He is not a hyperorthodox pianist—the type of musician who clings to the religious devotion of detail without meaning. Though there is restraint, it is

restraint with affection for the music. This makes
a worthy recorded experience. The sound is on
the pinched side, but not sufficient to mar the
value of the record.
—Artur Balsam. WASHINGTON WR-430 (with
*Sonatas No. 40, 44, 48 and 49*)

### No. 40, IN G ***

There is little to chose between Miss Long's
older recording of this graceful work and
Balsam's newer release. The London record has
richer sound engineering; Washington's lacks
roominess, without which the element of piano
tinkle enters the picture. Balsam's chamber-music
experience shines through his conception of
music. His Haydn is a clear response to the order
of classical design. Only in this respect do I prefer his playing to that of Miss Long.
—Artur Balsam. WASHINGTON WR-430 (with
*Sonatas No. 35, 44, 48 and 49*)

### No. 43, IN A-FLAT ***

Despite certain reservations Miss Reisenberg's
version is the superior one. Her habit of incul-
cating rubati are not minor to the major proposi-
tions of classically-ordered music. When a
performer yields to the ego of a rubato when
the punctuation of a phrase is very apparent it
only means that a yielding of tempo will stick
out, and mar the music's shape. Otherwise the
playing is controlled, elastic where it should be,
and the tempi in general keep matters moving

with proper care. Westminster's sound is full, resonant, and no explosiveness or room echo spoils the recording.
—Nadia Reisenberg. WESTMINSTER XWN-18358 (with *Sonatas No. 34 and 52*)

### No. 44, IN G MINOR ***

Balsam concentrates all his insight on the music. No ostentatious display or looseness of revamping Haydn is to be heard. The contrasts are not extreme, yet they offer as much explanation as the bombastic method of a virtuoso. In this respect Balsam *is* the pure virtuoso. A fine-grained, top-polished achievement.
—Artur Balsam. WASHINGTON WR-430 (with *Sonatas No. 35, 40, 48 and 49*)

### No. 48, IN C ***

Despite excellent performances of the other music on this recording of five Haydn piano sonatas, Balsam cannot obtain a clear bill of technical health for this reading. His left-hand figurations lack the fine-honed edge of those performed by the other hand. Though of minor percentage in reference to the total achievement, the blur reduces the effectiveness of the work. Haydn's piano sonatas occupy a reduced page in the concert ledger, and we hope that their rich values will be recognized and made evident. The more expert the renditions the quicker the attention. At least, Balsam plays without Chopinesque

vacillation of tempi. His engineers do not give him the wide range of proper sound.
—Artur Balsam. WASHINGTON WR-430 (with *Sonatas No. 35, 40, 44 and 49*)

### No. 49, IN E-FLAT ***

Many have taken sides in the arguments pertaining to Glenn Gould, some with a dim view of the prospects of this young man, others with enthusiasm almost amounting to cult-worship. I do not believe in the last, but I believe in the musical expertese of this chap. He plays a piano as it should be played—as a vocal-percussion-string amalgam. The ancient Greeks said "the beautiful is difficult." Gould's piano playing is of sheer beauty, wealthy with musical virtue, absent of sham, though almost on the verge of skyrocketing into stylistic display. He makes the piano a magnificent, uncomplex instrument. His articulation of figurations in this work (listed on the cover as No. 3) are the most published conception of this musical device possible. Let the statement stand: this is the only version to own, though Balsam's has no faults, save that it cannot match the penetration that is Gould's or make its effect as patently exciting as his. And Gould makes this without sensationalizing the Haydn music. A rare performance.
—Glenn Gould. COLUMBIA ML 5274 (with *Mozart: Sonata No. 10, K. 330 and Fantasia and Fugue in C, K. 394*)

—Artur Balsam. WASHINGTON WR-430 (with *Sonatas No. 35, 40, 44 and 48*)

### No. 52, IN E-FLAT ***

Mr. Burke suggests that we await the release of Nadia Reisenberg's version of this important sonata. His opinion is that previous recordings did not do justice to the work. I join him in full agreement, and with the postscript that neither does Miss Reisenberg fulfill the need for a total realization of this magnificent creation. Her playing can be termed poetically realized, but it is the "poetic" that one cannot accept. The tempi are too sustained, the inflection of romantic subjectivity is not for Haydn. Nor is this the report of a purist, who has the pontifical urge that total objectivity must rule.

On the other hand, Horowitz storms the Haydn citadel with the ax of a virtuoso. The music becomes transmuted into a bravura, *echt*-personalized recitation. Since the recording was made during a public performance the Horowitz falter accompanies the record. Also some audience noises. Also some Rachmaninovian pedal peals in the slow movement. Neither of these records fill the need for Haydn's Number 52.
—Nadia Reisenberg. WESTMINSTER XWN-18358 (with *Sonatas No. 34 and 43*)
—Vladimir Horowitz. RCA LM-1957 (*Horowitz in Recital*)

# MISCELLANEOUS

## DIVERTIMENTOS

CELLO AND PIANO, IN D (TRANSCRIBED BY PIATI-GORSKY

The three-movement arrangement is unidentified as to its original source. It deserves attention mainly through the cellist's handy translation. The playing of Shafran is not in the class of other Russian cellists of today. The sound is "close-in," and the roughage is not healthy sonority. Unsteady pitch is also to be heard in the higher positions.

—Daniel Shafran, Nina Musinian. VANGUARD VRS-6028 (with *Schumann: Concerto for Cello and Orchestra and Falla: Suite Populaire Espagnole: Ritual Dance of Fire*)

TWO OBOES, TWO HORNS, THREE BASSOONS AND SERPENT, IN B-FLAT, "ST. ANTHONY" ***

Similar to the beautiful Columbia recording, this version employs the traditional woodwind quintet grouping. It will require more than these capable Parisians to better the performance of the Philadelphians. Woodwind tone of American vintage was brought to fruition by French teachers. The pupil outranks the teacher now —the French sound is nasal, bitten and does not

fall as gently on the ears. The Paris ensemble also wavers its pitch placement.
—Paris Wind Ensemble. Epic LC 3461 (with *Vivaldi: Concerto in G minor and Mozart: Cassation in E-flat*)

## HAYDN:–HIS LIFE—HIS TIMES—HIS MUSIC

This is the first of Period's "Composer Series" within which will be found releases covering the "life, times and music" of Mozart, Beethoven, Mendelssohn, etc.—ten albums in all. The idea is good, the execution does not match. Bernard Lebow wrote the text and it is narrated by David Randolph. One gets the impression that the music is a necessary evil, similar to the use of music with silent films—necessary, it was learned, to eliminate the hum of the projection machine and other assorted noises that would distract. There are three points that jar the listener. First, the music is parceled out in snippets, mean nothing, so little is given. Second, the narration is good, but has no relationship to the music, the comparison of music to text is not paralleled. Last, the chronology of the music is completely opposite to the text. This is a sampling of Haydn's music (from the piano sonatas, quartets, masses, concertos, symphonies, etc.). It does not make one run to the nearest record shop and purchase anything. Not for adults, and in a way, not even for children. Just not.
—Period PCS 1

# ORCHESTRAL MUSIC

## CONCERTOS

### FLUTE AND ORCHESTRA, IN D ***

Despite the need for balanced authority, more light-faceted music is composed for wind solo instruments with orchestra than for any other combination. And the performers, at times, cling to this misconception that light-weight in facture, so feather-weight in performance. Wanausek has a sweet tone, but not a spirited, deep one. His neutrality of concerto viewpoint makes the Haydn (is it by Haydn?) resemble, quite often, the lifelike, but lifeless wax figures in Madame Toussaud's establishment. The best-played portion is the final movement. Not any better than previous recordings.
—Camillo Wanausek; Pro Musica Chamber Orchestra, Paul Angerer. Vox PL 10,150 (with *Leclair: Concerto and Pergolesi: Concerto*)

### KEYBOARD AND ORCHESTRA, IN C (1760)

A first-rate first performance on records of a beautiful work. The soloist controls her playing to a sensitive degree and the response she has to Haydn's music shows common sense and realization of creative logic. The orchestra has its moments of uncontrol (dynamically speaking), covers the solo instrument so that the figurations which are paramount become subsidiary. This fault cannot be pinned to the baton of the conductor. The reasons: the cover states Rolf Reinhardt as the conductor, while the reverse side credits Michael Gielen as the director. If the majority is to rule, then Reinhardt it is, since he is credited as the conductor on the record label. By the bye, why give almost as much space to Barchet, as a solo voice as to the harpsichordist? Possibly this is relative truth, not absolute.

—Helma Elsner; Pro Musica Chamber Orchestra, Rolf Reinhardt. Vox PL 10,300 (with *Harpsichord Concerto in F*)

### KEYBOARD AND ORCHESTRA, IN F ***

An especially welcome addition to the Haydn literature. The Period recording, discussed by Mr. Burke, employs the piano. It is immediately apparent how much is gained by use of the harpsichord. Clarity, formal outlines, and the total sonority become etched with clear perspective in the performance here discussed. Roesgen-Champion plays simply and artistically, but the advantage is with Elsner. Her registration is a delight, almost of organ quality in terms of the bass gamut.

—Helma Elsner; Pro Musica Chamber Orchestra, Rolf Reinhardt. Vox PL 10, 300 (with *Harpsichord Concerto in C*)

### KEYBOARD AND ORCHESTRA, IN D, OP. 21 ***

The choice offered by previous recordings of

this popular work indicates the Westminster release (with Veyron-Lacroix as soloist) as the best
in general, across-the-board terms of performance, sound, and other factors. I must now beg
that the gentleman move over and politely, and
musically, give his place to a lady. Miss Marlowe's performance can best be described as superb, and the engineers have seen to it that she
obtains the full-scale sonority denied to harpsi-
chordists in present-day concert halls. Haydn's D
major Concerto is rarely ever heard on a harpsichord in the concert hall, but history gives anyone the right to perform it "per il clavicembalo
o il forte piano." The orchestra is excellent
throughout.
—Sylvia Marlowe; Concert Arts Orchestra, Sylvia Marlowe. CAPITOL P-8375 (with *Bach: Concerto in D minor*)

### Oboe and Orchestra, in C ***

The decision is clear-cut: Mr. Pierlot's oboe playing is one of the possibilities of playing the oboe;
the plurality of all artistic truths (and triumphs)
belongs to the superb artistry of André Lardrot.
His tone floats, it sings, it is a joy to hear, and
makes Haydn's work of stature far beyond what
it actually is. In comparison, Evelyn Rothwell is
simply not of the major leagues. Her tone is
pinched, a petty imitation of the real thing. Performing genius makes this recording paradoxi-
cally prove the untruth, that music is an international language. It would seem impossible to

imagine anyone not enjoying this fruitful concerto dish.

—André Lardrot; Chamber Orchestra of the Vienna State Opera, Felix Prohaska. VANGUARD VRS-1025 (*The Virtuoso Oboe*)

—Evelyn Rothwell; members of the Hallé Orchestra, John Barbirolli. MERCURY MG 50041 (with *Dvořak: Serenade*)

### TRUMPET AND ORCHESTRA, IN E-FLAT ***

Once a rarity, now every trumpet player's helping of brassy food. The writer recalls when there was but one copy of the score in the country, jealously guarded by the solo-chair member of one of the major orchestras. Then another copy was uncovered, also in manuscript copy, in a New York radio station's library. From then on the gates were opened wide—concert performances multiplied, and now the number of recordings is ready to go past the half-dozen mark. And the publishers have made haste to issue their versions—four thus far, and one in the works whereby the trumpet part has been transcribed for trombone. Surely, a home without a copy of the trumpet concerto is not a place of artistic balance. The Haydn music is good—for the trumpet—naturally it is restricted by the instrument for which Haydn composed. But, with half of the string quartets still unrecorded one wonders why this overemphasis on a simple concerto.

The effort to get the jump on the market is exhibited by the Unicorn release. Voisin uses an E-flat clarino trumpet and the orchestration has been colored and stitched by Leslie Woodgate (why?). Thus authenticity (or the close attempt to obtain it) is bunted into foul territory by this attempt to play two games simultaneously. Voisin's is the best presentation of the releases described below. His dynamic over-regard for the increase-decrease punctuations is strongly stated in the trills. Holler's playing is smooth, but his tempi are too anchored. Least acceptable is the squeezed tone, the unequal quality and the partial intonational lapses that pertain to Longinotti's performance. He has fashioned the cadenzas that are heard in the end movements. Lest the record-purchaser be confused with all these varied revelations, one would recommend Eskdale's performance above all others. If the budget permits, then Voisin's would be worthy. But, in legal terms: Let the buyer beware!

—Roger Voisin; Unicorn Concert Orchestra; Harry Ellis Dickson. Unicorn UNLP 1054 (*Music for Trumpet and Orchestra*)

—Adolph Holler; Vienna Philharmonica Symphony, Hans-Swarowsky. Urania UX 104 (with *Symphony No. 100, Italian Overture and Toy Symphony*)

—Paolo Longinotti; L'Orchestre de la Suisse Romande, Ernest Ansermet. London LL 3020 (with *Mozart: Concerto for Flute; Schumann: Adagio and Allegro for Horn*)

## Violin and Orchestra, in C ***

A reissue and the resultant revised coupling is more attractive. In place of a Mozart sonata, the rich soil of his G major Concerto is surveyed. Stern does an artistic delivery of Haydn's music, but I too prefer the "soft pliancy" that is not part of Stern's fat tone.

—Isaac Stern; Columbia String Orchestra, Isaac Stern. COLUMBIA ML 5248 (with *Mozart: Concerto No. 3 in G major*)

## OVERTURES

### ITALIAN OVERTURE

The title offers no clue, neither does the liner copy. In this case it merely serves as a filler. No one, it is difficult to believe, would purposely purchase this record for the overture. Somewhere I read that Picasso had said that when one loves a woman he doesn't measure her limbs. If you like Haydn you will enjoy this overture—without measurement of title, place of composition, and the like.

—Vienna Philharmonica Symphony, Hans Swarowsky. URANIA UX-104 (with *Symphony No. 100, Trumpet Concerto and Toy Symphony*)

## SYMPHONIES

### No. 45, IN F-SHARP MINOR, "FAREWELL" ***

Not being cut to exact pattern, the "Farewell" has the elusiveness of mystery. Most of the stories pertaining to this symphony have a central point,

but few have the more important formal moral
that Haydn drew from the shaping of this ex-
tremely individual opus. Merely the final movement is necessary to documentate this highly individual method of the composer. The ending of
this movement is a listener's reward. The performances preferred by Mr. Burke are now aug-
mented by Reinhardt's reading with the Southwest German Radio Orchestra. Only a thin, edgy
upper string tone interferes with whole-hearted
recommendation of this release. Benjamin Britten's version is fully covered in conjunction with
Symphony No. 55 (*see* below). It is not proper
Haydn testimony.
—Southwest German Radio Orchestra, Baden-
Baden, Rolf Reinhardt. Vox PL 10,340 (with
*Symphony No. 82*)
—The Aldeburgh Festival Orchestra, Benjamin
Britten. LONDON LL 1640 (with *Symphony No.
55*)

## No. 55, IN E-FLAT, "SCHOOLMASTER" ***

No obscure paradox surrounds the release of this
recording. There is much more than the languid
interest in the art of the "hard sell." In the name
of authenticity, this and the "Farewell"—two
superb Haydn symphonies are served hot off the
performance griddle. The noise at the beginning
and end of the record does not mean a call to
the service man—it filters down to recognizable
applause, if one has patience. Since the point is
emphasized: "recorded during the actual per-

formance . . ." we recognize the recording for what it is—or we should recognize and be aware of the dangers. Especially, with a pick-up band and the high horn tessitura of the "Farewell" symphony.

Thus registered for posterity are the technically warm garnet jewels of Haydn's flawless symphonies. The display includes gritty reproduction, poor intonation, blatantly so in the case of unison and octave sounds, and a general carelessness over all. Britten, the composer, has been ill-advised.

—The Aldeburgh Festival Orchestra, Benjamin Britten. LONDON LL 1640 (with *Symphony No. 45*)

### No. 82, IN C, "THE BEAR" ***

Reinhardt's sharply-defined performance has vigor, and is sensitive to the textural changes that mark this symphony. Let not the auditor be confused by the fancy nickname assigned this work. There is no programmatic intent. Nonetheless the pedal insistence that brought the cognomen to be fastened to the work is drawn and quartered properly. Vox has given the recording excellent sound, and an authoritative liner to aid the listener.

—Southwest German Radio Orchestra, Baden-Baden, Rolf Reinhardt. Vox PL 10,340 (with *Symphony No. 45*)

### No. 86, IN D ***

Haydn's music is monumental by way of its

simplicity and genuineness. This symphony, rarely performed (what reasons can our conductors supply?) is no smattering of trivia. The full-length reportage of a proper symphony needs no apology. Yet, the same "famous fifty" symphonic works grace our symphonic programs, ad infinitum. Mr. Burke will be pleased to learn that the "atrocious" performances he mentions can be forgotten. The Angel release fills the gap of a needed, profitable performance. Yet, even in this case, the art of Haydn is mistaken—its wit, its homophonic gaiety, its refreshing musical manners—for Rossini. Perhaps this is because an Italian is viewing the score page. But otherwise all is well. The sound is average, while the strings seem to be of lesser quality than one expects from those trained in the Italian ways.

—Scarlatti Orchestra, Franco Caracciolo. ANGEL 35323 (with *Symphony No. 92*)

### No. 92, IN G "OXFORD" ***

Haydn's symphonies are so full of freshets of inspiration that only a volume of commentary could do them full justice. The "Oxford" Symphony is one of the perfect gems in the jewel case of Haydn. Its hybrid flow of joy and seriousness require the attention of a disciplined conductor, and as disciplined an orchestra. The Rosbaud version wins the honors for one of the best Haydn recordings in many a year. His tempi are fitting, the tone of the orchestra a delight, but a Haydn delight. The style fits the music, and the music fits Haydn's score. There is no doubt that this is one of the top performances in the catalogue. The Scarlatti Orchestra performs with clarity, but their depth is not of probing condition; and, as in the case of their rendition of Symphony No. 86, a little too much of light vino is mixed with the notes. The tempo of the minuet is especially uncompelling.

—Berlin Philharmonic Orchestra, Hans Rosbaud. DECCA DL 9959 (with *Symphony No. 104*)

—Scarlatti Orchestra, Franco Caracciolo. ANGEL 35325 (with *Symphony No. 86*)

## "LONDON" SYMPHONIES: Nos. 93-104***

The orchestras have been negligent in regard to numbers 93, 95, 98, and surprisingly, number 102. A single exception, however, has changed this lamentable matter. Just as this portion of the book was near conclusion the first of the pair of volumes containing the dozen "Salomon" (a substitute name for the better-known "London") symphonies was released by Capitol. Since the three records are not available singly (at present, in any event) they are discussed below as a unit. For the remainder of the symphonies there are eighteen additional versions. These releases are considered individually.

Music's spiritual and emotional content are not observed on the printed pages of the score. The notes and signs must be decoded—sonorous transmutation, it might be termed. In this aural translation the music itself is not the total consideration; the personality of the composer and the era in which he lived must be realized. The honest musician represents matters as they exist on the printed copy; the exceptional performer illuminates them, moves freely (thus artistically) within the composition, and yet respects every sound-duration, nuance, tempo and modification. When a conductor is concerned it is a mark of his ability how well he understands this premise. In the plethora of recordings, it is unfortunate how so many conductors are not even honest, let alone exceptional.

Beecham's versions of Mozart compositions have proven he is one of the giants in performing this master's music. We should now change this phrase to read "these masters," with the issuing of the first six of the "London" symphonies by Haydn. This is, indeed, a Haydn banquet, served by the Royal Philharmonic men under the *chef d'orchestre*, Sir Thomas, himself. There is a continuity of beauty in every movement, and not once is a phrase distorted. In choice of tempi alone, the performances make the release the definitive one. Quite often Haydn's allegros are merely furiously flamboyant instead of being fluidly fast, and the andantes are paced to the point of being almost paralyzed. Beecham's tempi are so proper that he transforms the well-known into discoveries.

For the first time the variational technique of the "Surprise" (slow movement) is understood to signify not chunks of music, but one solid piece. Plasticity of mood is conveyed—the C minor opus is not tossed off as a frothy tidbit, but is played with full seriousness, correctly so, even when the tonality is in the bright major. Both Paray's and Szell's performances of the symphonies numbers 96 and 97, respectively, are discriminating. But Beecham's versions are even better, simply because he has a sonority quotient which gives dynamic weight without extraneous gloss.

It will be noted that Mr. Burke spoke highly of Scherchen's performances of these symphonies. This conductor belongs in the exceptional category, respecting the creative viewpoint and responding with respect. His "Salomon" set must give place, however, to the more flexible, vividly true readings of Beecham. Capitol's magnificent treatment of the sound on the records could not be bettered. It permits the ideal for the orchestra —no interference with balance and contrast, and all clear from top to bottom gamut. This set will serve for many a day, it is safe to prophesy. (The second volume, containing symphonies numbers 99 through 104, is scheduled for release in the spring of 1959. There is no doubt it will be the equal of the initial volume.)
—The Royal Philharmonic Orchestra, Sir Thomas Beecham. Capitol-EMI CGR 7127 (*Symphonies 93 through 98*)

No. 94, IN G, "SURPRISE" ***
Krips offers a neutral—and therefore, tame read-

ing of the work. The sound is excellent, the music too firmly affixed to the instruments, or the conductor's baton. It has become fashionable to play Haydn with simple regard, but this disregards the essence of the composer's thought. Damn the Papa Haydn edict could well be a watchword for some conductors. The man had real intense creative juice. It must emerge in performance. Not in this case.
—Vienna Philharmonic Orchestra, Josef Krips. LONDON LL 3009 (with *Symphony No. 99*)

No. 96, IN D, "MIRACLE" ***

Paray's performance with the Detroit men can well go to the top of the list, as companion to the choices Mr. Burke makes. His tempi are correct, his Haydn demeanor is not patronizing, nor does he consider the composer of mamby-pamby characteristic. The clarity of the voices is precise, whereas Münchinger's viewpoint is not exactly as clear as it might be. In regard to tempo Paray moves matters, while the Viennese take a slower view of the Haydn music. Of the pair under discussion the Paray wins with sufficient margin not to require overemphasis. It also employs the full apparatus, for the sound is of the total variety —no mere fractioned orchestra here!
—Detroit Symphony Orchestra, Paul Paray. MERCURY MG 50129 (with *Mozart: "Haffner" Symphony*)
—Vienna Philharmonic Orchestra, Karl Mün-

chinger. LONDON LL 1756 (with *Symphony No. 104*)

## No. 97, IN C***

The success story of the Cleveland Orchestra under George Szell was no mere publicity dream. The orchestra's triumphs in a series of concerts in New York offered the proof. Now, Szell emerges as one of the first-rank conductors of the music of Haydn. What brings this ability? It is a simple matter: the mark of the true re-creative artist is the ability to stay within style and not blend varying sources. One bows to the profuse inspiration of a conductor who maintains the inexhaustible attention to all details without permitting one minuscule portion of style-change. Following these instructions is the instrument represented by the Cleveland Orchestra. There is no doubt that their performance of this symphony is number one on the books.
—Cleveland Orchestra, George Szell. EPIC LC 3455 (with *Symphony No. 99*)

## No. 99, IN E-FLAT ***

In my opinion Szell's impressive concern for shading, style, and dynamic balance places the Epic release ahead of Scherchen's. Robust performance tactics are not un-Haydnish at all, they proclaim the proper measurement of the composer. The sensitivity of change, requisite to any large-scaled work's performance is not absent—

note well the relaxed feeling of the trio to the minuet. And Epic has served this up with proper fidelity trimmings. Krip's methodical performance lacks the viewpoint of the colorist, and since when was Haydn a study of only black and white, plus neutral grey?

—Cleveland Orchestra, George Szell. Epic LC 3455 (with *Symphony No. 97*)

—Vienna Philharmonic Orchestra, Josef Krips. London LL 3009 (with *Symphony No. 94*)

No. 100, in G, "Military" ***

There is a militaristic sense in reference to this work, additional to the superficial ones of the larger array of percussion instruments. Haydn has reached the ultimate point of his symphonic development; he does not err; there is no false step; no miscalculated point or direction, nor is there pedantry. Symphony Number 100 displays the peak of the composer's brilliance and stylistic virtuosity.

Most desirable of the new recordings of this symphony is that conducted by Dorati. The sprightliness effectively clothes the composition and Mercury's sound is quality at its best. The Vox release has excellent sound, but the quality of the orchestra is not as good as that of the London aggregation. Swarowsky's orchestra is earthbound; the music is heard as if it were aged with creases.

—London Symphony Orchestra, Antal Dorati. Mercury MG 50155 (with *Symphony No. 101*)

—Bamberg Symphony, Edouard van Remoortel. Vox PL 9860 (with *Symphony No. 103*)

—Vienna Philharmusica Symphony, Hans Swarowsky. URANIA UX 104 (with *Italian Overture, Trumpet Concerto and Toy Symphony*)

### No. 101, IN D, "CLOCK" ***

Most critics affirm that, regardless of the type of music, the composer passes through three stages —imitation, reaching out, and finally, maturity. Naturally, the maturity quotient is in direct ratio to artistic growth in the individual concerned. In any event, the creative artist has some type of growth via experience, if not through actual innate ability and talent. These thoughts came to mind in listening to Dorati's interpretation of the "Clock" Symphony. Dorati understands classical fashions, though he may have gained his reputation from music of much later mintage. His performance is worth possessing—despite a very heady pace for the first movement (*Presto*, yes; but not *Presto possibile!*) and a rather tepid consideration of the final movement. One cannot fathom Horenstein's unenthusiastic demeanor with Haydn. This is not a virtue. Vox's sound, in this case, is not smoothly set forth, there is some buzz that does not aid the listener. The Crowell-Collier has its moments, too few to satisfy, too Frenchified to illustrate Joseph Haydn. Ormandy, Wöldike, and Scherchen hold the top rungs in the recorded performances of this work.

Mention must be made of the Toscanini performance released by RCA via its Camden label. Considering the year of recording—1929—the sound is fairly good. But despite the virtues of this great conductor the sonority of the orchestra, its ordinary quality, makes this report show a minus sign.

—London Symphony Orchestra, Antal Dorati. MERCURY MG 50155 (with *Symphony No. 100*)
—Pro Musica Symphony, Vienna, Jascha Horenstein. Vox PL 9330 (with *Symphony No. 104*)
—Pasdeloup Orchestra, Louis Martin. CROWELL-COLLIER RG 131 (with *Symphony No. 104*)
—Philharmonic-Symphony Orchestra of New York, Arturo Toscanini CAMDEN CAL-375 (with: *Wagner: "Preludes" to Acts 1 and 3 of "Lohengrin" and excerpts from "Die Götterdämmerung"*)

### No. 103, IN E-FLAT, "DRUMROLL" ***

The introduction to the symphony proclaims the thrilling place in symphonic literature this composition holds. The picture is almost gloomy, weighted with sadness, verges on the tragic. It is a clue to a conductor's ability whether he can make this preamble more than heavy, dark and bass-colored. The performance must intrigue and be related to the severe contrast that follows. Throughout the work Haydn's audacious creative slant makes the area of the work one for only the very best conductors and orchestras. Given sufficient time the young man who conducts the Pro Musica outfit may be a candidate—not by

this example, however. We are not intrigued.
—Pro Musica Symphony, Stuttgart, Edouard van
Remoortel. Vox PL 9860 (with *Symphony No.
100*)

### No. 104, IN D "LONDON" ***

It is considered opinion that Haydn's Number 104
is fast approaching the saturation point. Listening
to so many recordings of this music is not the
easy way of life. Nor do any of us love to see
conductors fall, like the movie comedian, by
slipping on a banana peel. But, unless our orchestra leaders spend some time studying the formal
conditions of music (as well as some technical
considerations) we will have to let go with the
"blast"—the critical form of invective. How contemporary the works of men such as Haydn,
Mozart, and Beethoven! Conductors could well
drink from the fountain of these old and truly
tried composers, by studying the workshop materials, the twists of the tools, the elements of
the music. Then, and only then, will music be
performed, if not totally perfect in correctness,
close to the proper mark.

Of the new releases I can only give one full
credit. Rosbaud's performance is true to Haydn,
performed with tonal beauty, correct style, and
pertinent sensitivity. Münchinger has a sensitive
orchestra and he is an able conductor. But this is
Haydn seen against Viennese backdrops. Horenstein's tempi drag and illustrate the perfect con-
travention of everything this symphony should

represent. The other performance is strictly sec-
ond-rate, the sound pinched, the playing not of
top-drawer variety. For the Horenstein and Martin records a critic requires the restraint of a
stoic.

—Berlin Philharmonic Orchestra, Hans Rosbaud.
DECCA DL 9959 (with *Symphony No. 92*)
—Vienna Philharmonic Orchestra, Karl Münch-
inger. LONDON LL 1756 (with *Symphony No. 96*)
—Pro Musica Symphony, Vienna, Jascha Horen-
stein. Vox PL 9330 (with *Symphony No. 101*)
—Pasdeloup Orchestra, Louis Martin. CROWELL-
COLLIER RG 131 (with *Symphony No. 101*)

TOY SYMPHONY ***

Habit persists—not by Haydn, this work is still
considered his. Urania's offering is good, Columbia's is better, and best of all is the careful and
musical presentation accorded the orchestral
sweetmeat by those virtuosi, the Zagreb group
of thirteen super-musicians. They do not regard
Haydn's (pardon, Leopold Mozart's) music as
laconic fancy, but as a serious setting of an un-
serious idea.

—I Solisti di Zagreb, Antonio Janigro. VANGUARD
BG-569 (*An 18th Century Christmas*)
—British Symphony Orchestra, Felix Weingart-
ner. COLUMBIA 4 ML-4776 (with *Mozart: Sym-
phony No. 39 and Eine Kleine Nachtmusik*)
—Orchestre Radio-Symphonique de Paris, René
Leibowitz. URANIA UX 104 (with *Symphony No.
100, Italian Overture and Concerto for Trumpet*)

# VOCAL MUSIC

## MASSES

### No. 9, in C (Missa in Tempore Belli; "Kettledrum" Mass) ***

Too long absent from the catalogue, it is welcome news that the Haydn Society has reissued this stunning work. It is performed with splendid assurance and style; the voices all of musical as well as vocal beauty. This is a genuine art work, worthy of being on every music-lover's record shelves.

—Jetti Topitz-Feiler, Herbert Handt, Giorgina Milinkovic, Hans Braun, Joseph Nebois, Orchestra of the Vienna State Opera and the Akademie Chorus, Vienna, Hans Gillesberger. HAYDN SOCIETY 9055